Women and Peacebuilding in Africa

This volume re-centres African women scholars in the discourse on African women and peacebuilding, combining theoretical reflections with case studies in a range of African countries.

The chapters outline the history of African women's engagement in peacebuilding, introducing new and neglected themes such as youth, disability, and religious peacebuilding, and laying the foundations for new theoretical insights. Providing case studies from across Africa, the contributors highlight the achievements and challenges characterising women's contribution to peacebuilding on the continent.

This book will be of interest to students and scholars of peacebuilding, African security and gender.

Anna Chitando is an associate professor in the Department of Languages and Literature, Faculty of Arts, Culture and Heritage Studies at the Zimbabwe Open University.

Routledge Studies on Gender and Sexuality in Africa

1. **The Tunisian Women's Rights Movement**
   From Nascent Activism to Influential Power-broking
   Jane D. Tchaicha and Khédija Arfaoui

2. **Disability and Sexuality in Zimbabwe**
   Voices from the Periphery
   Christine Peta

3. **Love, Sex and Teenage Sexual Cultures in South Africa**
   16 Turning 17
   Deevia Bhana

4. **African Women, ICT and Neoliberal Politics**
   The Challenge of Gendered Digital Divides to People-Centered
   Governance
   Assata Zerai

5. **Widow Inheritance and Contested Citizenship in Kenya**
   Building Nations
   Awino Okech

6. **Women, Agency, and the State in Guinea**
   Silent Politics
   Carole Ammann

7. **Women and Peacebuilding in Africa**
   Edited by Anna Chitando

Women and Peacebuilding in Africa

Edited by
Anna Chitando

LONDON AND NEW YORK

First published 2021
by Routledge
2 Park Square, Milton Park, Abingdon, Oxon OX14 4RN

and by Routledge
52 Vanderbilt Avenue, New York, NY 10017

Routledge is an imprint of the Taylor & Francis Group, an informa business

© 2021 selection and editorial matter, Anna Chitando; individual
chapters, the contributors

The right of Anna Chitando to be identified as the author of the editorial
material, and of the authors for their individual chapters, has been
asserted in accordance with sections 77 and 78 of the Copyright,
Designs and Patents Act 1988.

All rights reserved. No part of this book may be reprinted or reproduced or utilised
in any form or by any electronic, mechanical, or other means, now known or
hereafter invented, including photocopying and recording, or in any information
storage or retrieval system, without permission in writing from the publishers.

Trademark notice: Product or corporate names may be trademarks or registered trademarks,
and are used only for identification and explanation without intent to infringe.

British Library Cataloguing-in-Publication Data
A catalogue record for this book is available from the British Library

Library of Congress Cataloging-in-Publication Data
A catalog record has been requested for this book

ISBN: 978-0-367-43614-8 (hbk)
ISBN: 978-1-003-02604-4 (ebk)

Typeset in Bembo
by Newgen Publishing UK

Contents

	List of contributors	vii
1	African women and peacebuilding ANNA CHITANDO	1
2	Women in peacebuilding: Influencing Africa's peace and security architecture LUKONG STELLA SHULIKA AND JANET MUTHONI MUTHUKI	21
3	Women's participation in peacebuilding in Africa ESTHER TAWIAH	36
4	Young women and peacebuilding MAUREEN GUMA	49
5	Building sustainable peace in post-conflict settings in Africa: A case study of Liberia PEARL KARUHANGA ATUHAIRE	64
6	Women and peacebuilding in Madagascar GABY RAZAFINDRAKOTO	83
7	Women as religious citizens and peacebuilding in Kenya LOREEN MASENO	96
8	Women as agents of peace in the Midlands Province, Zimbabwe: Towards sustainable peace and development SOPHIA CHIRONGOMA	108

vi *Contents*

9 Women with disabilities, peacebuilding and development
in Adamawa State, Nigeria   124
JESSIE FUBARA-MANUEL AND JUSTINA MIKE NGWOBIA

10 Peacebuilding through health work: Opportunities and
challenges for women community health volunteers in Kenya   136
ROSEANNE NJIRU

11 Women, artisanal mining and peacebuilding in Africa   158
MAAME ESI ESHUN

12 A role analysis of women in the fight against terrorism
in Nigeria   173
GRACE ATIM

13 "Not all heroes wear caps": Women and peacebuilding in the
public sphere in Zambia through a narrative of Susan Sikaneta   186
NELLY MWALE

14 "Swimming against the current": Queen Labotsibeni, the
epitome of effective peacebuilding in Eswatini   199
SONENE NYAWO

15 *Pray the Devil Back to Hell* as a resource for appreciating
African women's contribution to peacebuilding   213
ANNA CHITANDO

Index   226

Contributors

Editor

Anna Chitando is an associate professor in the Department of Languages and Literature, Faculty of Arts, Culture and Heritage Studies at the Zimbabwe Open University. She holds a Doctor of Literature and Philosophy (English) from the University of South Africa. Her research interests include African literature, children's literature peacebuilding and gender studies.

Contributors

Grace Atim is a research fellow in the Directorate of Internal Conflict Prevention and Resolution at the Institute for Peace and Conflict Resolution, Ministry of Foreign Affairs, Abuja, Nigeria. She has a master's degree, with honours, in English Language from Ahmadu Bello University, Zaria. She also holds two other master's degrees: an MA in Mass Communication and an MSc in Gender Studies from Benue State University, Makurdi. In addition, she has a Post-Graduate Diploma in Development Administration (PGDA) from the University of Ibadan as well as a Certificate in Strategic Negotiation and Conflict Resolution from West End College, London. Her research interests include gender justice, security, human rights, peacebuilding, communication and development studies.

Pearl Karuhanga Atuhaire is a programme technical specialist with UN Women, Liberia. She holds a doctorate in Public Administration: Peace and Conflict Studies from the Durban University of Technology, South Africa. Her research interests include gender studies, sexual and gender-based violence in post-conflict situations and women in peace processes.

Sophia Chirongoma is a senior lecturer in the Religious Studies Department at Midlands State University, Zimbabwe. She is also an academic associate/research fellow at the Research Institute for Theology and Religion (RITR) in the College of Human Sciences, University of South Africa (UNISA). Her research interests and publications focus on the interface between culture, ecology, religion, health and gender justice.

viii *List of contributors*

Maame Esi Eshun is an economist and regulatory research analyst in the Research Department of the Public Utilities Regulatory Commission of Ghana. She holds an MPhil in Economics from the Kwame Nkrumah University of Science and Technology (KNUST). Her research interests include regulatory and energy economics, women in mining and energy, and gender responsive research.

Jessie Fubara-Manuel is a PhD student of World Christianity at the School of Divinity, University of Edinburgh, UK. She holds master's degrees in Legal Studies from Lagos State University, Ojo, Nigeria, and in World Christianity from the University of Edinburgh, UK. Her research interests include gender, disability and HIV.

Maureen Guma is an associate consultant with the Management Training and Advisory Centre and an alumnus of the Peace Building Institute (By Never Again Rwanda) in Kigali, Rwanda. Maureen is also an author of children's books. She believes that the foundation for sustainable peace starts at the smallest unit of a country, which is the family. She holds a bachelor's degree in Business Administration from Makerere University, Uganda.

Loreen Maseno is senior lecturer in the Department of Religion, Theology and Philosophy, Maseno University, Kenya, and a research fellow at the Department of Biblical and Ancient Studies, University of South Africa. Recently a Humboldt research fellow, her research interests include gender and religion, development, eco-theology and biblical studies.

Justina Mike Ngwobia is the Executive Director of the Justice, Peace and Reconciliation Movement (JPRM) and the founder/co-chair of the Women Peace Builders Network in Nigeria. She holds a master's degree in Peace and Conflict and is a PhD student in Peace and Conflict Studies at the University of Jos, Nigeria. Her research interests include women, peace and security.

Janet Muthoni Muthuki is a senior lecturer in Gender Studies in the School of Social Sciences, College of Humanities at the University of KwaZulu-Natal in South Africa

Nelly Mwale is a lecturer in the Department of Religious Studies, University of Zambia, and an associate researcher in the Faculty of Library and Information Centre, University of Johannesburg, South Africa. Her research interests include religion in the public sphere, religion and education, gender studies and African indigenous religions.

Roseanne Njiru is a lecturer in the Department of Sociology and Social Work, Faculty of Arts, at the University of Nairobi, Kenya. She holds a doctorate from the University of Connecticut, USA. Her research interests include gender, health, development studies, internal displacement and peacebuilding.

Sonene Nyawo is a senior lecturer in the Department of Theology and Religious Studies, Faculty of Humanities, at University of Eswatini. She

List of contributors ix

holds a Doctor of Philosophy (Gender and Religion) from the University of KwaZulu-Natal, South Africa. Her research interests include new religious movements in Africa, church history, religion and gender studies.

Gaby Razafindrakoto is secretary of the Federation pour la Promotion Feminine et Enfantine (FPFE; Federation of Women and Children), a Southern African Development Community Protocol Alliance focal point in Madagascar. Her research interests include gender-based violence, women's empowerment, peace and security. She also participated in the Global Media Monitoring Project with GEMSA.

Lukong Stella Shulika is a post-doctoral research fellow in the School of Management, IT and Governance, College of Law and Management Studies at the University of KwaZulu-Natal in South Africa.

Esther Tawiah is the founder and executive director of the Gender Centre for Empowering Development (GenCED) in Ghana. She has an MA in International Politics (International Relations) from the University of Manchester, UK. Her research interests as a gender expert span democracy, governance, elections, and peace and security.

1 African women and peacebuilding

Anna Chitando

There is a growing recognition of the critical role that women play in peacebuilding, globally. The United Nations Security Council Resolution (UNSCR) 1325 calls for women's equal participation and full involvement in all efforts for the maintenance and promotion of peace and security (Miller, Pournik and Swaine 2014). Other subsequent resolutions, namely 1820, 1888, 1889, 1960, 2106, 2122 and 2242, which are integral to the Women, Peace and Security framework, have contributed towards highlighting the role of women in peacebuilding. However, according to Machakanja (2016: 1), "women's participation in peace and security remains more symbolic than substantive, and their capacity to influence and engage in peace negotiations is often resisted by local cultural norms and patriarchal hierarchies." Although women are playing significant roles in peacebuilding in Africa, their efforts tend to be minimised or ignored. This is principally due to the patriarchal bias that pervades human societies, including those in Africa (Ilesanmi 2018). In her analysis of structural obstacles to women's African peacebuilding work, Nadine Puechguirbal (2005: 4) made this observation:

> Women are indeed defined according to what they are, not what they do, according to what French philosopher Simone de Beauvoir used to call "anatomy as destiny." Women are constructed as passive elements subordinated to a male power always apprehended within more active dynamics. As a result, women are very often associated with maternal capacity only, thus keeping them secluded from outside political activities and official peace negotiations.

African women scholars in peacebuilding have sought to resist this negative portrayal of women. They have shown that they are strategic players by publishing material that confirms the active involvement of women peacebuilding in Africa. This volume builds on the increasing interest in African women and peacebuilding, as well as the challenges that women face in conflict (Annan 2014; Cheldelin and Mutisi 2016). The field[1] is emerging as a viable and significant one. It is promising to have the same profile as its sister fields, African women's writings and African women's theologies. Both of these fields are

2 *Anna Chitando*

championing the voice of African women. Located within this context, this volume challenges the general silence and exclusion of African women scholars in peacebuilding. The volume reflects on the extent of women's participation in peace and security in different African countries/contexts and proffers recommendations from within these spaces. It is by no means the first volume to attempt this (see below). While recognising the earlier work done by various scholars and activists (for example, in sole authored books, edited volumes, reports, position papers, strategy reviews and policy briefs), the volume seeks to expand the boundaries of the field.

While acknowledging the horrendous pain and suffering that women experience in violent conflict, women scholars in particular have sought to highlight women's distinctive contribution to peacebuilding in Africa. Alongside the more established and consistent voices of women researchers from beyond the continent and from within it, new voices on women and peacebuilding in specific African contexts are emerging. In particular, African think tanks, such as the African Gender Institute (AGI), CODESRIA (the Council for the Development of Social Science Research in Africa) and OSSREA (Organisation for Social Science Research in Eastern and Southern Africa), have sought to encourage African women scholars to reflect on women and peacebuilding. They have been ably supported by the African Peacebuilding Network (APN) which has ensured that the theme receives a prominent place in its research agenda.

This volume combines theoretical reflections and case studies on women's peacebuilding activities in Africa. It seeks to describe the achievements and challenges characterising women's contributions to peacebuilding on the continent. The volume recognises the need for more in-depth analyses of women's roles in peacebuilding in Africa in general and in well-defined contexts in particular (for example, Ball 2019). It is a partial response to the following observation and invitation by Hendricks (2011: 22):

> We need to begin to collate data on the experiences of women and document and analyse the contributions of women who have been part of peace negotiations, peace missions, security-related parliamentary portfolio committees, and the few who have made it to the upper levels of security institutions.

Speaking for ourselves: African women scholars on African women's contribution to peacebuilding

As has been acknowledged already, there is a notable increase in publications on women and peacebuilding in general, and African women and peacebuilding in particular. Some of the publications have a global outlook. For example, the *Palgrave Handbook of Global Approaches to Peace* (Kulnazarova and Popovski 2019) is a very well conceptualised and creative resource. It broadens approaches to peace by ensuring contributions and case studies from the Global South. More importantly, it carries a notable number of essays by women. The main challenge, however, is that it completely leaves out African women scholars from the conversation. Even though there are some essays by African male scholars, the total exclusion of African women's voices is a highly significant issue, at least from the perspective of an African woman scholar and peace activist. It perpetuates the struggle that African women (scholars and those not in academia) have always faced, namely, that of not having space within which to articulate themselves. This exclusion and significant minimisation of African women scholars and activists in peacebuilding also characterises the voluminous *Oxford Handbook of Women, Peace, and Security* (Davies and True 2019).

One effort at providing a comprehensive list of "key scholars and practitioners for women and peace and security" (Gakiya et al. 2016, Appendix 3) falls terribly short. On the African side, it includes only Phumzile Mlambo-Ngcuka, Executive Director, UN Women (at the time of writing). The book *Narrating War and Peace*, co-edited by an African scholar fully committed to Africa, Toyin Falola (Falola and Ter Haar 2010), has the same problem as the other works referred to above, namely, that of silencing/minimising African women's voices (probably because it emerged from a conference in the United States which most African women scholars would not have been able to attend).

This volume is distinctive in that it consists of black African women reflecting on black African women's contributions to peacebuilding in Africa. In this regard, it represents an assertive intervention by mostly relatively young and emerging black African women scholars and activists reclaiming/staking a claim to have a voice in the discourses on African women and peacebuilding in Africa. It is an effort to temper the domination of Euro-American women scholars and, to a lesser extent, black African male scholars.

The marginal voice of African women scholars in the field is consistent with the exclusion of African women scholars in many different academic disciplines. Historical and cultural factors, particularly the preference for the boy child ahead of the girl child in accessing educational opportunities, feature prominently. This does not apply only to black women in societies that have been organised on the principle of race, such as South Africa's (Ramohai 2019), but cuts across all African countries.

African feminists have challenged continental think tanks such as CODESRIA to be more purposeful in ensuring that women participate in higher education. For example, Amina Mama (2003) bemoaned the very slow pace at which women were accessing higher education in Africa. This exclusion persists, although African women scholars are making steady progress (Yacob-Haliso and Falola 2020). This progress can be seen in how African women scholars are contributing to the different disciplines, including Science, Technology, Engineering and Mathematics (STEM), where they have been even more marginalised. More work needs to be done at home, at school and in society to motivate more girls and young women to take up STEM (Ndirika and Agommuoh 2017: 54).

4 *Anna Chitando*

The field of African women and peacebuilding has seen African women scholars announcing their presence in a clear way. As I explain below, a number of factors have enabled African women scholars to contribute to the field. By reclaiming their voices, African women scholars in the field of peacebuilding are sustaining an emerging trend in African studies. This is the notion that platforms must be availed where African women speak for themselves. In the area of African literature, African women writers are challenging the image of a quiet and "decent" African woman who must only be seen and not heard. They are writing books where African women exercise agency and articulate themselves clearly (Chitando 2012; Iboroma 2017).

Some critics have argued that there is a wide gap between African women scholars and grassroots African women peacebuilders. They often cite differences in professional and academic accomplishment, education, social class, place of residence (urban versus rural) and other variables. According to this argument, African women scholars are somehow not "the real African woman" (Okech and Musindarwezo 2019). This argument is problematic in that it is clear that there are some people who have given themselves the authority to define who is a "real African woman" and who is not. In reality, although there are differences among African women, there is also lot that they share in common. This includes the reality of a shared gender identity and the exclusions that come with it. Further, there are close ties between many African women scholars and African women peacebuilders. They are united in their call for women-led, locally owned peace processes. However, they are also aware of the regional, continental and global implications of such engagements.

African women and peacebuilding: An emerging field of study

This volume is consistent with observations that women are defying victimhood (Schnabel and Tabyshalieva 2012) and are employing their agency in different areas in order to contribute to peacebuilding. Although this section will not provide a detailed account of the emergence of the field of African women and peacebuilding (this task requires separate studies), it endeavours to signal some of the major developments and challenges. It is surprising that although publications in this field have been available since the 1990s, there have been very few attempts to map the field. This would be by way of drawing attention to the enabling factors, acknowledging some of the consistent voices, identifying recurrent and new themes, and discussing some of the key challenges.

Enabling factors

Fields of study do not emerge out of nothing. They are shaped by various historical, ideological, political and other factors. The interest in women and peacebuilding in Africa should be placed in this context. It should be acknowledged, however, that the systematisation attempted below is the responsibility of the author. The field itself is not as systematic as the well-defined boundaries might suggest.

Global security concerns

The global interest in security, with particular emphasis on the United Nation's Women, Peace and Security agenda (for the African response, see the African Union Commission 2016), is noteworthy. The adoption of UNSCR 1325 on Women, Peace and Security in October 2000 represents a watershed moment when states undertook to ensure the active and meaningful participation of women in peacebuilding.[2] African women, however, have encountered major problems relating to the implementation of this resolution (Ilesanmi 2020). This global interest in the full participation of women in local, national and global development issues (Konte and Tirivavi 2020) was to be pursued through the earlier Millennium Development Goals (MDGs), and, from 2015, the Sustainable Development Goals (SDGs). The Global North's growing interest in security is linked to the United States' concerns after the events of September 11, 2001. Africa, which had been long ignored, was integrated into the global security matrix (Walker and Seegers 2012: 22).

Linking the crystallisation of the field of women and peacebuilding in Africa to global security concerns in the 2000s does not imply there was no interest, research and publication on this theme. Many scholars had shown an interest in this area and there were numerous publications, especially in relation to women's role in peacebuilding in traditional Africa. Further, African feminists have explored the positive leadership roles of women in precolonial Africa, their determination in the anti-colonial movements in the 1950s and 1960s, and the postcolonial period (Shulika 2016).

However, the upsurge in the number of books, journal articles, manuals and other publications focusing on women and peacebuilding globally and in Africa is closely linked to the global context noted above. These publications include Rehn and Sirleaf (2002), Bouta et al. (2005), Pankhurst (2007), Shteir 2013, Kirby and Shepherd (2016), Warren et al. (2018), Krause et al. (2018), Scheuerman and Zürn (2020) and others. There is also a willingness to analyse whether women shine light on specifically "women's issues" when they participate in peacebuilding. According to Goyol (2019: 133), "… an important question is whether it is the fact that they are women that matters or just that they are members of civil society willing to work for peace?" An overwhelming number of women peacebuilding researchers answer this question positively. Castillejo's (2016: 1) affirmative reply to this question is expressed as follows:

> Indeed, women frequently bring important issues to the peacebuilding agenda that male elites tend to overlook, e.g. the inclusivity and accessibility of processes and institutions, the plurality of citizens' voices, or the importance of local and informal spheres.

6   *Anna Chitando*

Many of the publications mainly focus on women's positive contribution to peacebuilding, women's experience of violence in conflict (Baaz and Stern 2013), and the historical and structural barriers that they face in their peacebuilding work. Others link the theme of women and peacebuilding to the call for women's leadership. One can also discern an interest in applying feminist principles, critiquing liberal peace and identifying women's contributions to peacebuilding in specific countries.

Nevertheless, the bulk of the literature is by researchers in North America and central Europe, writing about women's peacebuilding work in "the rest of the world." The unfortunate impression that this creates is that peace abounds in the "centre" and chaos reigns in "the rest of the world." Thus, there are much fewer resources on women and peacebuilding in North America and central Europe. It also suggests that there is no peacebuilding work for women in the powerful countries of the world. The reality, however, is that investing in women's peacebuilding work in countries that are members of the UN Security Council, for example, would contribute greatly towards global peace and security.

United Nations bodies, including UNIFEM, UNESCO and UN Women, have invested in research into women and peacebuilding in Africa. Central to their concern has been to promote women's participation in peacebuilding and leadership. Some African women scholars and activists have benefited from their engagement with these UN bodies. In keeping with its interest in heritage, UNESCO supported the publication of the volume *Women and Peace in Africa: Case Studies on Traditional Conflict Resolution Practices* (2003). UN Women has been interested in post-conflict recovery, peace processes, mediation and conflict resolution and other related themes in Africa.

Institutions and organisations

African women scholars researching into African women and peacebuilding have also benefited from the presence of institutions and organisations that have prioritised this area of study in Africa. These include independent research institutes and universities such as[3] (in no particular order): the Africa Gender Institute at the University of Cape Town, South Africa; the University for Peace Africa Regional Programme in Addis Ababa, Ethiopia; the Institute for Security Studies Africa (ISS Africa) in Pretoria, South Africa; the Institute of Peace, Leadership and Governance (IPLG) at Africa University in Mutare, Zimbabwe; Institute for Peace and Security Studies (IPSS) at Addis Ababa University, Addis Ababa, Ethiopia; Kofi Annan International Peacekeeping Training Centre in Accra, Ghana; Africa Institute of South Africa (AISA) in Pretoria, South Africa; the Institute of Peace and Strategic Studies at the University of Ibadan, Nigeria; Nigerian Institute of International Affairs in Lagos, Nigeria; Centre for Peace and Conflict Studies at Makerere University, Kampala, Uganda; and the African Leadership Centre (ALC) in Nairobi, Kenya. These institutes and others have

African women and peacebuilding 7

inspired, hosted and facilitated the success of African women researchers with interest in women/gender and peacebuilding in Africa.

Studies on African women and peacebuilding are not confined to research institutes that were set up shortly after the turn of the century. Many women researchers in different university departments housed in Faculties of Arts, Humanities and Social Sciences, including Gender Studies, Languages and Literature, Political Science (particularly International Relations units), History, Religious Studies, Education, Theatre Arts and others have been actively involved in research and publication on the contributions by African women to peacebuilding in Africa. The inspiration by initiatives such as the African Gender Institute (AGI) at the University of Cape Town and the earlier (late 1980s) focus on gender by the Southern African Political and Economic Series (SAPES) must be acknowledged. The steady progress being made by gender/women's studies in Africa (see, for example, Ampofo et al. 2004; Mama 2011; Etim 2016 and, Yacob-Haliso and Falola 2020) is also a major factor behind the popularity of women and peacebuilding in Africa.

The rapid expansion of higher education in Africa has also seen many institutions offering undergraduate and postgraduate courses in Peace and Security in general, and Women, Peace and Security in particular. Both state and private universities across the different regional zones in Africa are offering such courses. The availability of doctoral studies in this area at some universities in Africa has also added to the popularity of the theme. Further, the harsh reality of multiple conflicts in Africa (Elbadawi and Samanis 2000) and women's roles in them has been another motivating factor. Research and publication on African women and peacebuilding has, therefore, tended to be interdisciplinary due to the diverse backgrounds of the contributors. This has added to its vibrancy.

Some organisations have also invested in the area of African women and peacebuilding. Reference has already been made to organisations such as CODESRIA, OSSREA and the APN. The Next Generation Social Sciences in Africa Fellowship Program of the Social Science Research Council (SSRC) and the Southern Voices for Peacebuilding Network at the Wilson Center in Washington have provided scholarships and research opportunities for African women researchers on peacebuilding. Further, there is also a consortium that includes the Center for Research on Gender and Women of the University of Wisconsin–Madison, USA, the Chr. Michelsen Institute (CMI) in Bergen, Norway, and Isis-Women's International Cross-Cultural Exchange (Isis-WICCE), in Kampala, Uganda, undertaking research on, "Women and Peacebuilding in Africa." Such initiatives have equipped emerging and experienced African women researchers with additional resources, knowledge, skills and exposure.

The interest in African women and peacebuilding extends beyond Africa. A number of African studies institutes in Europe and North America offer, in particular, postgraduate courses and doctoral degrees in aspects of women/

8 *Anna Chitando*

gender and peacebuilding in Africa. In many instances, the pressure brought by African intellectuals is beginning to yield positive results and these programmes are taught by African women scholars. However, the debate on African studies outside Africa persists in terms of how knowledge about and on Africa is produced, by whom, and how it is, or must be, presented.

The availability of consultancy opportunities, the chance of having lively community engagement, the scope for innovation, and the need to enhance career opportunities have also contributed towards the increase in the number of women scholars researching into African women and peacebuilding. Greater internet access and the emergence of more journals, some of which have published special issues on this theme, have seen the area expanding notably.

Consistent voices and dominant themes

Some of the consistent voices in the field of African women and peacebuilding[4] include Funmi Olonisakin (for example, 1995 and 2017); Edith Natukunda-Togboa (for example, Rodríguez and Natukunda-Togboa 2005); Jean Izabiliza (for example, Mutamba and Izabiliza 2005); Pamela Machakanja (for example, 2012); Awino Okech (for example, 2016); Ecoma Alaga (2010); Pearl Karuhana Atuhaire (for example, 2015); Yasmin Jusu-Sheriff (for example, 2000); Sidonia Angom (for example, 2018); Esther Lubunga (for example, 2016), Rirhandu Mageza-Barthel (for example, 2015), Olajumoke Yacob-Haliso (see for example, 2011), and many others.

The list can definitely be extended (especially to reflect younger and emerging African women researchers), but the sole purpose of this section is to illustrate that there is now a notable number of African women scholars publishing on African women's contributions to peacebuilding for it to be considered a unique field in its own right. The contributors to this area include pioneers who have been consistently in the trenches and emerging voices. In order to reach a wider audience and in keeping with the changing information and communication technologies, some of the contributors use social media to communicate their views. Some of these scholars have remained in academia in Africa; others have combined scholarship with peace activism in Africa; yet others have joined non-governmental organisations or have joined organisations and research institutes outside Africa. What unites them is their consistency in drawing attention to African women's strategic role in peacebuilding.

There are some notable themes and approaches that can be discerned from analysing the works of the above scholars (and others writing in the field). In the first instance, authors tend to concentrate on women and peacebuilding in particular countries (or provide regional overviews). Some of the countries that get greater coverage include Liberia, Sierra Leone, Nigeria, Kenya, Rwanda, Mozambique, Uganda, the Democratic Republic of Congo, South Africa, Zimbabwe among others. These countries have generally experienced intense levels of conflict and women have used their expertise to contribute towards achieving peace.

African women and peacebuilding   9

African women scholars and activists have also assisted global scholarship by sharpening the definitions of conflict and peacebuilding. In their different writings (in articles, books, blogs and so on), they have expanded on definitions that have received popular acclaim. Due to their lived realities (for example, knowing that women and girls are caused to be vulnerable[5] to rape even when the guns have been silent), they have sought to play a critical role in redefining peace. One of the leading activists, Leymah Gbowee (2019–2020: 13), who received the Nobel Peace Prize in 2011, says:

> We need to reframe our notion of peace. Peace is not the absence of war; it is the full expression of human dignity. Peace is an environment in which human needs can be met. It means education for our children, health systems that function, a fair and unbiased justice system, food on the table in every home, an empowered, recognised, appreciated and fully compensated community of women and a lot more.

They have also focused on the interface between gender and peacebuilding at the practical and theoretical levels. A study of their publications also shows their commitment towards having an impact at the level of policy. Through strategy papers and policy briefs, contributors to the field seek to change the lives of women and girls at the grassroots level (see, for example, Kezie-Nwoha and Were 2018).

Works by African scholars consistently demonstrate the positive contributions of women to peacebuilding. They show that African women are actively engaged in the search for peace and security in their local, national (see, for example, Adeogun 2016) and regional settings. They have emphasised the socialisation role of women as mothers in inculcating "cultures of peace" among boys and young men. They have also examined the various strategies that women have used in their peacebuilding. For example, Esther Tawiah (2018, online) has explored the role of African women in peacebuilding, which she elaborates as follows:

> Women activists also promote a vision of peace that goes beyond the negotiating table. Women have contributed to stopping violence and alleviating its consequences in a range of ways: providing humanitarian relief, creating and facilitating the space for negotiations through advocacy, and exerting influence through cultural or social means. They have also spearheaded civil society and reconciliation activities. Even though some women activists faced numerous injustices for trying to protect women's rights, they have played a vital role in promoting women's rights and their place in the society. Women activists have unequivocally rejected the patriarchal language which denotes women as daughters, wives or sisters entitled to protection in that capacity rather than as human beings who will assert themselves as change agents of peace and change in their communities.

10 *Anna Chitando*

Other themes that African women scholars and activists have explored in relation to African women's peacebuilding include connections with grassroots[6] African women, gendered approaches to security (see for example, Adeogun and Muthuki 2018) and elaborating on women's roles in conflict. For example, when expanding on the latter dimension, Fébé Potgieter-Gqubule says,

> The literature on women's roles in conflict therefore lists not less than seven "roles" of women in conflicts: as combatants; victims of (sexual) and other forms of violence; peace activists; participants in "formal peace politics"; coping and surviving actors; head of households; and as part of the labour force.
>
> (Potgieter-Gqubule 2010, online)

Agbaje (2018) has raised the red flag over the instrumentalisation of women in peacebuilding in Africa. She fears, rightly, that the socially constructed "feminine" qualities ascribed to women are often used against them during and after conflict. One consistent theme that runs across most of the publications in the field relate to the numerous "roadblocks" that African women involved in peacebuilding face. There are historical, cultural, economic, political, capacity and other factors that result in African women's peacebuilding work being extremely difficult (Garba 2016). Mutisi (2016) takes time to reflect on the implications of women's quotas to the struggle for equality.

African women scholars on peacebuilding have brought out details relating to women's leadership and the use of new information and communication technologies in young women's peacebuilding (see, for example, Chitando 2019: 8). While reflecting on women's vulnerability to sexual and gender-based violence in conflict, African women scholars have expanded on the meaning of women's security (see, for example, Okech 2016). Responding to the gruesome murders of women in South Africa, women scholars and activists engaged in demonstrations that called for serious action in order to address this epidemic. Under the hashtags #NotInMyName, #AmINext and #SAShutDown, they ensured that women's security became a national security issue. This was highly significant. However, African women researchers will need to do more to highlight the role of women in the military/security agencies and their contribution to peace keeping in Africa and outside the continent.

Some key challenges

Despite making such notable strides, the field of African women and peacebuilding (by African women scholars) still faces some key challenges. One of the biggest of these relates to the field's self-awareness. Currently, most of the contributors are housed elsewhere and do not self-consciously locate themselves within the field of African women and peacebuilding. The active women scholars come from diverse areas within the arts/humanities and social sciences. While this diversity is a source of strength, it is a weakness in that it limits the possibility of the field defining itself with greater precision. Additionally, conversations across generations of African feminists on the struggle for women's dignity need to be undertaken urgently (for example, Clark, Mafokoane and Nyathi 2019).

The field is also weakened by the absence of regional and transregional networking among women scholars and practitioners. West African women peace activists are more coordinated than their East and Southern African counterparts. Closer interaction among scholars across the regions would contribute towards giving the field a more definite shape (although there is some informal interaction due to the fact of some women scholars having taken up teaching and research positions in South African institutions). A deliberate effort to support women scholars in Mozambique and Angola, for example, is required. Most of the publications on women and peacebuilding in these countries are mostly by scholars who are not based there (or by male scholars from these countries).

Africa-based and overseas-based organisations are investing in the training of African women scholars who have shown an interest in researching into African women and peacebuilding. However, there are limited publications that focus on methodology in this field (for example, Yacob-Haliso 2018). Sharing field research experiences is very important as it prepares younger women scholars as they venture into this field, which is full of problematic ethical issues. Scholars and practitioners who have been in the field for a longer period can mentor younger African women scholars.

Chapters in this volume

In Chapter 1, Anna Chitando introduces the concept of peacebuilding and how women are deployed as a resource in peacebuilding in Africa. Machakanja (2016: 1) notes that, "women's participation in peace and security remains more symbolic than substantive, and their capacity to influence and engage in peace negotiations is often resisted by local cultural norms and patriarchal hierarchies." This chapter explores the extent of women's participation in peace and security in different African countries/contexts. It also explores the growth of the field.

In Chapter 2, Lukong Stella Shulika and Janet Muthoni Muthuki address the question regarding the role of African women in peacebuilding. They argue that in Africa, civil conflicts and wars often instigate the formation and rise of women's agency. Shulika and Muthuki draw from several African experiences that embody both the narratives and agency of women's pursuit of peace. They assert that women's drive to build peace is not a new phenomenon. They say that it is as old as the term conflict itself and is underpinned by historical perspectives that are invariably interconnected to the present. The two scholars also recognise the importance of demystifying misconceptions about women, and integrating their lived experiences into peacebuilding, as vital for the effectiveness and sustainability of post-conflict initiatives.

12 Anna Chitando

Africa has been at the forefront of normative developments around Women, Peace and Security. In Chapter 3, Esther Tawiah examines a number of legislative and policy instruments that address conventional security issues as part of the Women, Peace and Security agenda. Due to stereotypical notions of gender, women's participation in war-related work can be overlooked or hidden away when disarmament, demobilisation and reintegration processes begin. Despite their active engagement in all aspects of social life in times of conflict, when post-war reconstruction begins, along with the appointment of transitional governments, women do not often gain positions of leadership. Women play important roles as custodians of culture and nurturers of families, yet in times of conflict, they are not represented at the peace negotiating table, or in community reconstruction efforts. Therefore, Tawiah maintains that it is important to have women participate in the peacebuilding process in Africa as they are in the majority.

For Maureen Guma, it is not a secret that young women across Africa are faced with gender-based discrimination in all spheres of life, such as education and participation in political and leadership processes, compared to their male counterparts. In December 2015, the UN passed the 2250 Resolution on Youth, Peace and Security, recognising that youth play an important and positive role in the maintenance and promotion of peace and security. This resolution urges member states to give youth a voice in decision making at all levels and to establish mechanisms and systems that enable young people to participate meaningfully in peace processes. Nonetheless, in many African countries, young women are restricted by certain oppressive traditional gender roles. In Chapter 4, Guma thus argues for the creation of equal training opportunities for both young women and men in civic education, peace education, conflict resolution, mentoring, mind-set change and critical thinking as part of the greater solution to achieving sustainable peace and development in Africa.

Chapter 5 examines the nature of current peacebuilding and reconstruction efforts in post-conflict settings in Africa. Despite the growing desire by post-conflict countries to sustain peace through various strategies, much is still required. In this chapter, Pearl Karuhanga Atuhaire evaluates the practical implementation of the different strategies, with a specific focus on their impact on human security dimensions in post-conflict settings with regard to Agenda 2030 on achieving sustainable peace. Atuhaire deals with two key human security issues: sexual and gender-based violence (SGBV) and sexual exploitation and abuse (SEA) in post-conflict settings. She articulates the gaps and challenges faced in implementing strategies for peace. Atuhaire draws from field experiences and insights from thematic analyses, as well as country experiences from the African context, and offers recommendations to address the challenges.

In Chapter 6, Gaby Razafindrakoto argues that the development of Madagascar cannot be achieved without peace and security. Though the country has not been the field of armed and open conflicts, the population is living in permanent anxiety. Various forms of law-breaking and criminal offences are taking place both in rural and urban areas. This is a serious obstacle to sustainable development and peace. Since the Reform of the Security Sector was initiated in 2014, Madagascar has achieved some steps. It has mainstreamed gender in the recruitment process of the armed forces, taking into consideration women's qualifications and specific needs, without discrimination. On the other hand, non-government bodies and peace associations are forming coalitions to foster peace culture and education. The key questions are: To what extent are all these efforts efficient? How can women bring about changes and tangible results in this area? And, what is their impact in the implementation of peace in the country? As she addresses the key questions raised above, Razafindrakoto focuses on three points: the reform of the security sector, UN Resolution 1325, and women's access to decision-making circles related to peace talks in Madagascar.

Using the analytical perspective on positions of the religious citizen, in Chapter 7, Loreen Maseno demonstrates how women in Kenya as religious citizens promote peacebuilding. She examines how religious women in Kenya are agents of peacebuilding. Maseno points to Kenyan women's peacebuilding responsibility in society as including the communication of messages of peace, as well as listening to, and supporting the people affected by violence, all of which are a means to psychological healing. Further, she analyses the different roles that these religious citizens in Kenya perform in peacebuilding.

In Chapter 8, Sophia Chirongoma contends that women have not been spared from brutal repression, beatings, rape and torture during times of war and political violence. Be that as it may, women have gone beyond their trauma, suffering and pain to look for alternatives and connections to resolve conflict. In this chapter, Chirongoma illustrates the fact that in order to achieve meaningful peace, reconciliation and sustainable development, Zimbabwe needs to empower women and promote their participation in governance and political leadership. Tapping from the field research conducted in the Midlands Province of Zimbabwe, the author illuminates women's initiatives and contribution towards peacebuilding and self-empowerment. She sustains the argument that there is ample evidence that women can work effectively to improve their communities if they are empowered.

Jessie Fubara-Manuel and Justina Mike Ngwobia, in Chapter 9, tackle the participation of women with disabilities in peacebuilding. They assert that, as in most issues of response, the voices and perspectives of women with disabilities are often neglected or ignored on matters relating to conflict, peace and development. Fubara-Manuel and Ngwobia examine the interrelatedness of development and peacebuilding in facilitating a culture of peaceful postconflict existence. They explore the multifaceted roles of women with disabilities as parties in development and peace projects. These two authors further illustrate how intentioned inclusion requires the participation of all persons in policies and programmes to ensure accessibility of aid to all displaced persons. They argue that peacebuilding does better when the elements of development are taken seriously, and all vulnerable parties are treated as veritable peacebuilders.

14   *Anna Chitando*

Roseanne Njiru focuses on women community health workers (CHWs) in Kenya in Chapter 10. While there is growing recognition of women's roles in peacebuilding in Kenya, the place of women community health workers in the peacebuilding infrastructure is not accounted for. Njiru examines the potential of women community health workers in peacebuilding and the challenges that exist to fulfil this prospect. Njiru interrogates how the features of health care, including legitimacy, trust and accessibility, advance CHWs' knowledge on community life and violence, which may be significant for local–national peacebuilding efforts. Overall, she argues that women CHWs are valuable resources for peacebuilding and there is a need to recognise and include their insights in Kenya's peace architecture.

Chapter 11, by Maame Esi Eshun, is an exploration of the involvement of women artisanal miners. The artisanal mining sector continues to grow, with women sharing the mining space with men. These women artisanal miners (WAMs) mostly take employment in dangerous working conditions often fraught with violence and conflicts. Nonetheless, their contributions to peace discussions are often overlooked. By excluding WAMs at the peace table, the prospect of dealing with the core drivers of conflicts, caused especially by mineral resources, is weakened. In this chapter, Eshun justifies and rationalises the participation of WAMs in the sector for peacebuilding. She further identifies the factors hindering WAMs from participating in peacebuilding. She examines the ways of engaging and empowering WAMs to partake in dialogues pertaining to conflict resolution, mediation, and peacebuilding. Looking forward, Eshun anticipates the ways in which participation of WAMs in peace processes will be more pronounced so greater efforts can go into anchoring peacebuilding in gender equality.

In Chapter 12, Grace Atim tackles terrorism, focusing on Nigeria. Terrorism is a serious menace that has been disturbing the Nigerian state. The origin of this problem can be better appreciated against the backdrop of ethnic and religious chauvinism, where groups at one point or another take up arms against the Nigerian state. The problem has been compounded by the governance crisis, which bred socio-political violence, unemployment, high levels of poverty, hunger, diseases, abduction, kidnapping, corruption and the like in a country that has plenty of human and mineral resources. These Hydra-like problems account for the emergence and intensity of terrorism in contemporary Nigeria. Thus, Atim interrogates the role of women in the fight against terrorism. She establishes the different ways in which women fight or counter terrorism in Nigeria. Atim discovers that, even though women have been playing crucial roles in combating terrorism, they are not recognised by the Nigerian state. She therefore recommends the recognition and inclusion of women by the Nigerian state in all strategies for counter-terrorism if this battle is to be waged successfully.

Nelly Mwale, in Chapter 13, upholds the view that despite growing calls for women's recognition and participation in peacebuilding in Zambia, women have not only continued to be marginalised, but also, the few women's contributions to peacebuilding have remained undocumented. Informed by narrative research in which data were collected through document analysis and recorded interviews, Mwale trails Susan Sikaneta's contributions to peacebuilding in the public sphere. She shows that Sikaneta contributed to peacebuilding through her long service in Zambia's public and diplomatic service until her retirement early in 2019. In this chapter, Mwale argues that Sikaneta's narrative, while symbolising heroines without caps, represents what women can do in peacebuilding, and how women can be beacons of peace at the local, national, and regional levels.

In Chapter 14, Sonene Nyawo advances the viewpoint that peacebuilding is an amorphous concept defined differently, depending on the context. While most definitions restrict the scope of peacebuilding to post-conflict interventions, common to all is the agreement that it seeks to improve human security by ensuring that people are safe from harm and that they have access to law and justice. It also strives to protect people from political decisions that may adversely affect them, and it enables them to have access to better economic opportunities and better livelihoods. Though originally conceived in terms of post-conflict recovery efforts in war-torn countries, Nyawo uses the term peacebuilding more broadly in the context of a non-violent conflict between Emaswati and European settlers over the land. She presents a scenario of a Liswati woman-leader, visionary and strategist who, in the 36 years of her reign beginning in 1889, employed peacebuilding processes to regain tracts of land that her husband, the king, had lost to European settlers. Nyawo asserts that Emaswati women can derive strength to swim against the tide of cultural barriers and make their voices heard in peacebuilding and decision-making processes.

Anna Chitando affirms that there is a growing acknowledgement of the significant role that women play in peacebuilding across the globe. The United Nations Security Council Resolution 1325 calls for women's equal participation and full involvement in all efforts for the maintenance and promotion of peace and security. In Chapter 15, Chitando interrogates the extent of African women's participation in peace and security, and their potential to influence and engage in peace negotiations in cultural and patriarchal contexts. She utilises the movie *Pray the Devil Back to Hell* as a basis/resource for African women's participation in the continent's peacebuilding endeavours. Chitando examines the movie's portrayal of the role played by the women of Liberia in ending the Second Liberian Civil War of 1999–2003. The movie depicts women who speak in one voice as they bring out everyday meanings of peace and security, and the desire to have peace and security. Nonetheless, there is never a neat struggle as portrayed by the women's movement in the movie. Therefore, in her discussion, Chitando critiques such representation of women in peacebuilding to establish their impact. She contends that the movie is a helpful resource and calls for the adoption of more genres in teaching women and peacebuilding in Africa.

16   *Anna Chitando*

Conclusion

African women scholars and activists have refused to allow the many conflicts in Africa to deflate them. They have instead emerged as very creative actors in contributing towards peace. Even if many of the official histories of peacebuilding in Africa neglect to tell the story of women, the reality is that African women have been and are actively involved in peacebuilding. African women scholars in different parts of the continent are putting together the stories of African women's contributions to peacebuilding. This chapter has sought to emphasise some of the major factors that are relevant to the emergence of the field of African women and peacebuilding. It is envisaged that this volume is contributing towards the ongoing telling of the stories of courage and agency that African women have demonstrated in their peacebuilding.

Notes

1 Although I have preferred the term field in this chapter due to its breadth, others might want to use "discipline." Yet others might argue that the term "area" is more appropriate.
2 This should also be located in the larger global history of feminism and the struggle for women's rights. For a helpful outline, see for example Gakiya et al. (2016), Appendix 2, "Key moments contributing to women in peace and security (since Beijing)."
3 The listing here is indicative and not exhaustive. Further, due to the constant reconfiguration of departments and institutes in universities, some of the names continue to change. With the field expanding, it can be projected that more institutions focusing on the theme of gender/women and peacebuilding, or "Women, Peace and Security," in Africa will emerge.
4 Different scholars in different African countries need to carry out research to identify the major contributors in particular countries.
5 The active role of men in violating women's rights and dignity needs to be named, although some women have also brutalised some women and men.
6 The concept is politically charged and has many disempowering connotations. It is used here due to its recurrence in the literature reviewed for this chapter.

References

Adeogun, Tolulope J. 2016. "Nigerian women in peacebuilding processes and its implication on peacebuilding," in Dhikru Adewale Yagboyaju (Ed.), *Reflections on Politics, Governance and Economy in Contemporary Nigeria.* Ibadan: University of Ibadan Press.
Adeogun, Tolulope J., and Janet M. Muthuki. 2018. "Feminist perspectives on peacebuilding: The case of women's organisations in South Sudan," *Agenda* 32(2), 83–92.
African Union Commission. 2016. *Implementation of the Women, Peace, and Security Agenda in Africa.* Addis Ababa: Office of the Special Envoy on Women, Peace and Security of the Chairperson of the African Union Commission (AUC).

African women and peacebuilding 17

Agbaje, Funmilayo Idowu. 2018. "The challenges of [an] instrumentalist approach to the involvement of African women in peacemaking and peacebuilding," *International Journal of Humanities and Social Science* 8(8), 99–105.

Alaga, Ecoma. 2010. "Challenges for women in peacebuilding in West Africa." *AISA Briefing*, No. 18, June.

Ampofo, Akosua Adomako, et al. 2004. "Women's and gender studies in English-speaking sub-Saharan Africa: A review of research in the social sciences," *Gender & Society* 18, 685–714.

Angom, Sidonia. 2018. *Women in Peacemaking and Peacebuilding in Northern Uganda.* New York: Springer.

Annan, Nancy. 2014. "Violent conflicts and civil strife in West Africa: Causes, challenges and prospects for stability," *International Journal of Security & Development* 3(1), 1–16.

Atuhaire, Pearl K. 2015. "The role of women in peace and security." Available at: www.peacewomen.org/node/91591, accessed 27 January 2020.

Baaz, Maria E., and Maria Stern. 2013. *Sexual Violence as a Weapon of War? Perceptions, Prescriptions, Problems in the Congo and Beyond.* Uppsala: Nordic Africa Institute.

Ball, Jennifer. 2019. *Women, Development and Peacebuilding in Africa: Stories from Uganda.* New York: Palgrave Macmillan.

Bouta, Tsjeard et al. 2005. *Gender, Conflict, and Development.* Washington, DC: The International Bank for Reconstruction and Development / The World Bank.

Castillejo, Clare. 2016. *Women Political Leaders and Peacebuilding.* Report 16. Oslo: Norwegian Peacebuilding Resource Centre (NOREF).

Cheldelin, Sandra, and Martha Mutisi. (Eds.). 2016. *Deconstructing Women, Peace and Security: A Critical Review of Approaches to Gender and Empowerment.* Cape Town: HSRC.

Chitando, Anna. 2012. *Fictions of Gender and the Dangers of Fiction in Zimbabwean Women's Writings on HIV and AIDS.* Harare: Africa Institute for Culture, Dialogue, Peace and Tolerance Studies.

Chitando, Anna. 2019. "From victims to the vaunted: Young women and peace building in Mashonaland East, Zimbabwe," *African Security Review*, (28)2, 110–123.

Clark, Jude, Shula Mafokoane and Talent N. Nyathi. 2019. "'Rocking the rock': A conversation on the slogan '*Wathinta abafazi, wathint' imbokodo!*': Intergenerational feminisms and the implications for women's leadership," *Agenda* 33(1), 67–73.

Davies, Sara E., and Jacqui True. (Eds.). 2019. *The Oxford Handbook of Women, Peace, and Security.* Oxford: Oxford University Press.

Elbadawi, Ibrahim, and Nicholus Sambanis. 2000. "Why are there so many civil wars in Africa? Understanding and preventing violent conflict," *Journal of African Economies* 9(3), 244–269.

Etim, James. (Ed.). 2016. *Introduction to Gender Studies in Eastern and Southern Africa: A Reader.* Rotterdam: Sense Publishers.

Falola, Toyin, and Hetty Ter Haar. (Eds.). 2010. *Narrating War and Peace in Africa.* Rochester, NY: Rochester University Press.

Gakiya, Mariko, et al. 2016. *Women's Leadership and Empowerment for Peacebuilding.* Tokyo: Sakawa Peace Foundation. Available at: www.spf.org/publication/upload/Women%27s%20Leadership%20and%20Empowerment%20for%20PeacebuildingII.pdf, accessed 6 January 2020.

Garba, Gladys K. 2016. "Building women's capacity for peacebuilding in Nigeria," *Review of History and Political Science* 4(1), 31–46.

18   *Anna Chitando*

Gbowee, Leymah. 2019–2020. "We must involve women in the peace process: They are the ones sustaining peace and nurturing society," *Africa Renewal,* December 2019–March 2020. New York: Strategic Communications Division of the United Nations Department of Global Communications. Available at: www.un.org/africarenewal/sites/www.un.org.africarenewal/files/A_R33_3_EN.pdf, accessed 7 January 2020.

Goyol, Yilritmwa I. 2019. "The role of women in peacebuilding: Liberia in focus," *International Journal of Development and Management Review* 14(1), 123–135.

Hendricks, Cheryl. 2011. *Gender and Security in Africa: An Overview.* Uppsala: Nordic Africa Institute.

Iboroma, Ibiene E. 2017. "The 'generalized other': Good woman in African fiction," *European Journal of English Language and Literature Studies* 5(8), 63–72.

Ilesanmi, Oluwatoyin. 2018. "Women's visibility in decision making processes in Africa: Progress, challenges, and way forward," *Frontiers in Sociology* 3, 38. doi: 10.3389/fsoc.2018.00038

Ilesanmi, Omotola. 2020. "UNSCR 1325 and African women in conflict and peace," in Olajumoke Yacob-Haliso and Toyin Falola (Eds.), *The Palgrave Handbook of African Women's Studies.* Cham, Switzerland: Palgrave Macmillan.

Jusu-Sheriff, Yasmin. 2000. "Sierra Leonean women and the peace process," in David Lord (Ed.), *Paying the Price: The Sierra Leone Peace Process.* London: Conciliation Resources.

Kezie-Nwoha, Helen, and Juliet Were. 2018. "Women's informal peace efforts: Grassroots activism in South Sudan." *CMI Brief,* No. 7. Bergen, Norway: CMI.

Kirby, Paul, and Laura J. Shepherd. 2016. "The futures past of the Women, Peace and Security agenda," *International Affairs* 92(2), 373–392.

Konte, Maty, and Nyasha Tirivayi. (Eds.). 2020. *Women and Sustainable Development: Empowering Women in Africa.* Cham, Switzerland: Palgrave Macmillan.

Krause, Jana, et al. 2018. "Women's participation in peace negotiations and the durability of peace," *International Interactions: Empirical and Theoretical Research in International Relations* 44(6), 985–1016.

Kulnazarova, Aigul, and Vesselin Popovski (Eds.). 2019. *The Palgrave Handbook of Global Approaches to Peace.* Cham, Switzerland: Palgrave Macmillan.

Lubunga, Esther. 2016. "The impact of conflict in the Democratic Republic of Congo on women and their response to peace-building," *Stellenbosch Theological Journal* 2(2), 347–364.

Machakanja, Pamela. 2012. *Mapping Women's Needs in Zimbabwe's National Healing Process.* Wynberg, South Africa: Institute for Justice and Reconciliation.

Machakanja, Pamela. 2016. "Is UNSCR 1325 empowering African women to negotiate peace? Insights and policy options," *APN Briefing Note,* No. 6, 1–2.

Mageza-Barthel, Rirhandu. 2015. *Mobilizing Transnational Gender Politics in Post-Genocide Rwanda.* Farnham, UK: Ashgate.

Mama, Amina. 2003. "Restore, reform but do not transform: The gender politics of higher education in Africa," *JHEA/RESA* 1(1), 101–125.

Mama, Amina. 2011. "What does it mean to do feminist research in African contexts?" *Feminist Review,* 98(1), e4–e20.

Miller, Barbara, Milad Pournik and Aisling Swaine. 2014. "Women in peace and security through United Nations Security Council Resolution 1325: Literature review, content analysis of national action plans, and implementation," *IGIS WP 13/GGP WP 09.* Institute for Global and International Studies, Georgetown University.

African women and peacebuilding 19

Mutamba, John, and Jeanne Izabiliza. 2005. *The Role of Women in Reconciliation and Peacebuilding in Rwanda: Ten Years after Genocide 1994–2004 – Contributions, Challenges and Way Forward*. Kigali: The National Unity and Reconciliation Commission.

Mutisi, Martha. 2016. "Add women and stir: Implications of gender quotas," in Sandra Cheldelin and Martha Mutisi, (Eds.), *Deconstructing Women, Peace and Security: A Critical Review of Approaches to Gender and Empowerment*. Cape Town: HSRC.

Ndirika, Maryann C., and Patience C. Agommuoh. 2017. "Investigating factors influencing girls participation in science and technology education in Nigeria," *IOSR Journal of Research & Method in Education* 7(3), 50–54.

Okech, Awino. 2016. *Gender and Security in Africa*. Accra: African Women's Development Fund.

Okech, Awino, and Dinah Musindarwezo. 2019. "Building transnational feminist alliances: Reflections on the post-2015 development agenda," *Contexto Internacional* 4(2), 255–272.

Olonisakin, Funmi. 1995. "'Liberia,' (collection of interviews)," in Olivia Bennett and Jo Bexley (Eds.), *Arms to Fight, Arms to Protect: Women Speak Out about Conflict*. London: Panos.

Olonisakin, Funmi. 2017. "Towards re-conceptualising leadership for sustainable peace," *The Journal of Leadership & Developing Societies*, 2(1), 1–30.

Pankhurst, Donna. (Ed.). 2007. *Gendered Peace: Women's Struggle for Post-War Justice and Reconciliation*. London: Routledge.

Potgieter-Gqubule, Fébé, 2010. "Peacebuilding, protocols and policy: women and conflict in Southern Africa," *Genderlinks*. Available at: https://genderlinks.org.za/programme-web-menu/peace-building-protocols-and-policy-women-and-conflict-in-southern-africa-2010-11-24/, accessed 7 January 2020.

Puechguirbal, Nadine. 2005. "Gender and peacebuilding in Africa: Analysis of some structural obstacles," in Dina Rodríguez and Edith Natukunda-Togboa (Eds.), *Gender and Peacebuilding in Africa*. San Jose: University of Peace.

Ramohai, Juliet. 2019, "A black woman's perspective on understanding transformation and diversity in South African higher education," *Transformation in Higher Education* 4(1). doi: 10.4102/the.v4i0.58

Rehn, Elisabeth, and Ellen Johnson Sirleaf. 2002. *Women, War and Peace: The Independent Experts' Assessment on the Impact of Armed Conflict on Women and Women's Role in Peacebuilding*. New York: United Nations Development Fund for Women

Rodríguez, Dina, and Edith Natukunda-Togboa. (Eds.). 2005. *Gender and Peacebuilding in Africa*. San Jose: University for Peace.

Scheuerman, Manuela, and Anja Zürn. (Eds.). 2020. *Gender Roles in Peace and Security: Prevent, Protect, Participate*. Cham, Switzerland: Springer Nature Switzerland AG.

Schnabel, Albrecht, and Anara Tabyshalieva. (Eds.). 2012. *Defying Victimhood: Women and Post-Conflict Peacebuilding*. Tokyo: United Nations University Press.

Shulika, Lukong S. 2016. "Women and peacebuilding: From historical to contemporary African perspectives," *Ubuntu: Journal of Conflict and Social Transformation* 5(1), 7–31.

Shteir, Sarah. 2013. "Gendered crises, gendered responses: The necessity and utility of a gender perspective in armed conflicts and natural disasters – an introductory overview." *Civil-Military Occasional Papers*. Canberra: Australian Government/Australian Civil-Military Centre.

Tawiah, Esther. 2018. "Women's participation in promoting peace and security in Africa." Available at: www.acdhrs.org/2018/07/women-participation/, accessed 7 January 2020.

20 *Anna Chitando*

UNESCO. 2003. *Women and Peace in Africa: Case Studies on Traditional Conflict Resolution Practices*. Paris: UNESCO.

Walker, Robin E., and Annette Seegers. 2012. "Securitisation: The case of post-9/11 United States Africa policy," *Scientia Militaria: South African Journal of Military Studies* 4(2), 22–45.

Warren, Roslyn, et al. 2018. *Women's Peacebuilding Strategies Amidst Conflict: Lessons from Myanmar and Ukraine*. Washington, DC: Georgetown Institute for Women, Peace and Security (GIWPS).

Yacob-Haliso, Olajumoke. 2011. "The illusion of home and the elusion of peace: Framing the 'return' of Liberian refugee women," *Africa Peace and Conflict Journal* 4(2), 42–53.

Yacob-Haliso, Olajumoke. 2018. "Intersectionalities and access in fieldwork in postconflict Liberia: Motherland, motherhood, and minefields," *African Affairs* 118(470), 168–181.

Yacob-Haliso, Olajumoke, and Toyin Falola. (Eds.). 2020. *The Palgrave Handbook of African Women's Studies*. Cham, Switzerland: Palgrave Macmillan.

2 Women in peacebuilding

Influencing Africa's peace and
security architecture

Lukong Stella Shulika and Janet Muthoni Muthuki

Introduction

The final three decades of the 20th century and most notably the present 21st century have been strengthened by efforts to harmonise and advance the participation of women in affairs of peace and security. Significant developments in this light have included policy blueprints such as the Beijing Declaration of 1995; the Protocol to the African Charter on Human and Peoples' Rights on the Rights of Women in Africa of 2003; and most notably, the United Nations Security Council Resolution (UNSCR) 1325 of 2000 on Women, Peace and Security. However, these developments have led to interrogations that seek clear responses and insight into theoretical and practical questions, such as: Why is there a particular emphasis to incorporate and heighten women's participation in peace and security agendas? What are the dynamics underpinning their roles, perspectives and interests in the field?

Probing these questions has engendered significant justifications and scholarship to the effect that, in conflict, women take-up active roles as actors, combatants, caregivers, and peace activists. Likewise, women remain disproportionately victimised and marginalised because of the "gendered nature of conflicts" and the sexist nature of society (McKay 2004). For Alaga (2010), women through their distinctive and sometimes shared experiences of conflict also provide a gendered specific and transformative perspective to the peace and security agendas, both at the structural and practical levels. As such, the attainment of sustainable peace is said to be considerably contingent on women's inclusion and participation as active stakeholders in the process. Firstly, this is because gender, as advocated by feminist peace philosophy, must be made visible in peace processes in order to bring to light the centrality of women's contribution to the advancement of durable peace (Sharoni 1994). So, women's exclusion or absence from peace processes is bound to render these processes incomplete, as not all gendered interests and views would have been included in the inventory of considerations. Secondly, inclusivity, which connotes the acknowledgement of people's human rights to belong, is crucial to attaining peace and development objectives. Further, women's rights as an expression

22   Lukong Stella Shulika et al.

of these rights cannot be isolated from the general undertone of human rights as provisioned in the Universal Declaration of Human Rights adopted by the United Nations in 1948. Basically, the UN conceives human rights as the foundation for all global (political, economic, social and security) development goals. Thirdly, conflicts, either directly or indirectly, severely trespass on the human rights of women as they come under attack as victims of sexual and gender-based violence (Human Security Baseline Assessment 2012). Consequently, women's activism for peace emanates from their experiences of conflict, which fuels their passion and resolve to ensure society's return to the state of normalcy – namely, peace and security (Shulika 2016).

In keeping with these developments, strategising for peace and security in the contemporary world has been gradually met with the inclusion of women in the processes. African countries such as Liberia, Sierra Leone, South Africa, and Rwanda are among the many examples of contexts where women are constantly organising for peace under the auspices of civil society and non-governmental organisations (NGOs). Accordingly, studies by Rehn and Sirleaf (2002) and Mutamba and Izabiliza (2005) highlight that by locating their rightful place and organisational significance in society, women in these countries have embraced their human/civil rights and responsibilities to pursue and engender meaningful responses and approaches to peace and security processes. Therefore, through widespread advocacy and activism, these women are living up to their potential as agents and architects of peace, security, socio-political and economic development. This notwithstanding, the effectiveness of their peacebuilding efforts remains a challenge. Pankhurst and Anderlini (1998), and Mpoumou (2004) contend that this is because of several factors, including, but not limited to: prevailing institutional, traditional and socio-economic barriers that hinder them from charting the way forward to peace; the inability of most governments to translate adopted policies on women's inclusion in peace and security agendas into viable projects (Rehn and Sirleaf 2002; Alaga 2010); and the politicisation and over-centralisation of the women, peace and security policies at national levels leading to the minimal inclusion of the grassroots women, where the bulk of women's activism and motivation for peace resides (CARE International 2010).

In view of these challenges and seeking to advance long-term peace, security and development in Africa, the African Union in consultation and partnership with African organisations, have engaged "a global strategy to optimize the use of Africa's resources for the benefit of all Africans" (African Union Commission 2015). The African Agenda 2063 reiterates its goals of "The Africa We Want" by recognising and emphasising the significance of women's involvement in driving the peace, security and development agenda in Africa. Building on this, this chapter explores the role of African women in Africa's current/future peace and security agendas. In essence, it advances the argument that women's success in influencing sustainable peace and development goals in Africa is contingent on the meaningful support and acknowledgement they receive at all levels of their involvement as equal owners and participants in the processes meant to

Women influencing peace and security 23

impact on their well-being and future. Taking on the Agenda 2063 theme of "a peaceful and secure Africa," the chapter further builds on the thesis that the realisation of this theme is, inter alia, dependent on a well-defined implementation of strategic policies that are inclusive, people-driven, and trust the abilities of women, as outlined in said Agenda.

The women and peacebuilding discourse: A review

The past two decades have witnessed a remarkable focus on and publication of topical literature on women's role in peacebuilding. However, the importance and dynamics of their role in the subject field cannot be fully understood without spelling out a conceptual and practical understanding of peacebuilding. For the most part, literature on peacebuilding often attempts to expound the concept as a framework of integrated processes. In this context, peacebuilding can be defined as a comprehensive set of activities correlated to engender meaningful responses to resolve conflicts in a non-violent manner, reduce direct violence, transform conflict relationships, and strengthen national capacity at all levels of the society (Schirch 2008). Practically, it involves four major transformative pillars, which are: security sector reform and transformation, justice and reconciliation, socio-economic welfare, as well as governance and political participation (Hamre and Sullivan 2002).

Note is also taken that peacebuilding is a comprehensive agenda that dovetails with a wide range of issues, and realising the agenda entails undertaking it in sequence, from the bottom-up, top-down and middle-out (Lederach 1997). However, several studies indicate that the role of women within the agenda is obfuscated as a consequence of their limited engagement in the initial adoption of peacebuilding policies and strategies (Woroniuk 2001). Likewise, the minimisation of women's role is heightened by society's continuous marginalisation and biased portrayal of women as feeble victims of conflicts and the vulnerable of society (Puechguirbal 2005). This consideration is further illuminated by Women for Women International (2010: 2):

> Sadly, in times of war a woman's burdens only get heavier, her vulnerabilities more pronounced. She remains locked in poverty, often losing the protection of home and husband, coping with fear and suffering devastating rights violations and violence, including torture, rape, sexual slavery, enforced prostitution and mutilation. Despite these grim realities, she brings enormous energy, leadership and resilience to protecting families and rebuilding fractured communities. Yet, her essential voice remains absent from formal peace negotiations and her needs remain on the margins of reconstruction, development and poverty reduction programmes.

This perspective on the predicaments women face has been at the nucleus of the debates on women and peacebuilding. Accordingly, Wibben (2003) and McCarthy (2011) theorise that these dilemmas emerge from women's

24   *Lukong Stella Shulika et al.*

repression by gender inequality and power hierarchies, which permeate society. However, it would seem the role of women in peacebuilding dates as far back as their experience of violence and transcends cultures, histories, political divides and geographic space (Shulika 2016). It was not until the 1970s that the introduction of "women's issues as global issues" attracted widespread international deliberations and awareness, leading to the declaration of the United Nations Decade for Women (UNDW), 1975–1985 (Reardon 1993).

The UNDW was spurred by women's vision for their struggle for peace and human dignity and was marked by three international conferences held in Mexico City in Mexico (1975), Copenhagen in Denmark (1980), and Nairobi in Kenya (1985). The Mexico conference adopted a World Plan of Action that called for the "full participation of women in all efforts to promote and maintain peace"; the Copenhagen conference on Equality, Development and Peace concluded on the objectives of the UNDW; and the Nairobi conference reviewed and evaluated the achievements of UNDW and, by agreement, adopted sets of principles – *The Nairobi Forward Looking Strategies for the Advancement of Women* – for the emancipation of women as a point of departure for a peaceful society (Reardon 1993). As a result, this epoch signified a chapter in history when women and society started to fully acknowledge the supportive roles women play and have played in the war settings, the devastating impacts wars have and have had on humanity—particularly on women and girls, and their potential to contribute to world peace by influencing peace and security policies (Reardon 1993).

Beyond the 1970s, women's role in peacebuilding gained growing legitimacy through popular activism, instrumental rights-based frameworks and relevant scholarship. One example was the 1979 UN Convention on the Elimination of All forms of Discrimination against Women (CEDAW), followed by the Optional Protocol of 1999, which committed signatory states to protect women's rights, especially in decision-making processes. In addition, the Beijing Declaration and Platform for Action of 1995 calls attention to the importance of women's right to participate in decision-making and peace programmes. Similarly, the UNSCR 1325 of 2000, underpinned by the decisions of the UN Commission on the Status of Women (CSW) in 2004, underscores the centrality of gender mainstreaming and women's practical role in sustaining peace and security in all the phases and ambits of peacebuilding. Article 10(2)(b) of the 2003 Protocol of the African Charter on the Rights of Women in Africa includes provisions for states to put in place all measures necessary for strengthening the participation of women in the areas of conflict prevention, conflict management and conflict resolution at all levels of society, from the local to the international. Similarly, UNSCR 2122 of 2013 puts forth precise recommendations on approaches to support and strengthen women's participation and the works of women's organisations in areas of peace and security, and underscores the importance of collaborative mechanisms for sustainable peacebuilding.

Furthermore, scholarly perspectives on this discourse affirm that participating in peace and reconstruction processes presents women with the platform for convalescence following their human security impairment as a result of their experiences and society's gender discriminatory practices (McKay 2004). Others contend that women as agents of change possess unique and strategic abilities to resolve conflicts non-violently, rally actors from across all sectors of society, and influence warring parties to work on overcoming their divisions for the greater good of peace (Ernest 1997). Purportedly, and in consonance with the views of essentialist feminists, Johan Galtung—recognised as the father and proponent of Positive and Negative Peace—also posited that women's overall peacebuilding ability derives from their instinctive peace-loving nature (Galtung 1996: 40). Furthermore, an ever-present and shared urge has been the easy affiliation of women with reconciliation and peacebuilding.

However, these assertions are problematic and stereotypical because not all women possess that instinctive capacity to build peace (Weber 2006). According to Coulter, Persson and Utas (2008), Cohen (2006), and Specht (2006), women also take up arms during conflicts and commit vicious acts of violence, as in the case of the conflicts in Uganda, Sudan, Rwanda and Liberia. Often, this form of activism by women in response to conflict is seen as an exception to the generic essentialising perception of political agency and engagement accessible to women (Kaufman and Williams 2013). On the one hand, the acts of violence as a response mechanism to conflict can be empowering for some women. On the other hand, it conveys the understanding that not all forms of women's political activism, especially in times of conflicts, is perceptibly feminist. Conclusions have arisen from these different thoughts that women ostensibly epitomise that indispensable element needed to advance and maintain peace (Isike and Okeke-Uzodike 2010). Women, just like all other citizens of the world, are endowed with inalienable, civic and fundamental human rights as outlined in the Universal Declaration of Human Rights. These rights normally should constitute the primary basis for recognition, inclusion and participation of women in peace, security, and development agendas.

Within these scholarly perspectives, the question of how women coordinate their roles and plan activities also constitutes an important factor in appraising this current discourse. In Africa, as in most parts of the world, the general operationalisation of women's peacebuilding efforts is effected through the aegis of civil society organisations (CSOs). Notably, CSOs operating as NGOs or women's organisations and groups have over the past 20 years and more developed as influential driving forces in peace and security discourses across the globe (Ekiyor 2008). Scholars assert that these women's organisations serve as a platform for women's activism and a foundation for advancing their participation in decision-making processes. Most importantly, their goals, basic and strategic, are appropriately and collectively defined through women's organisations and initiatives (Molyneux 1985).

As a consequence of having oriented and defined strategic goals, women are ideally positioned to engage in long-term processes focusing on their and their communities' welfare, human rights, justice, anti-poverty strategies and socio-economic empowerment (Massaquoi 2007). In this context of women

26   *Lukong Stella Shulika et al.*

organising, therefore, a common underlying factor articulated by scholars is that their efforts are particularly noticeable at the level of grass-roots initiatives, which, though often excluded or marginalised in practical decision-making processes, still remain at the forefront of local peacebuilding activities (McKay and Mazurana 2001). The motivation for these women's initiatives for peace and security resonates with their interests and understanding that building peace entails creating sustainable environments for their families, safeguarding a future for their children, and addressing socio-economic challenges of poverty and deprivation that confront them and their communities (McKay and Mazurana 2001).

Further insight on the women and peacebuilding debate explores literature on the complex reality of their peacebuilding roles. As argued by some scholars, the challenges that confront women in their roles as peacebuilders emanate from the failure of post-conflict peacebuilding policies to equally address the socio-economic injustices faced by women in pre- to post-conflict conditions (True 2013). This reality not only inhibits women's active involvement in the field, but is noted to also increase institutional and structural gender disparities between men and women, especially in the area of security engagements. What's more, security has traditionally been perceived as a male-dominated undertaking, and this continues to be the case. After all, several policy domains, institutions and structures tend to treat women as a homogenous group, thus overlooking the diversity of their interests, approaches and roles in the processes of post-conflict recovery (Domingo et al. 2013).

Given this, some scholarly approaches have also noted the tendency to present the case of women's peacebuilding roles as a whole, defining their activities within specific confines of building social cohesion, ensuring economic revitalisation and political legality, as stated by a United Nations report (2010). In addition to this, there are assertions that from 1990 to 2010, of those involved in the facilitation of peace processes worldwide, only 8% were women (Butler, Mader and Kean 2010). Moreover, following the 10-year review of UNSCR 1325, the United Nations Development Fund for Women (UNIFEM) acknowledged and noted that women's participation and representation in negotiating major peace processes remained remarkably minimal. Given these challenges, uncertainty remains over how and whether women's interests are addressed when discussing peace processes, and whether widespread consensus about their importance in decision making, as ratified through policy instruments, has in practice created a wider space for their inclusiveness.

Advancing from these scholarly views, Africa provides a good case in point for this debate, analyses and perspectives on women's roles in fulfilling peace and security objectives. In actuality, several African women's peace narratives chronicle that women's peace and security experiences in Africa, progressively undertaken under the aegis of women's organisations and projects, have been and remain prominent in the areas of advocacy, capacity building and community mobilisation for reconciliation, justice and peace projects (Ernest 1997).

Focusing on African experiences, therefore, allows for considerations of "best practices" (informative case studies), as well as the challenges women face in participating and shaping peace and security policies. Sourcing methods that enhance women's roles as a precondition for sustainable peace in the continent is critical. Realising this necessitates strategies for actions that are inclusive and supportive of women's integration and contributions in matters of peace and security, and draws attention to the need for the processes to be ingrained in fostering their peacebuilding efforts locally, and especially at the grass-roots levels.

Women in peacebuilding: Experiences from Africa

There is no gainsaying that women are proactive exponents of peace and security in Africa. Through relentless efforts, African women are demonstrating their ability to improve the prospects for sustainable peace by providing those living in conflict areas with positive female role models; facilitating good relations between traumatised civilians and security services; giving authority a female face; offering an alternative perspective on conflict resolution; building momentum to reduce poverty and enhance development; and mobilising support for increased women's representation in decision-making processes (Norville 2011). Drawing from Liberian and Rwandan experiences, this section expands on the ways women have been influencing Africa's peacebuilding processes. These countries, just like many others on the African continent, present cases where the surge of conflicts meant that women were not only overburdened with a disproportionate share of protecting and supporting families but also suffered the brunt of the abuse that came with those civil wars. Despite the odds stacked against them, women in these countries demonstrated enduring resilience and determined resolve to cope with the seemingly insurmountable challenges of war, and in the aftermath embarked with enthusiasm on the path to (re)building new lives and preventing the reoccurrence of conflicts.

The Liberian experience

Liberia is a nation-state that suffered a long history of civil war, lasting 14 years, which eventually ended in 2003, owing greatly to the influential role of women. The Liberian Women's Initiative (LWI) and Women of Liberia Mass Action for Peace Movement played leading roles in the negotiation and peace process. Mobilising for the purpose of ensuring effective ceasefire processes that would bring an end to the conflict and revitalise peace for all, exposed Liberian women to positions of political influence as well as participation in decision making. As such, Liberian women under the auspices of women's organisations, women-led initiatives and institutions have made significant strides at various levels of the country's peacebuilding and reconstruction initiatives, in addition to the disarmament, demobilisation and reintegration (DDR) and electoral processes (Shilue and Fagen 2014). For example, Women in Peacebuilding

28   *Lukong Stella Shulika et al.*

Network (WIPNET), through its advocacy, conflict/violence management, civic education, empowerment and peace training campaigns, has remained a key participant in the advancement of these post-conflict recovery strategies (PeaceWomen Project 2006).

Likewise, civil society organisations, such as the Women NGOs Secretariat of Liberia (WONGOSOL), have been strategically involved in the Truth and Reconciliation Commission (TRC), the Independent National Human Rights Commission (INHRC), and other innovative peacebuilding activities in the arena of rule of law and transitional justice in Liberia (Von Gienanth and Jaye 2007). At the grass-roots level, the contributions of women in peacebuilding continue to be promoted and realised through advocacy programmes organised by groups like the Sinoe Women Peace Network (SWPN) in Liberia. By way of popular activism, SWPN has been at the forefront of increasing grass-roots women's participation in decision making through campaigns and rallies that demand better service delivery at the local and grass-roots level (Fründt et al. 2012). This has also been realised through civic education, peace training programmes, and problem-solving workshops that discuss challenges confronting women, such as women's inheritance and gender-based violence, among others, and strategies for moving forward (Fründt et al. 2012).

Against the background of women's vital roles and commitment to peace, the Liberian government in support thereof ratified a number of African Union, Economic Community of West African States and UN conventions on women's rights and gender equality (Shulika 2016). In same vein, the government adopted legal policies to amend the widow inheritance customary convention; safeguard the rights of women to own property and land under state and customary regulations; and increase incarceration terms for rape offenders (Caesar et al. 2010). In addition, the United Nations Mission in Liberia (UNMIL) Office of the Senior Gender Adviser also instituted a framework for gender mainstreaming in Liberia's DDR programme, as did the government in its policies and agendas. Through collaborative efforts, both UNMIL and the Ministry of Gender and Development have been and remain prominent in promoting women's active participation and representation in democratic processes and rule of law (Shulika 2016). Consistent with women's peacebuilding efforts, the government also adopted a National Action Plan (NAP) for implementing UNSCR 1325 in 2009, and instituted the 1325 (Women, Peace and Security) bureau within the Ministry of Gender and Development.

It is worth noting that the above changes are major historic achievements of women's organising and activism in Liberia. These accomplishments are also greatly signified by women's massive support in the holding of national votes that resulted in the 2005 election and 2011 re-election of the first female African head of state, President Ellen Johnson Sirleaf. In her person as a leader, a woman, and "mother of the nation," Ellen Johnson Sirleaf continued to promote women's rights, participation and gender equality, as was evident under her regime in that, among others, 26% of ministries, agencies and corporations were headed by women; 44% of the Truth and Reconciliation Committee members were women; and women held ambassadorial positions as foreign relations and international organisation representatives worldwide (Government of Liberia 2014). It is in these contexts of women's leadership and participation in Liberia that Ellen Johnson Sirleaf and Leymah Gbowee (founder of WIPNET) were honoured in 2011 with the Nobel Peace Prize for their human rights and peace activism roles.

Nevertheless, the impetus of sustainable peace in Liberia remains subject to a number of complexities, as does women's resolve for peace and security. Conventional perceptions of patriarchy and other cultural aspects that place men at the higher echelons of society, as strong and able compared to women, continue to instigate exclusionary practices against women in their efforts for peace. Liberian women are still unequally represented and marginalised in democratic governance and decision-making processes of the state. As of 2009 to 2011, women accounted for just 14% of the national legislature, 0.8% of government departments and agencies, and 10.3% of those in government ministries (Cole 2011). Also, while women organising at the grass-roots level (like SWPN and WIPNET) are making significant strides in their peace efforts, they remain challenged by their limited or lack of access to resources; constraints due to domestic duties; lack of employment and sufficient education and training to engage in economic or income generating activities; and lack of support and collaboration from and between national and grass-roots women's organisations and groupings (Cardona et al. 2012). Overall, these challenges impeding women's efforts are further heightened by the prevalence of gender-based violence against young girls and women, and society's superficial acceptance of the reality that women, like every other citizen, possess equal rights that should be respected and reinforced (Shulika 2016).

The Rwandan experience

If anything, the 1994 Rwanda genocide and conflict represented the most unpleasant kind of crime against humanity that not only had devastating effects on its citizenry but also, in particular, left many women and girls with the scars of rape and widowhood. However, Rwandan women still played a vital role in influencing an end to the conflict by convincing both their husbands and children to give up their arms for peace (Balikungeri and Ingabire 2010). In the post-conflict era, these women have risen above the pains of conflict and taken progressive steps in leading and contributing to the country's peacebuilding, reconciliation and development initiatives. Through networks such as Unity Club, Forum of Rwandan Women Parliamentarians, and Pro-Femmes Twese Hamwe, Rwandan women and women in positions of political leadership have continued to mastermind reconciliation, confidence building and peace empowerment projects that also enlist grass-roots women to share in decision making (Mutamba and Izabiliza 2005). Noteworthy in the Rwandan case is the fact that women's growing activism and involvement in post-conflict processes not only resulted in the government's commitment and support for women's

30 *Lukong Stella Shulika et al.*

political leadership roles but also secured them an overwhelming 56.3% and 34.6% representation in the lower and upper houses of parliament, respectively, in 2010 (Cole 2011). As per the recent ranking, Rwanda continues to lead the world's rankings in terms of representation of women in parliament, which now stands at 61.3% in the lower house and 38.5% in the upper house (Inter-Parliamentary Union 2019).

Promoting gender equality and women's empowerment countrywide has been and remains one of the strategies for sustainable political, economic and social development invested in by the government of Rwanda. Evidently, the government, mindful of the challenges that Rwandan women (especially genocide survivors, widows and spouses of detainees serving sentences for the 1994 genocide crimes against humanity) faced in the aftermath of the conflict, set in place a fund to assist them through the process of social and economic transformation (Balikungeri and Ingabire 2010). Likewise, the government conceived a traditional grass-roots-based restorative and participatory court system – the gacaca – of which women made up 35% of the panel of people with honour enough to be designated to judge the 1994 genocide offences and acts committed against humanity (East African Community Secretariat 2009). In the same manner, the government of Rwanda also endorsed and implemented several international as well as regional agreements that underscore the importance of gender mainstreaming and the operationalisation of gender-inclusive planning in all areas of decision making of the state as central to attaining sustainable development goals. These included, among others, the Beijing Platform for Action, CEDAW, the Millennium Development Goals, UNSCR 1325, the Universal Declaration of Human Rights of 10 December 1948, the New Partnership for Africa's Development, Southern African Development Community, and Common Market for Eastern and Southern Africa (East African Community Secretariat 2009).

Within this framework of commitment to enhance and sustain women's participation and gender equality in society, the Rwandan government also enacted laws to curb customs and systems that promoted the marginalisation of women's human and civic rights in relation to land and property ownership, and laws to punish rape and sexual offences as crimes against humanity (Balikungeri and Ingabire 2010). It also established the Ministry of Gender and Family Promotion to build the capacity of women, manage and oversee the execution of government gender policies, empower families and communities to cooperate in working towards ensuring sustainable development and building of secured societies (Balikungeri and Ingabire 2010), and so on. Rwanda's Constitution also provisions for gender inclusiveness in all spheres of national leadership, such that a National Gender Policy and the country's Vision 2020 roadmap for imminent sustainable development underscored the importance of gender integration and women's participation in decision making in development agendas.

While the Rwandan experience of women's roles in peacebuilding and support thereof from the government and institutions is evidence of women influencing current and future peace and security goals, significant challenges still stand to hinder their efforts. These are anchored on the fact that society, especially at the grass-roots level, still holds stereotypical views about women's abilities to actively drive and influence peace and reconciliation processes; thus there is a lack of support and motivation from society, which in most part stems from women's male counterparts (Mutamba and Izabiliza 2005). Also, the prevalence of rape and sexual violence against women and girls, and the problems of poverty and lack of food or sustenance means for families, particularly in the rural areas, have been identified as some of the factors thwarting women's peacebuilding efforts in Rwanda (Mutamba and Izabiliza 2005). These challenges have been attributed to the fact that women are subject to limited educational opportunities, and educational curricula in learning institutions have failed or not adequately incorporated gender and peace education, which can play an important role in transforming societies to embrace the culture of peace and prevent the recurrence of conflict.

Conclusion

The question, "how do we address the challenges impeding women's peacebuilding efforts and reinforce their participation towards a peaceful and secure Africa?" forms the basis of this conclusion. Basically, the understanding derived from examining the experiences of women's peacebuilding roles in Liberia and Rwanda is that African women have the potential not only to transform the political and socio-economic landscape of conflict and post-conflict societies, but also to advance sustainable peace and development goals in the continent. Both states and societies have been acknowledging the importance of women's roles as imperative to preventing conflicts from recurring, especially as women actively seek to prioritise, direct, and coordinate policy making at all levels of society. Regardless of this, women's participation, as indicated above, remains constrained by a number of factors. Putting these complexities side by side with the vision of "The Africa We Want" in Agenda 2063 (African Union Commission 2015) calls for action to create wider space for women's engagement and support in Africa's peace and security towards a realisation of this aspiration.

Unquestionably, women's involvement in peace and security, and advancing their roles, requires more than adopting policies. It entails empowerment, viable and accountable political, economic and social structures, and institutions that can support women's efforts without discrimination or limitations. The successful and effective realisation of women's efforts towards a peaceful and secure Africa must, therefore, be guided and driven by the context of the greater freedoms and respect of human and civil rights, solidarity, tolerance, justice and equality under which societies should function. While it is true that Africa, just like other regions in the world, is host to many patriarchal societies and cultures that are discriminatory towards women's position and role in society, transforming them and promoting equality and participation

32 *Lukong Stella Shulika et al.*

in decision-making processes remains imperative to attaining sustainable peace and development.

Working towards "a peaceful and secure Africa" where development is people-driven, and likewise reliant on the "potential of women and youth" as premised in Agenda 2063, demands that the African Union, its partner organisations, governments and peoples establish transparent and accountable systems and networks of institutions with which to collaborate on long-term peace, security and development programmes. These should include engaging societies in peace education, capacity building and advocacy that seeks to empower and enhance awareness, and support, not only for women's roles as equal partners and contributors to the processes, but also society's role in advancing their socio-political, economic and development welfare. Operationalising these processes also entails joint efforts of governments and civil society to work with communities to embrace the culture of peace and non-violence, both nationally and locally, especially at the grass-roots level where women activism is more prominent. There is also the need for governments to institutionalise the capacity and involvement of grass-roots women's initiatives to contribute to peace and security processes, given their resourcefulness in the field at local community levels in reconciliation, stabilisation, social and economic rehabilitation processes.

References

African Union Commission. 2015. *African Agenda 2013: "The Africa We Want."* Addis Ababa, Ethiopia: AU Commission. Available at: https://au.int/sites/default/files/documents/36204-docagenda2063_popular_version_en. pdf

Alaga, E. 2010. *Challenges for Women In Peacebuilding in West Africa.* Policy Brief, No. 18. Africa Institute of South Africa.

Balikungeri, M., and Ingabire, I. 2010. *Security Council Resolution 1325: Civil Society Monitoring Report.* A Project of the Global Network of Women Peacebuilders.

Butler, M., Mader, K., and Kean, R. 2010. *Women, Peace, and Security Handbook: Compilation and Analysis of United Nations Security Council Resolution Language 2000–2010.* Geneva, Switzerland: Women's International League for Peace and Freedom.

Caesar, R. G., Garlo, C. K., Nagarajan, C., and Schoofs, S. 2010. *Implementing Resolution 1325 in Liberia: Reflections of Women's Associations.* Initiative for Peacebuilding Gender Cluster.

Cardona, I., Justino, P., Mitchell, B., and Müller, C. 2012. *From the Ground up: Women's Roles in Local Peacebuilding in Afghanistan, Liberia, Nepal, Pakistan and Sierra Leone.* University of Sussex, UK: Institute of Development Studies.

CARE International. 2010. *From Resolution to Reality: Lessons Learned from Afghanistan, Nepal and Uganda on Women's Participation in Peacebuilding and Post-Conflict Governance.* Available at: www.carefrance.org/images/CARE-FROM_RESOLUTION_TO_REALITY1.pdf

Cohen, S. 2006. "Integrating diplomacy and development in building civil society in post-conflict environment: From the micro to the macro," *Occasional Paper Series,* Issue 1, November. Woodrow Wilson International Centre for Scholars.

Women influencing peace and security   33

Cole, S. 2011. *Increasing Women's Political Participation in Liberia: Challenges and Potential Lessons from India, Rwanda and South Africa.* International Foundation for Electoral Systems.

Coulter, C., Persson, M., and Utas, M. 2008. *Young Female Fighters in African Wars, Conflict and its Consequences.* Uppsala, Sweden: Nordic Africa Institute.

Domingo, P., Holmes, R., Menocal, A. R., Jones, N., Bhuvanendra, D., and Wood, J. 2013. *Assessment of the Evidence of Links between Gender Equality, Peacebuilding and Statebuilding: Literature Review.* Overseas Development Institute Report.

East African Community Secretariat. 2009. *Gender and Community Development Analysis in Rwanda.* Available at: http://cleancookstoves.org/resources_files/gender-and-community.pdf

Ekiyor, T. 2008. "The role of civil society in conflict prevention: West African experiences." United Nations Institute for Disarmament Research, Disarmament Forum, No. 4, pp. 27–34.

Ernest, A. (Ed.), 1997. *Documented Best Practices in Peacebuilding and Non-violent Conflict Resolution.* Addis Ababa Workshop. Geneva, Switzerland: UNHCR, UNESCO, UNDP, UNFPA, UNICEF and UNIFEM.

Fründt, S., Hayes, C., Notz, S., and Seifert, I. 2012. *Making Women's Voices Heard: A Handbook for Training Participants of the Project for Political Participation of Women.* Cologne, Germany: Medica Mondiale.

Galtung, J. 1996. *Peace by Peaceful Means: Peace and Conflict, Development and Civilization.* Oslo, Norway: International Peace Research Institute.

Government of Liberia. 2014. *National Review Report on Beijing+20.* Available at: www.unwomen.org/~/media/headquarters/attachments/sections/csw/59/national_reviews/liberia_review_beijing20.ashx

Hamre, J. J., and Sullivan, G. R. 2002. "Toward post conflict reconstruction," *The Washington Quarterly,* 25(4), pp. 85–96, 89.

Human Security Baseline Assessment. 2012. *Women and Armed Violence in South Sudan.* Available at: www.smallarmssurveysudan.org/fileadmin/docs/facts-figures/south-sudan/womens -security/HSBA-women-and-armed-conflict.pdf

Inter-Parliamentary Union. 2019. *Women in National Parliaments: World Classification,* 1 February. Available at: http://archive.ipu.org/wmn-e/classif.htm.

Isike, C. A., and Okeke-Uzodike, N. 2010. "Moral imagination, Ubuntu and African women: Towards feminizing politics and peacebuilding in KwaZulu-Natal (South Africa)," *Gandhi Marg,* 31(4), pp. 679–709.

Kaufman, J. P., and Williams, K. P. 2013. *Women at War, Women Building Peace: Challenging Gender Norms.* London, UK: Kumarian Press.

Lederach, J. P. 1997. *Building Peace: Sustainable Reconciliation in Divided Societies.* Washington, DC: United States Institute of Peace Press.

Massaquoi, W. N. 2007. *Women and Post-Conflict Development: A Case Study of Liberia.* Cambridge, MA: Massachusetts Institute of Technology, Department of Urban Studies and Planning.

McCarthy, M. K. 2011. "Women's participation in peacebuilding: A missing piece of the puzzle?" CUREJ: *College Undergraduate Research Electronic Journal.* Philadelphia, PA: University of Pennsylvania. Available at: http://repository.upenn.edu/curej/132

McKay, S. 2004. *Women, Human Security, and Peacebuilding: A Feminist Analysis.* IPSHU English Research Report Series, No. 19.

34 Lukong Stella Shulika et al.

McKay, S., and Mazurana, D. 2001. "Gendering peacebuilding." In Christie, D. J., Wagner, R.V., and Winter, D.A. (Eds.) *Peace, Conflict, and Violence: Peace Psychology for the 21st Century*. Englewood Cliffs, NJ: Prentice Hall.

Molyneux, M. 1985. "Mobilization without emancipation? Women's interests, the state and revolution in Nicaragua," *Feminist Studies*, 11(2), pp. 227–254.

Mpoumou, D. 2004. "Women's participation in peace negotiations: Discourse in the Democratic Republic of the Congo." In Ballington, J. (Ed.) *The Implementation of Quotas: African Experiences*. Stockholm: International IDEA.

Mutamba, J., and Izabiliza, J. 2005. *The Role of Women in Reconciliation and Peacebuilding in Rwanda: Ten Years after Genocide 1994–2004 – Contributions, Challenges and Way Forward*. Kigali, Rwanda: The National Unity and Reconciliation Commission.

Norville, V. 2011. *The Role of Women in Global Security*. Special Report. Washington, DC: United States Institute of Peace.

Pankhurst, D., and Anderlini, S. N. 1998. *Mainstreaming Gender in Peacebuilding: A Framework for Action – From the Village Council to the Negotiating Table*. London: International Alert.

PeaceWomen Project. 2006. *Liberia Elects Africa's First Woman President: What Does That Mean for the Women?* Available at: www.peacewomen.org/portal_resources _ resource.php?id=731

Puechguirbal, N. 2005. "Gender and peacebuilding in Africa: Analysis of some structural obstacles." In Rodríguez, D., and Natukunda-Togboa, E. (Eds.) *Gender and Peacebuilding in Africa*. Ciudad Colón, Costa Rica: University for Peace.

Reardon, B.A. 1993. *Women and Peace: Feminist Visions of Global Security*. New York: State University of New York Press.

Rehn, E., and Sirleaf, E. J. 2002. *Women, War and Peace: The Independent Experts' Assessment on the Impact of Armed Conflict on Women and Women's Role in Peacebuilding*. New York: UNIFEM.

Schirch, L. 2008. "Strategic peacebuilding: State of the field," *Peace Prints: South Asian Journal of Peacebuilding*, 1(1), pp. 1–17.

Sharoni, S. 1994. Toward feminist theorizing in conflict resolution. Available at: web. pdx.edu/~ingham/ syllabi/Perspectives/SharoniFemCR.doc

Shilue, J. S., and Fagen, P. 2014. *Liberia: Links between Peacebuilding, Conflict Prevention and Durable Solutions to Displacement*. Washington DC: Brookings Institution.

Shulika, L. S. 2016. "Women and peacebuilding: From historical to contemporary African perspectives," *Ubuntu: Journal of Conflict and Social Transformation*, 5(1), pp. 7–31.

Specht, I. 2006. *Red Shoes: Experiences of Girl Combatants in Liberia*. Geneva, Switzerland: ILO Office.

True, J. 2013. *Women, Peace and Security in Post-Conflict and Peacebuilding Contexts*. Policy Brief. Oslo, Norway: The Norwegian Peacebuilding Resource Centre (NOREF).

United Nations. 2010. *Report of the Secretary-General on Women's Participation in Peacebuilding*. Available at www.un.org/ga/search/view_doc.asp? symbol=A/65/354

Von Gienanth, T., and Jaye, T. 2007. *Post-Conflict Peacebuilding in Liberia: Much Remains to Be Done*. Report of the Third Annual KAIPTC/ZIF Seminar, Accra, Ghana, 1–3 November.

Weber, A. 2006. "Feminist peace and conflict theory." In *Routledge Encyclopaedia on Peace and Conflict Theory*. Available at: www.uibk.ac.at/peacestudies/downloads/ peacelibrary/feministpeace.pdf

Wibben, A. T. R. 2003. "Feminist international relations: Old debates and new directions," *The Brown Journal of World Affairs*, X(2), pp. 97–114.

Women for Women International. 2010. *Gender, Conflict and the Millennium Development Goals*. London, UK: Women for Women International.

Woroniuk, B. 2001. *Gender Equality and Peacebuilding: An Operational Framework.* Gatineau, Canada: Canadian International Development Agency (CIDA).

3 Women's participation in peacebuilding in Africa

Esther Tawiah

Background

The unanimous adoption of the United Nations Security Council (UNSC) Resolution 1325 in October 2000 brought about international, regional and national recognition of the significant roles played by women with regards to issues of security, war, conflict prevention, resolution, management and reconstruction. However, the role played by women with respect to peacebuilding and conflict resolution is still mainly marginal in formal peace processes and the political establishments put in place after civil wars. Women are largely relegated to the background and are marginalised in the peace and security processes. Women peace activists are also faced with challenges at different levels from the international community, the national political settings and the highly patriarchal nature of society. The highly patriarchal nature of African society makes issues of security, war, conflict prevention and resolution management, and reconstruction highly gendered. There is an urgent need to fully enrol women in the formal space of peacebuilding and conflict resolutions. Even though Africa has made great strides with regards to the Women, Peace and Security agenda, at continental and regional levels, there is more room for improvement in relation to women's participation in peacebuilding processes.

List of abbreviations

AU: African Union
CEDAW: Convention on the Elimination of all forms of Discrimination Against Women
CRF: Continental Result Framework
GBV: Gender-based violence
HIV and AIDS: Human immunodeficiency virus and acquired immunodeficiency syndrome
NAP: National Action Plan
NGO: Non- governmental organisation
PCRD: Post-Conflict Reconstruction and Development framework
RAP: Regional Action Plan

RECs: Regional economic communities
STIs: Sexually transmitted infections
UN: United Nations
UNSCR: United Nations Security Council Resolution
WPS: Women, Peace and Security
WSRs: Women's Situation Rooms

Context and setting

The post-Cold War period saw an increase in protracted intra-state wars, along with numerous civil conflicts and other forms of violence and insecurity on the African continent. These wars have had, and still have, grave effects on civilians, particularly women and children. Women are victims of awful atrocities and injustices during conflict. Women and men have different experiences during conflicts. Women hardly possess the same rights, resources and authority over their setting in comparison to men. Also, their domestic and caregiving tasks largely limit their ability and mobility to protect themselves during wars. During conflicts, women experience high levels of violence, sexual abuse, kidnapping, slavery, forced pregnancy, while some are deliberately infected with sexually transmitted infections (STIs) such as HIV and AIDS and the bodies of others used as tools for sending messages to supposed adversaries (United Nations Development Fund for Women 2002).

These violent conflicts within both the global and African spaces have raised the awareness of women on the need to take the initiative. This has brought about an increasing global appreciation of the important roles that women can, and do, play in conflict resolution and the peacebuilding processes. Drawing on lessons from Liberia, Ivory Coast, Sierra Leone and Guinea Bissau, among others, it is clear that sustainable peace can only be attained with the full inclusion and participation of women at all levels of society. Women bring about a different and gendered view to peacemaking and peacebuilding, resulting in a transformation at the structural and practical level (Alaga 2010). Women's full participation in peacebuilding processes bridges indomitable divides and also integrates actors from the space of civil society (since women are chief players in the NGO space) and families, instead of the battlefield, with the aim of creating a lasting and sustainable peace (McCarthy 2011). This shows that there exists a connection between gender, peace and security, and development.

Women peace activists are also faced with challenges at different levels, from the international community, the national political setting and the highly patriarchal nature of society. Other challenges arise from women's low confidence levels and their lack of skills, capacity and resources. Women's efforts in peacebuilding have not been institutionalised, which explains why they have had hardly any influence on nationwide and international strategies and instruments regarding peace and war; their stories, knowledge, concepts and experiences remain relegated and all but invisible. In this regard, the highly patriarchal nature of African society makes issues of security, war, conflict

38 *Esther Tawiah*

prevention and resolution, management, and reconstruction highly gendered. These roles are regarded and treated as the preserve of men and, in turn, they are associated with gender disparities and inequalities that perpetuate violence against women (Alaga 2010).

Despite the progress made by women in peacemaking and peacebuilding, women are largely marginalised in the peace and security processes, mainly at the official and technical levels where their roles tend to be invisible. This has, however, been acknowledged internationally. The growing efforts by women and advocacy groups to eliminate the violence faced by women in conflicts, promote women's participation in the peacebuilding processes, and deal with gender-based violence, among other issues, have resulted in substantive legal frameworks and policies at the global, regional and national levels. With regards to peace and security, the United Nations Security Council Resolutions (UNSCRs) 1325 and 1820, which build on several other interventions – such as the United Nations Convention on the Elimination of all forms of Discrimination Against Women (CEDAW), the Beijing Declaration and Platform for Action, and the Windhoek Declaration – signified a great milestone for women's representation and participation in peace and security activities (Institute for Security Studies 2008). However, the role played by women in issues of security, war, conflict prevention and resolution, management, and conflict reconstruction is still marginal, particularly in formal peace processes and the political establishments put in place after civil wars.

The United Nations Security Council Resolution 1325

The international community affirmed and recognised the significance of women's participation in issues of security, war, conflict prevention and resolution, management, reconstruction and in creating the conditions for peace on 31 October 2000 through the adoption of United Nations Security Council Resolution 1325. UNSCR 1325 affirms the significance of women in peacebuilding and calls on its member states to "to ensure increased representation of women at all decision-making levels in national, regional and international institutions and mechanisms for the prevention, management and resolution of conflict."[1] It also calls on all actors involved

> when negotiating and implementing peace agreements, to adopt a gender perspective, including, inter alia: the special needs of women and girls during repatriation and resettlement and for rehabilitation, reintegration and post-conflict reconstruction; measures that support local women's peace initiatives and indigenous processes for conflict resolution, and that involve women in all of the implementation mechanisms of the peace agreements.[2]

The resolution further mandates the UN to solicit and take into consideration views on gender issues in order to increase the role of women in the peacebuilding processes among others. However, the role played by women in peacebuilding processes is still minimal. UN Women also argue that the percentage of women in peace talks has stagnated at single digits since the passage of the resolution. This reflects a devastating impact on the lives of women (UN Women 2012).

Also, the UNSC in its attempt to prevent sexual violence in conflict, adopted Resolution 2467 on Women, Peace and Security (WPS) on the 23 April 2019. The resolution emphasises accountability for acts of sexual violence in conflict situations and also includes, among others, measures on a survivor-centred approach to prevent and respond to acts of sexual violence during conflicts.[3] UNSCR 1325 and its subsequent resolutions have provided member states and regional organisations with a normative framework for driving the agenda, action and advocacy on Women, Peace and Security.

The Women, Peace and Security agenda in Africa

The African Union's Agenda 2063 is geared towards achieving an integrated, people-centred, united, peaceful, and prosperous Africa. Apart from silencing the guns, the AU's Agenda 2063 also seeks to create positive peace throughout the continent. However, this goal of the AU can only be achieved holistically if women, who constitute more than half of Africa's population, are secured to be a part of peace-related activities on the continent. The AU has a long way to go in order to achieve full women's inclusion in peace processes. Women in the sub-region are faced with sexual and gender-based violence, poor representation in leadership, high rates of economic marginalisation and poor access to justice, among other things. These issues faced by women in the sub-region continually challenge the AU's realisation of its goal. This calls for a lot of work to be done by the regional organisation to fast-track the implementation of its obligations, which will change the state of affairs of women in the region in the long run.

The AU's Protocol to the African Charter on Human and People's Rights on the Rights of Women in Africa, and its Post-Conflict Reconstruction and Development framework (PCRD) are major regional instruments which seek to give effect to the participation of women in peacebuilding (Institute for Security Studies 2008). These instruments have helped in the promotion and growth of women's organisations and peacebuilding initiatives. In spite of progress made in creating a conducive legal environment for the participation of women in peacebuilding, women are still largely relegated in contemporary peace processes.

The regional economic communities (RECs) of the African continent have also made great strides with regards to normative frameworks around Women, Peace and Security. These RECs – such as the Economic Community of West African States (ECOWAS), Economic Community of Central African States (ECCAS), Common Market for Eastern and Southern Africa (COMESA), East African Community (EAC), Intergovernmental Authority for Development

40   *Esther Tawiah*

(IGAD), Southern Africa Development Community (SADC), and the Great Lakes – have several policy and legislative instruments subsequent to Resolution 1325. Nevertheless, there also exist "regional particularities" which focus on different sectors across the continent. For example, among other things, the Great Lakes focuses on the prevention of sexual and gender-based violence; IGAD and SADC on the other hand have focused on participation in decision making; and COMESA focuses on redressing gender inequalities. Some regions have also focused mainly on policy frameworks.[4]

United Nations Security Council Resolution 1325 signifies a global initiative on Women, Peace and Security which was given birth by Africa. The AU and the African continent have taken a large step to fully embed UNSCR 1325 in their continental, regional and national legal and policy instruments and outlined programs. In order to fully address the issues of African women with regards to peace and security, the AU has provided for an annual reporting scheme on the empowerment of women through the solemn Declaration on Gender Equality in the continent.

The AU's acknowledgement of the significance of women's participation on issues of peace and security in the region led to the creation of a Women, Peace and Security Envoy, which is a part of the comprehensive approach to prevent, mediate and resolve conflicts in Africa. The union's framework and the envoy show their continuous commitment to implement the Women, Peace and Security agenda in Africa. The AU's development and adoption of the Continental Result Framework (CRF) for monitoring and reporting on the implementation of the Women, Peace and Security agenda signifies a great landmark in advancing the domestication and implementation of the transformative goals of UNSRC 1325 in Africa.[5]

However, out of the 55 member states of the African Union, only 23 have adopted Resolution 1325 and developed their National Action Plans (NAPs). The West African sub-region is said to have the highest concentration of Resolution 1325 Action Plans, with 13 of its member states having NAPs. There is, therefore, the need to interrogate the relationship between the existence of Regional Action Plans (RAPs) and the adoption and implementation of NAPs in the same region and the outcomes and interactions between the two.[6]

Even though strategies and policies for implementing the peace and security agenda have been developed, the case is totally different with regards to actual implementation. The implementation process is one which is poor, slow and denies women the dividends of the transformative goals promised by the agenda. Several factors mitigate against the implementation of the policies and strategies. However, the major hindrance is lack of funds. Member states fail to allocate funds to the implementation of the policies and strategies developed. Member states tend to rely heavily on donors for funds to execute the implementation of their strategies and policies.[7] For instance, in Ghana, the Gender Centre for Empowering Development (GenCED) led the implementation of the "Women's Situation Room" following the development of the National Action Plan. However, this initiative was 100% funded by donors and other development partners. This is also the case in countries like Liberia, Sierra Leone, Uganda and Nigeria, which have also implemented the Women's Situation Room.

Again, within the peace and security space, several governments are not held accountable due to inadequate monitoring systems and lack of transparency within the space. Several states fail to monitor the processes, achievements and weaknesses with regard to the implementation.

The Continental Result Framework is a strategic tool aimed at bridging the gap between developing policies on Women, Peace and Security and implementing them. It provides member states a systemic and focused way of regularly tracking and reporting on implementation of the policies using common tools and parameters. The indicators are structured around four pillars on Women, Peace and Security, namely prevention, participation, protection, relief and recovery. With this, it makes it easy to identify the implementation gap as financing at all levels, institutional culture and leadership, which if well addressed will contribute to the actualisation of the Women, Peace and Security agenda objectives and goals.

Women's participation in peace processes in Africa (1992–2011)

Table 3.1 shows that women's participation in peace processes and negotiations in a variety of official roles is very low. Even though there has been advocacy that seeks to see an increase in women's participation at the table, research shows that, influence or timing of participation or not only presence is significant in changing the outcomes of the peace agreements and their provisions. Some important strategies noted for influence include the manner in which women mobilise outside the formal space and the availability of opportunities for women's participation. Mediators have a major role to play with regards to this. The UN has also developed guidelines for the inclusion of women in peace processes. Women's participation in even the UN and AU peace processes and operations shows that women are woefully under-represented with regards to the military and higher level participation. However, there has been an improvement in the reporting of sexual assaults. They have also set up units that provide protection to civilian victims of abuse.

The role of feminists, civil society organisations, and gender-based organisations in the Women, Peace and Security agenda

In the African context, women have played both an active and passive role with regards to the restoration of peace. Even though women have been relegated to the margins during peacemaking processes in their communities as a result of cultural stereotypes, political favouritism and hegemony, women have still played important and selfless roles in some aspects of conflict situations. Undoubtedly,

42   Esther Tawiah

Table 3.1 Women's participation in peace processes (1999–2011)[1]

Countries	Women signatories	Women lead mediators	Women witnesses	Women in negotiating teams
Sierra Leone (1999):	0%	0%	20%	0%
Burundi (2000): Arusha Peace and Reconciliation Agreement for Burundi	0%	0%	–	2%
Somalia (2002): Eldoret Declaration on Cessation of Hostilities	0%	0%	–	0%
Cote D'Ivoire (2003): Linas-Marcoussis Peace Accords	0%	0%	0%	–
Democratic Republic of Congo (2003): The Sun City Agreement	5%	0%	0%	12%
Liberia (2003): Accra Peace Agreement	0%	0%	17%	–
Sudan (2005): Naivasha Comprehensive Peace Agreement	0%	0%	9%	–
Darfur (2006): Darfur Peace Agreement, Abuja	0%	0%	7%	8%
Democratic Republic of Congo (2008): Goma – North Kivu, Acte D'Engagement	5%	20%	0%	–
Democratic Republic of Congo (2008): Goma – South Kivu, Acte D'Engagement	0%	20%	0%	–
Uganda (2008): Juba Peace Agreement	0%	0%	20%	9%
Kenya (2008): Nairobi Agreement on the Principles of Partnership of the Coalition Government	0%	33%	0%	25%
Central African Republic (2008): Accord de Paix Global	0%	0%	0%	–
Zimbabwe (2008): Agreement between ZANU-PF and MDC	0%	0%	0%	–
Somalia (2008): The Djibouti Agreement	0%	0%	0%	–
Central African Republic (2011): Accord de cessez-le-feu entre l'UFDR et le CPJP	0%	0%	0%	–

[1] UN Women (2012: 4–5).

not all women groups desire to be at the table if it involves negotiating with the warlords or tyrants who created the conflict; however, most peace activists opine that the presence of women in such processes is of essence.

With regards to Liberia, Leymah Roberta Gbowee, a women's rights and peace activist, and Nobel Peace Prize Laureate in 2011, has spoken publicly on several occasions regarding the issue of women in conflict situations. Also, the ex-Liberian president, Ellen Johnson Sirleaf, another peace activist, who shared the Nobel Peace Prize with Leymah Gbowee, has contributed immensely to the advocacy of women's participation in peace processes. She has outlined the important roles women can play in promoting peace and security in Africa.

African women teach their children the ethics of society and appropriate behaviour, and impress on their children the significance of values such as honesty, uprightness and the necessity to compromise. This indicates that women have always been active advocates of peace in their communities, which can be called "culture of peace." This natural role[8] played by women is not exclusive to an ethnic group; rather, it is a virtue which is generalised throughout the African continent. A similar trend of emphasis with regards to the notion of "mothers as peace builders" can be seen among women who have exhibited the zeal to train their young boys, who will be the adults of future society. They teach their young boys the rules of leadership, mainly norms relating to human relations and conflict resolution. Consequently, women remain a rich reservoir of knowledge to be tapped during peace agreements in times of conflict situations.

Women activists also promote a vision of peace that is far beyond the negotiating table. Women have contributed immensely to bringing an end to violence and dealing with the consequences of violence in several ways. This includes the provision of human relief, the creation and facilitation of the space for negotiations through advocacy, and the exertion of influence through cultural or social means. They have also spearheaded civil society and reconciliation activities. Though some women activists face several injustices in their attempt to protect women's rights, nonetheless, they have played significant roles in promoting women's rights and place in society. These activists have collectively rejected the patriarchal culture which symbolises women as daughters, wives or sisters entitled to protection rather than humans who can assert themselves as agents of change in relation to peace and security in their communities.

The grassroots roles played by women are visible in their communities. Women organise to bring an end to violence and build the necessary skills for peacebuilding and conflict reconstruction. These grassroots organisations boost possibly different but shared interests and aspirations of women. Thus, there is an opportunity to add diverse views and ideas. Women's grassroots organisations also help in building networks of solidarity combining feminism and anti-militarism. Despite the progress, it remains important to review the progress made in terms of the Women, Peace and Security agenda in Africa.

Status of the implementation of the Women, Peace and Security agenda in Africa

Most African countries have embraced Resolution 1325 and 16 African states now have relevant NAPs in place. The AU has also made great strides in integrating commitments to the idea of Women, Peace and Security into its own security architecture, crisis response, human rights and peacebuilding efforts. The AU also trains women as mediators, election observers and advisers in relation to gender.

Whilst some countries are performing poorly with regards to women's participation in peace processes, other countries, such as Liberia, Sierra Leone and Rwanda, have made great strides. In the case of these countries, women have played vital roles in issues of peace and security. In Senegal, the establishment of platforms like the Women's Situation Rooms for women for peaceful elections has contributed immensely to early warning and conflict prevention. Also, in the Great Lakes, Mano River, IGAD and ECOWAS regions, positive strides were made with regards to the adoption of Regional Action Plans geared towards the implementation of Resolution 1325.

Some centres, research institutions and training centres, such as the Pan Africa Centre for Gender and Development in Senegal and the Kofi Annan International Peacekeeping Training Centre's Women, Peace, and Security Institute in Ghana, have added Women, Peace and Security initiatives to their programming in areas of research, capacity building and documentation.

Also, the United Nations Office for West Africa and the Sahel (UNOWAS) established a platform called the "Women, Youth, Peace and Security Working Group" in West Africa and the Sahel in April 2009 with the goal of facilitating the implementation of the Resolution 1325, which emphasises the significance of women's active and equal participation in conflict prevention and resolution. The group is coordinated by UNOWAS and UN Women.[9] UNOWAS focuses on gender mainstreaming in conflict prevention, management and peacebuilding processes. For example, UNOWAS in collaboration with UN Women trains women mediators at the community, national and sub-regional levels. Thirty-two women mediators were trained in 2011, with two from each of the West African countries and the Sahel, 60 women from Mali, and 16 men and women who are members of the working group were trained on "Conflict analysis for mediation programme design" in 2014. UNOWAS also supports the creation and running of Women's Situation Rooms and the management of working group solidarity missions in several states. It also launched an online database on "Gender, Women, Peace and Security" in the West African sub-region and the Sahel in 2014, as well as sharing best practices, information and knowledge with stakeholders in the sub-region.[10]

In addition, the establishment of networks by women's groups and civil society have shown that they are capable of convening, mobilising and organising to ensure their active participation in myriad issues relating to conflict prevention, resolution, and peacebuilding activities. The recognition of the significance of

Women's participation in peacebuilding 45

strategic and collective agencies has resulted in the creation of more permanent and official platforms for the promotion of women's participation in peace and conflict processes. For instance, in 2000, the Mano River Women's Peace Network was launched to complement nationally driven activities to consolidate peace in the sub-region. COCAFEM is a regional alliance of women's groups in the Great Lakes which was established in 2000 out of the recognition of the causes and dangers of conflict in the region and the desire of women to play a more official role in addressing and managing conflict, and advocate with key authorities with regards to the impact of insecurity on women. At the national level, platforms such as Planete Femme in the Central African Republic, the South Sudan National Platform for Peace, and the Platform for Women Leaders in Mali are examples that signify how women have organised to build consensus on major issues and priorities, and also advocate for their participation during the process of peace negotiations and processes.

With regards electoral violence, it is important to acknowledge the role of Women's Situation Rooms (WSRs), a women's group that mobilises both women and youth and also helps in addressing the gendered nature of electoral violence against women political candidates and voters. Electoral violence hinders women's participation in the electoral space and serves as a risk to peace and security within a country and locally. WSRs, with slight variations and contextual adaptations, have been established in several countries during elections. These countries include Liberia, Senegal, Sierra Leone, Kenya, Zimbabwe, Mali, Guinea Bissau, Ghana and Nigeria. This process, acknowledged as best practice, encompasses several activities that result in women's direct and full participation in ensuring peace and stability before, during, and after elections. It involves peacebuilding activities, including consultations, training, monitoring and advocacy; bringing together women, youth, media, electoral stakeholders, professionals, religious and traditional leaders and institutions to ensure a transparent and peaceful electoral process.

Also, at the UN and AU peacekeeping missions, there has been an increase in women military and police officers in peacekeeping missions. There is also an improvement in the reporting of sexual assaults faced by women. Units have also been established to protect civilians who are victims of abuse. Similar units that shelter victims of gender-based violence (GBV) are available in Somalia and the Darfur region of Sudan. Also, the UN supports victims of GBV in Rwanda, Liberia and the DRC.

Sadly, there are some nation-states that still have discriminatory laws that mitigate against women's participation in peace and security processes. For example, in Ghana there is a clause in the labour law which prevents women in the security forces from getting pregnant within the first 3 years of employment. Even though there is an increase in women's representation in the military, there exist serious human rights violations within the workforce. There is still an increased use of masculine uniforms. There are also instances where women have to wear men's boots since there are no provisions for women's boots. This shows that more needs to be done to deepen implementation of

46   *Esther Tawiah*

commitments and bring about an on-the-ground impact and true change to the situation of women in Africa.

The way forward in Africa

Moving forward, it would be highly important for the AU and RECs to increasingly push for the inclusion of more women in the peace and conflict resolution space. Also, the capacities of women should be built in leadership, mediation, negotiation, and election observation, and more women should be encouraged to take up roles in the peacebuilding and conflict management space. Further, there should be a development of rosters at the national, regional and global levels to ensure that member states and RECs have access to qualified women they can deploy during conflict prevention, management, and resolution efforts.

In addition, governments must be fully committed to the allocation of funds towards the implementation of the policies and strategies developed. Governments must also look for alternative sources of funding rather than relying heavily on donors for funds to execute the implementation of their strategies and policies.

There is also the need for nation-states who are yet to implement Resolution 1325 to do so, and implement the resolution in their National Action Plans. Also, member states who have already adopted the Resolution 1325 need to be regularly reminded of their commitments and accountability with regards to monitoring and reporting on the implementation of the resolution. Member states should also share information and document best practices, organise regional training and also monitor and report on progress with regards to the implementation of the resolution.

Furthermore, governments must support national statistical bodies to incorporate the WPS agenda into their existing national surveys or data collection mechanisms, and provide wider national-level data for monitoring and reporting purposes. This would help countries streamline and harmonise data for various national reporting requirements, as well as assessing the impact of interventions.

There is the need to support the development of regional plans which do not only mainstream gender internally within the AU and REC's peace and security architecture but also highlight coherence and synergy with NAPs, and implement regional-level programming through the identification of high-impact flagship projects to increase women's engagement in peacebuilding.

Finally, it is important to provide funding and build the capacity of women with regards to peace and security issues at the national, regional and continental levels, with the purpose of acquainting them with knowledge on issues of peace and security, to enable them to fully participate in conflict prevention, management, mediation, reconciliation, and peacebuilding, as well as in post-conflict reconstruction and development.

Conclusion

Despite the plentitude of policies and resolutions put in place to ensure the effective participation of women in the peacebuilding and conflict space, not much has been done to open up the space for women to fully participate in these fields. Some nation-states still have discriminatory laws that mitigate against women's participation in peace and security processes. There is the need to regard women as agents of peacebuilding rather than mere vulnerable citizens. This is because women have played important roles with regards to being mothers, educators, mediators, peace activists and community leaders, coping and surviving actors, breadwinners and decision makers. Also, the majority of peacebuilding activities conducted and initiated by women peace activists and community leaders have been done outside the official peacebuilding processes space. There is the need to fully enrol women in the formal space of peacebuilding and conflict resolutions. Even though Africa has made great strides with regards to the WPS agenda, at continental and regional levels, there is still room for improvement in relation to women's participation in peacebuilding processes.

Notes

1 Resolution 1325: Security Council Resolution 1325 (SCR1325), 2000.
2 Ibid.
3 Resolution 2467, Women, Peace and Security: Sexual Violence in Conflict, 2019, (S/RES/2467 (2019)) (Reference for Security Council Resolution 2467).
4 African Union Commission Implementation of the Women, Peace and Security agenda in Africa, July 2016.
5 Ibid.
6 Ibid.
7 Ibid.
8 The dimension of socialisation is also important.
9 https://unowas.unmissions.org/women-youth-peace-and-security-working-group-west-africa-and-sahel-evaluates-its-10-years-action.
10 https://unowas.unmissions.org/gender-women-peace-and-security.

References

Alaga, Ecoma. 2010. *Challenges for Women in Peacebuilding in West Africa*. Policy Brief, No. 18. Africa Institute of South Africa.
Institute for Security Studies. 2008. *Workshop Report: Women and Peacebuilding in Africa*. Pretoria, South Africa: Institute for Security Studies.
McCarthy, Mary K. 2011. "Women's participation in peacebuilding: A missing piece of the puzzle?" *CUREJ: College Undergraduate Research Electronic Journal*. Philadelphia, PA: University of Pennsylvania. Available at: http://repository.upenn.edu/curej/132
United Nations Development Fund for Women. 2002. *Women, War and Peace: The Independent Experts' Assessment on the Impact of Armed Conflict on Women and Women's Role in Peacebuilding*. New York: United Nations Development Fund for Women.

48 *Esther Tawiah*

UN Women. 2012. Women's Participation in Peace Negotiations: Connections between Presence and Influence. New York: UN Women.

Online resources

http://databank.worldbank.org/data/reports.aspx (World Bank Gender Statistics Databank)

www.peacewomen.org/resource/african-union-commission-implementation-women-peace-and-security-agenda-africa

www.peacewomen.org/content/role-women-promoting-peace-and-development-horn-africa

www.providingforpeacekeeping.org/contributions/ (International Peace Institute's Peacekeeping Database)

www.un.org/africarenewal/magazine/december-2015/women-peace-security

www.who.int/gender/violence/womenfirtseng.pdf

4 Young women and peacebuilding

Maureen Guma

Introduction

This chapter provides an overview of the various roles young women play in conflict situations and peace processes, as well as the different ways they are affected by armed conflict in Africa. We look at how young women are affected differently in conflict (as compared to young men) and the different roles that they play in armed conflicts. We also look at the different ways in which young women in Africa have managed to beat the odds and raised their voices to be heard in post-conflict and peacebuilding processes. We are conscious that women in Africa are not homogenous and that we need to acknowledge differences brought about by class, race, religion (Agbaje 2018: 103), age and other factors. We are also aware that Africa is a massive continent, characterised by numerous differences. However, when it comes to young women's participation, some commonalities can be identified.

This chapter also identifies gaps and barriers to the full engagement, recognition and contributions of young women in building sustainable peace in Africa. It analyses the various challenges that young women in Africa face in their contribution to peacebuilding. By highlighting these existing gaps, we hope that they will influence policy making in regard to including young women in decision-making and peacebuilding processes on the continent. This is vital, as young people are the most strategic age group in Africa.

After describing the strategic position of young women in Africa, the chapter summarises the United Nations Security Council Resolution (UNSCR) 2250 on Youth, Peace and Security, adopted in 2015, and how it relates to young women in Africa. This is followed by a discussion of the experiences of young women in conflict situations in Africa. The section that follows highlights the activities that young women involved in peacebuilding in Africa undertake. An analysis of the challenges is undertaken in the subsequent section, followed by a conclusion.

Young women as key players in Africa

According to the Gap Report 2004 on adolescent girls and young women, there are 1.8 billion young people (10–24 years old) in the world. Approximately half

50   *Maureen Guma*

of them – 880 million – are adolescent girls and young women. In 2015, the UN Security Council adopted the Resolution 2250 on Youth, Peace and Security (YPS), which recognises the contributions of young people to peacebuilding efforts and calls for the inclusion of youth in planning, programme design, policy development and decision-making processes for conflict prevention, resolution and recovery.

This resolution urges member states to give youth a greater voice in decision making at the local, national, regional and international levels and to consider setting up mechanisms that would enable young people to participate meaningfully in peace processes. Yet in African societies many engagements and activities that target the young often favour young men while ignoring young women. As a result, young women end up being left out. However, passing this resolution while generalising the word "youth" to mean both young men and women in a way puts the young women at a disadvantage.

Worse still, young women are also excluded from activities and engagements that target women in leadership, conflict resolution and decision making, as they are seen as unknowledgeable and too young. They end up facing a double discrimination. Society has made young women believe that they lack knowledge, are ignorant of political processes, and cannot engage in constructive peacemaking without the involvement of older people or politicians (United Nations 2018: 10).

This double discrimination results in young women's exclusion from participation, protection, and access to funding and programmes because of their age and sex. Efforts to include young women in peacebuilding processes, that is, post-conflict agreements, and decision making in Africa have been made, but are proving to be inadequate. In peace processes involving the youth in Africa, we find that the percentage of young men is larger than that of young women. This is attributed to the different gender roles and cultural norms in African society, which usually relegate women to the bottom. Young women should be fully included in peacebuilding processes in order to achieve sustainable peace because in areas where they *have* been engaged they have proved to be successful peace agents/ambassadors (Chitando 2019).

UNSCR 2250 defines youth to mean young women and men between the ages of 18 and 29. However, in many African countries, the definition of youth depends on the society or cultural norms because most young women in this age group are already married off in exchange for bride wealth. This could only mean that in Africa (as elsewhere), we have different categories of young women. Future policies and resolutions on young women should be more specific and more inclusive. Extensive research should be done to ensure that no category of young women is left out.

The Women, Peace and Security (WPS) and Youth, Peace and Security (YPS) agendas need to work hand in hand because they complement each other. Thus, WPS must groom the youth in YPS, especially the young women, as they later graduate into women who are actively involved in WPS. Having a good background and effective mentoring, these young women will definitely be the peace and change agents that the world needs. Consequently, it is important to note that these two need to work together.

Summarising the UN Security Council Resolution on Youth, Peace and Security

In order to put this discussion into its proper perspective, it is important to highlight the major calls that are made by Resolution 2250. The UN Security Council Resolution 2250 on Youth, Peace and Security calls for the following:

Participation: Member states should take youth's participation and views into account in decision-making processes, from negotiation and prevention of violence to peace agreements.

Protection: Member states should ensure the protection of young civilians' lives and human rights and investigate and prosecute those responsible for crimes perpetrated against them.

Prevention: Member states should support young people in preventing violence and in promoting a culture of tolerance and intercultural dialogue.

Partnership: Member states should engage young people during and after conflict when developing peacebuilding strategies along with community actors and UN bodies.

Disengagement and reintegration: Member states should invest in youth affected by armed conflict through employment opportunities, inclusive labour policies and education promoting a culture of peace.

This chapter will highlight the status of young women in Africa in relation to some of the key processes that the resolution draws attention to.

The participation of young women

According to the findings of the progress study on Youth, Peace and Security (United Nations 2018), young women and men consistently raised two important and related frustrations: their exclusion from meaningful civic and political participation and their mistrust of systems of patronage and corrupt governance that lack the will and capacity to address their exclusion. Young people are consistently marginalised in African politics (Mengistu 2016). This has driven young people's demand for greater participation in electoral processes and policy making through youth councils, assemblies and parliaments, as well as decision-making forums at the local, national, regional and global levels.

However, for many young people, their mistrust has triggered scepticism and a loss of confidence in democratic governance itself. In response, many young people have withdrawn from formal politics, electoral systems and other institutions, instead creating alternative avenues for participation. Although spaces for political participation are often severely narrowed in contexts of ongoing or escalating violent conflict, young people can and do play important

52 Maureen Guma

political roles. These roles may more often be adaptive rather than transformative. Nonetheless, they contribute to the political positioning and standing of youth and their organisations (UN Women online).

Protection of young women

In most African countries, the protection of young women's rights and lives is still lacking. Owing to the fact that most of them lack access to quality education, as a result of gender-based discrimination, they are unqualified for jobs. The trend lately is that some of them are lured by middlemen and trafficked as sex slaves in the Middle East (Woldemichael 2013). Little is being done to curb this human rights crime as the perpetrators are left to roam freely. Further, young women continue to be violated in the various wars and conflicts in Africa (Ogbonna-Nwaogu 2008).

Prevention of violence against young women

Resolution 2250 enjoins member states to support young people in preventing violence and in promoting a culture of tolerance and intercultural dialogue. However, most states in Africa have not channelled resources towards the prevention of violence against young women. This applies to peace time, as well as times of intense conflict and war. In addition, gender-based violence and harmful cultural practices continue in different parts of the continent. Although there is some progress, more needs to be done so that young women do not experience violence in any of its forms.

Partnership with young women

Most African countries have not invested in engaging young women in decision making and post-conflict peacebuilding. Young women are discriminated against, usually in favour of young men, due to patriarchal tendencies. In many organisations, young women are denied jobs because they will cause "inconvenience" by going for maternity leave and various antenatal visits. Employers see this as being unproductive. Young women, therefore, end up being sidelined.

In some African cultures, young women are always told that speaking loudly is disrespectful. Such beliefs and practices shape how young women are supposed to behave in public and make them shy away from partnerships or engaging in decision making or taking up leadership. However, it is important to acknowledge that there are positive values within the cultures that can be leveraged to promote partnership with young women (Falimusi 2012).

Disengagement and reintegration

Some governments in Africa have tried to empower young people in post-conflict situations by empowering them with skills and knowledge so that they are able to be economically empowered. However, in some settings, corruption leads to these programmes being unproductive. Corruption is a threat to justice and sustainable peace in Africa (Nduku and Tendamwenye 2014).

Young women are also disadvantaged in attending these training programmes because they are usually caregivers to the family; some would have been impregnated during the conflict and consequently be young mothers. In Rwanda, the government has sought to do post-conflict training after the genocide, wherein people are taught about how to forgive and live together. In addition, the younger generation is being taught about the past so that they learn from it for the better. Women-led non-governmental organisations have been contributing towards peacebuilding in Rwanda (Mwambari 2017).

Young women in conflict areas in Africa

As noted previously, conflicts expose young women to the risk of sexual abuse, not only by insurgent groups but also by government forces and civilian males who take advantage of the situation that they are in to carry out these acts. The sexual abuse of young men is not as widespread as that of young women, although it is a reality which is often understated. Young women often fall victim to individual, repeated or gang rapes, sexual exploitation, enforced prostitution, witnessing the rape of family members and enforced participation in sex acts with relatives.

The financial strains on families during and after conflict often sees families trade off these young women for marriage in exchange for dowry or bride price to make ends meet. Early marriage not only exposes them to conditions such as HIV and AIDS, but can also bring about shame, rejection, physical abuse and early pregnancies. Being confined to early marriages makes them sole caregivers to their families and therefore fail to participate in any other activities outside the home, such as leadership and decision-making roles. As the adage goes, "They remain behind the curtains as the show goes on." In this regard, the celebration of motherhood in Africa (Siwila 2015: 62) needs to consider the extent to which early motherhood can restrict young women's opportunities in life.

As highlighted earlier but, for emphasis, it must again be underscored that peace interventions targeting youth usually take on more males rather than females. Yet in cases of conflict, both males and females are affected, but the young women face twice as much violence as their male counterparts because they are at risk of rape, other gender-based violence, discrimination, and the threat of being taken as sex slaves for the rebels. For example, 139 girls from St Mary's College Aboke Girls School in Northern Uganda were taken as wives by the Lord's Resistance Army in 1996. In Nigeria, it is estimated that Boko Haram has kidnapped over 1,000 girls. The kidnap of the Chibok girls on the nights of 14 and 15 April 2014 raised a global outcry that called on the world to intervene and have the young women returned home. Efforts to bring all the affected girls home continue to be undertaken, with the media taking different positions on the responses (Dunu and Okafor 2017: 126).

54 *Maureen Guma*

In Internally Displaced Peoples (IDP) camps, many young women are subjected to sexual violence, rape and harassment from officials. In Uganda, the *Daily Monitor* (26 March 2018), a leading newspaper in the country, reported how a refugee scandal involving officials in the Office of Prime Minister (OPM) and the UN agency for refugees, the UNHCR, unfolded. The report showed how young women refugees from Ethiopia, Somalia, and Sudan were being sexually trafficked because of the instability in their home countries.

In other areas, young women are kept in the background, away from prying eyes of the public or from danger, "to protect" them. This, therefore, limits their networks and they actually never get to know of any opportunities, if any, where they could share their opinions or show their potential. According to one study participant in Nigeria, "I restricted myself from going to places, and [was] sitting down doing nothing; this is all as a result of fear of attacks" (United Nations 2018). For young people – and young women in particular – notions of peace and security were inextricably tied to issues of gender equality and problems of gender-inequitable norms.

However, with current trends in technology and internet use, we have seen more women, particularly young women, engage more on the internet's social media platforms like Facebook and Twitter. These give them a veil, and they are therefore able to air out their views without any fear. This is, however, not good enough because these young women are trolled online and bullied, as there is also the challenge of online gender-based violence.

However, young women have sometimes expressed their agency by taking part as armed combatants. In countries such as Liberia, we have seen young women actively joining the armed groups in fighting/conflict. In other cases, young women are abducted against their wishes and forced to join but here we saw young women joining voluntarily. When these young women join, sometimes they are looking to gain some equality and for the protection of their families. When they are actively taking part in armed fighting groups, they are not as vulnerable as before. Some are married to male combatants for protection. In many of these fighting groups, there are rules to protect the female fighters (Specht 2006).

The Global Study on the Implementation of UNSCR 1325 (UN Women 2015) shows that when women are included in peace processes, there is a 20% increase in the probability of a peace agreement lasting at least 2 years. After the war in Liberia, young women who fought alongside boys in the bush were not regarded as decent. They are deemed to have crossed the line of femininity, the norms in society on how women should behave. They are generally not regarded as potential candidates for marriage and most employers are reluctant to hire them. They tend to become reclusive, as they seek to hide their past and start new lives.

In emergencies and conflict contexts, girls and young women often forgo meals or are given less food than male family members and livestock. They are forced to marry early or engage in unsafe livelihoods, including transactional sex, and are at risk of sexual exploitation by armed actors. Conflict and post-conflict situations also increase early and unintended pregnancies, unsafe abortions, the prevalence of HIV and AIDS and other sexually transmitted infections, with grave consequences to young women and girls' reproductive health. Recovery programmes often neglect or bypass girls and young women, because disarmament programmes do not see them as combatants or members of armed groups, and aid distribution does not reach young women and girls confined to the home because of social norms or insecurity. Furthermore, the stigma associated with sexual violence prevents girls and young women from reporting rape and abuse. For example, "Many returning female combatants are the subject of excessive labelling and stereotyping abuse, with these women often treated as outsiders by members of the community in comparison to their male counterparts" (Maina 2012: 5).

Young women's participation in peacebuilding processes in Africa

Despite the impact of the conflict and post-conflict contexts on young women in Africa, they remain active in peacebuilding. For example, UN Women recognises young women's agency and works to enhance their inclusion, participation, and protection in research, advocacy, policy and programming. UN Women invites young women to participate in high-level meetings and panels to influence decision making and to challenge their marginalisation. UN Women contributed to the Progress Study on YPS with a background paper on young women in peace and security (UN Women online). Young women in Africa have been involved in some of the following activities relating to peacebuilding.

Young women in the arts, music, dance and drama

Young women in Africa have come up with creative ways to raise their voices about peacebuilding and be heard. Some have taken up the arts, music, dance and drama, while others have not given up trying to get into positions of influence, like being representatives in parliament, blogging, using social media and writing about their role in decision making in society.

In 2018, a young female Somali poet, Nacima Qorane, was sentenced to 3 years in jail for writing a poem calling for the reunification of Somaliland with Somalia. According to a court ruling, she was found guilty of bringing the state into contempt by advocating for Somaliland to reunite with Somalia. The use of non-violent means by young women in calling for peace is highly significant. It shows that there are many non-violent ways in which one's voice can be heard.

Alaa Salah, the young woman from Sudan (aged 22 in 2019) who became the face of the Sudan uprising against the then presidency of Sudan Bashir, is a relevant case study. According to an interview she gave to *The Guardian*, a British daily newspaper (10 April 2019), she went out every day and read out

56   *Maureen Guma*

a revolutionary poem to over 10 groups. One line of the poem that generated the most reaction is: "The bullet doesn't kill. What kills is the silence of people." This shows how young women, if exposed, involved, accepted and allowed, can contribute to the peace processes in non-violent and creative ways. Alaa used poetry as her contribution to the revolution in Sudan. How phenomenal!

Young women in peacekeeping missions

The UN deploys more than 100,000 troops, police and civilians from 124 countries to its peacekeeping missions around the world. Many of these peacekeepers are young, in their 20s or early 30s. It is worth acknowledging these brave young men and women who have left their home countries to work in some of the harshest and most dangerous places in the world to protect some of the world's most vulnerable people and achieve peace. It confirms that young people must always be taken seriously.

Although women have demonstrated that they can fill the same roles as men in military settings, the number of young women in the peacekeeping missions is still low. South Africa's contribution of troops to peace missions is the 13th largest in the world, and the country has the largest women's contingent deployed in Peace Support Operations (PSOs). On average, only 2.4% of signatories to peace agreements are women and no women have been appointed chief or lead peace mediators in UN-sponsored peace talks (UN Women 2012), although the African Union appointed Graca Machel as one of three mediators in the Kenyan crisis of 2008. Women comprise only 8% of the police contingents in international peace operations. Increasing the number of women in mediation and peacekeeping is strategically beneficial (Okech 2016).

Young women and the internet and media

According to the World Bank (n.d.) two-thirds of the world's internet users are aged under 35 years, and half are under the age of 25. Today's youth have higher expectations than the generations before them for self-direction, freedom and opportunity. The information age has taught them their human rights and given them a broader vision of what their lives could be (UNFPA, 2014: 79).

The World Youth Report demonstrates that these cyber technologies offer unique organisational tools for peace and positive forms of digital organisation, as well as platforms for civic participation among youth (United Nations Department of Economic and Social Affairs, 2016). Unfortunately, the internet can also serve as a platform for disinformation and hate speech, both "enable[ing] and inhibit[ing] the spread of violent conflict" (World Bank and United Nations 2017: 10).

In 1994, prior to the genocide in Rwanda, journalists at the government-owned Radio Television Libre des Mille Collines broadcast messages inciting genocide and encouraging Hutus to rape Tutsi women and then either to kill them or leave some alive to bear so-called Hutu children. In the massacre that enveloped the country, many women were affected by rape or the real threat of being raped. The media played a negative role in generating hatred and as a coordinating device (Yanagizawa-Drott 2012).

Although journalism is a profession that is largely male, many young women in Africa have taken it up as an avenue where they can contribute to peacebuilding. This is because the media reaches far and wide. The young women use it to counter the negative deployment of the media by credibly informing audiences on relevant issues in society and spreading messages of peace and unity. Thus, "Women are the backbone of the society, have a better understanding of their communities and great love for people. Female journalists are in a better position to come up with the best programmes on peace and development," says Leyla Osman Mohamud, a young female journalist who uses media to advocate for peace in Somalia (EU-UNDP 2017).

On social media, young women can challenge gender stereotypes by building narratives to reach others, including men, who would not normally be exposed to such points of view. Indeed, the surge of female bloggers globally (and in Africa) has helped attract a younger generation of activists in many countries who represent a key target audience to begin dismantling established stereotypes and help advance gender equality. In conflict contexts, social media also offers a means for women to take action to mobilise and protect themselves, in the absence of more formal mechanisms and support structures.

Young women in Africa have sought to expose and challenge gender stereotypes, which reinforce the notion that women are inferior and serve to perpetuate discriminatory practices that limit women's access to resources like education. In addition, many civil society organisations are working together with governments to ensure that all young women get a chance at education. Education puts young women at an advantage as they can gain not only knowledge and skills, but also confidence to voice their concerns.

Young women in parliament

According to the Parliamentary Union report on youth's participation in parliaments across the world, the share of young parliamentarians has risen among young men since 2016 but not among young women. Because young women are the least represented of all age/gender groups, each target should be accompanied by a provision for gender parity. The report further states that 72 countries organise youth parliaments to educate and engage greater numbers of young people in parliamentary work (Inter-Parliamentary Union 2016).

In Uganda, an annual Youth Moot is held and the main objectives of the initiative include enhancement and catalysing multidisciplinary approaches to effecting meaningful participation of young people in decision-making and governance processes, build their confidence and further create an informed mass of young citizenry for responsive policy and legislative recommendations for national development. The 2019 youth moot saw a young woman, Miss

58 Maureen Guma

Winnie Adur, take the floor as the speaker. This is a form of effective training and empowerment of young women.

The Inter-Parliamentary Union (2018: 9) report also discovered an interesting pattern that only five African countries – The Gambia, Ethiopia, Seychelles, Cape Verde and Equatorial Guinea – make the top 20 across all three lists of members of parliament under 30, 40 and 45. Yet, according to the United Nations, Africa has the world's youngest population, with 200 million people between 15 and 24 years of age. This points to a sizeable deficit in the political representation of youth in the region, where young people are clearly disengaged from politics (Inter-Parliamentary Union 2018). Generally, young people in Africa, particularly young women, are not visible and active in politics (at all the different levels).

Some African states have sought to address youth apathy in politics by coming up with different initiatives. For example, in South Sudan, UN Women, in collaboration with the University of Juba and the Ministry of Gender, established a National Transformational Leadership Institute (NTLI) with the mandate of training women and grooming young women leaders. The training focuses on peacebuilding, transformational leadership and economic empowerment.

The Global Study on Women, Peace and Security (UN Women 2015) highlighted in its findings that peace processes inclusive of civil society have a greater chance of success, and societies with higher gender equality markers were proven to be more stable and less at risk of conflict. The same logic of inclusive processes and agency extends to the YPS agenda. *Peace and stability cannot be built without young women and young men, and it cannot be built for them without them.*

Young women and transitional justice

As noted previously, young women in Africa endure marginalisation and exclusion when it comes to contributing to peacebuilding, although they are making significant strides forward. However, there has been considerable innovation that is changing the trend. For example, the gacaca courts of Rwanda that were instituted after the genocide facilitated open consultation and the inclusion of all. This enabled the young women's voices to be heard. As there were too few lawyers or judges for the trials and as the courts were intended as community courts, lay members of the community would serve as judges (*inyangamugayo*). In October 2001, the first round of elections for gacaca judges began. Legal training was not required to serve as a judge. Instead, judges were selected based on their commitment to justice, truth and a spirit of sharing. They were required to be 21 years or older, have no previous criminal convictions, and could not have been serving in a government or political leadership role. They also should have never been suspected of committing crimes against people during the genocide (Organic Law 40/2000). More than 250,000 male and female judges were elected, and in April 2002, the elected judges underwent training.

Young women and peacebuilding 59

Although the gacaca courts were ridiculed by some, they were all inclusive and did not discriminate on gender. They, just like the formal judicial courts, aimed at bringing about sustainable peace in the country. It should be noted that transitional justice processes are most successful when they build upon and balance the common objectives of justice and peace, acknowledge the disparate impact of conflict on women and girls, and holistically address the full range of human rights violations, including violations of social, economic and cultural rights. Although some critiques have been levelled against the gacaca courts' failure to transform gender norms completely (Lorentzen 2016), it is still important to acknowledge that the innovation allowed women to express themselves openly, as well as to preside over cases.

In Liberia, some of the young women that participated in the civil war were involved in the post-conflict processes. Creativity and innovation can be discerned in the idea of creating peace huts, which acted as safe spaces for young women and women in mediating local disputes, serve as vigilant watchdogs on the police and justice services, prevent gender-based violence (GBV), refer GBV survivors to support services, raise community awareness of peacebuilding priorities, and mobilise on other critical issues such as elections and the importance of women's political participation, and governance.

Despite all these positive contributions, young women in Africa face several challenges in peacebuilding. The following section summarises some of these key challenges.

Challenges that young women face in peacebuilding in Africa: Stakeholders' laxity

Due to societal norms, most stakeholders do not take young women seriously. Such stakeholders include governments, non-governmental organisations and civil society organisations.

According to the International Crisis Group (2006), the international community's knowledge of how women build peace in Sudan, Congo and Uganda remains shallow, and there has been little commitment to including women as sources of information in the conduct of baseline security assessments, small arms surveys and joint assessment missions. Although there have been more efforts to understand African women's contribution to peacebuilding, there is still need for greater investment in this direction.

Governments in many African countries too often have failed to include young women in decision-making processes and post-conflict agreements. Instead, more males have taken up these roles. No measures are being taken to ensure that these young women are involved.

Young women, HIV and AIDS

According to the 2010 UNAIDS report on the global AIDS epidemic, the imbalance (particularly in sub-Saharan Africa, where 76% of all women living

60 Maureen Guma

with HIV are found and 13 women become infected for every 10 men) reflects not only the heightened physiological vulnerability of girls and young women but also a high prevalence of intergenerational sexual partnerships, the lack of woman initiated prevention methods, and broader social and legal inequality that impedes the ability of young women to reduce their sexual risk. According to UNAIDS (2010), the disparities are even more extreme in many conflict-affected regions where gender inequalities and all forms of violence against women and girls increase their vulnerability to HIV. HIV prevalence among young women 15–24 is typically much higher than among young boys in the same age group in conflict-affected countries. This has compromised young women's participation in peacebuilding.

Poor economic conditions and low levels of literacy

Poor economic conditions limit most young women in Africa from actively participating in peacebuilding. They cannot afford the associated expenses involved given that most of them are the sole breadwinners in their families.

Young women may not fully participate in peacebuilding processes if they are still struggling to meet their basic needs and those of their families. Poverty levels in Africa are still high. Further, women have higher overall work burdens than men and low-income women have longer working days than low-income men (Bardasi and Wodon 2010). Their responsibilities for care and household production make it difficult for women to "switch" into higher return activities (World Bank 2011) in order to move out of poverty. Health and education deprivations comprise other factors underpinning women's greater vulnerability to poverty. Educational deprivation impedes female upward mobility (World Bank 2011). Further, the lower nutritional status of women and girls is correlated with poverty contemporaneously and across generations (World Bank 2011).

Young women in the diaspora

Young African women who are able to enter the international arena are frustrated by their inability to retain influence at home and fear being thought of as having opted out. Women also face significant challenges when they try to assume leadership positions, especially the risk of being co-opted (International Crisis Group 2006: 16).

Male chauvinism

According to the International Crisis Group report (2006), in all of the three countries studied (Uganda, Congo and Sudan) peacebuilders face entrenched, male-dominated institutions in which elites cling to power, often violently. A male Ugandan peace activist said: "Men here generally like to be identified with coercive measures and force. You cannot be a man unless you have power, so you cannot talk about a non-violent approach" (International Crisis Group 2006: 16). Since peacebuilders work under difficult conditions, and the space given to their issues is restricted, women often organise separately from other post-conflict civil society groups. This partly explains why it often is easy for those who oppose women's empowerment to ignore the violence against them and dismiss their contributions, while excluding them from decision-making structures that might enhance their security. A South Kivu woman activist said: "Some male leaders cried out that the application of Resolution 1325 would give too much power to women who do not deserve it. 'Women remain women,' they said, 'and they have no experience to deserve such posts'" (International Crisis Group 2006: 16).

Women peace activists in all three countries complained about vague and inappropriate programs that, they believe, are designed less to empower women than as a sop to donors, international observers and, all too frequently, local women themselves. A Ugandan woman human rights specialist asserted:

> Donors interest themselves only in the politics of the day. They talk about democracy, but they do nothing to make it participatory, restorative or based on care. They give aid but they don't monitor how it gets spent. No wonder 1325 is ignored.
>
> (International Crisis Group 2006: 16)

Delayed or no justice for women

The lack of access to justice for survivors of sexual assault is a challenge for women in peacebuilding in Africa. Violence against women in the private sphere is drastically under-reported, even in countries with a vigorous women's movement and an advanced commitment to judicial and security sector reform. When law and order break down in war, as in Sudan, Congo and Uganda, few records are kept of how women's security, including their health and nutrition, is impacted. This contributes to impunity for male violators – especially those in the security sector or governmental authority – which directly undercut women's ability to enter positions that might allow them to change public policy or get laws against sexual crimes enforced (International Crisis Group 2006: 17).

Recommendations and conclusion

The critical roles that young women in Africa play in peacebuilding have been repeatedly highlighted and it is vital for African (and other) states to recognise the value of their input. If young women are empowered, they can contribute to sustainable peace and economic development in their countries and the continent at large, and their participation and decision making in political processes should be encouraged. This can be achieved if cultural norms that frustrate their participation are challenged, as well as ensuring that young women in Africa

62 Maureen Guma

benefit from effective mentorship programmes. Directing funding towards young women at grassroots levels is also strategically beneficial. Further, member states should design and implement young people-focused peacebuilding strategies and programmes. Young women are already demonstrating their leadership potential in the area of peacebuilding; all they need is a more enabling environment for them to express their knowledge and skills more effectively. In turn, this will transform Africa in dynamic and exciting ways.

References

Agbaje, Funmilayo I. 2018. "The challenges of instrumentalist approach to the involvement of African women in peacemaking and peacebuilding," *International Journal of Humanities and Social Science* 8(8), 99–105.

Bardasi, Elena, and Quentin Wodon. 2010. "Working long hours and having no choice: Time poverty in Guinea," *Feminist Economics* 16(3), 45–78.

Chitando, Anna. 2019. "From victims to the vaunted: Young women and peacebuilding in Mashonaland East, Zimbabwe," *African Security Review* 28(2), 110–123.

Daily Monitor. 2018. "Officials extort sex from refugee girls," Kampala, 26 March.

Dunu, Ifeoma V., and Godfrey E. Okafor. 2017. "The Chibok girls kidnap controversies: Analysis of Nigerian newspapers' coverage," *Global Journal of Applied, Management and Social Sciences* 14, 126–140.

EU-UNDP. 2017. "Young female journalist uses the power of media to advocate for peace in Somalia." Available at: https://somalia.ec-undp-electoralassistance.org/2017/06/02/young-female-journalist-uses-the-power-of-media-to-advocate-for-peace-in-somalia/, accessed 18 January 2020.

Falimusi, Olumuyiwa O. 2012. "African culture and the status of women: The Yoruba example," *Journal of Pan African Studies* 5(1), 299–313.

Guardian. 2019. "'I was raised to love our home': Sudan's singing protester speaks out," London, 10 April.

International Crisis Group. 2006. "Beyond victimhood: Women's peacebuilding in Sudan, Congo and Uganda," *Africa Report*, No. 112. Brussels: International Crisis Group.

Inter-Parliamentary Union. 2016. Youth Participation in National Parliaments. Geneva: Inter-Parliamentary Union. Available at: http://archive.ipu.org/pdf/publications/youthrep-e.pdf, accessed 18 January 2020.

Inter-Parliamentary Union. 2018. Youth Participation in National Parliaments. Geneva: Inter-Parliamentary Union. Available at: www.ipu.org/resources/publications/reports/2018-12/youth-participation-in-national-parliaments-2018, accessed 18 January 2020.

Lorentzen, Jenny. 2016. "Gender and culture in transitional justice: Rwanda's gacaca courts," *Gender-Just Peace and Transitional Justice Working Paper No. 2.* Lund: Lund University.

Maina, Grace. 2012. "An overview of the situation of women in conflict and post-conflict Africa," *ACCORD Conference Paper*, Issue 1. Available at: https://media.africaportal.org/documents/ACCORD_Conference_-_An_overview_of_the_situation_of_women_in_conflict.pdf, accessed 17 July 2020.

Mengistu, Muhabie Mekonnen. 2016. "The quest for youth inclusion in the African politics: Trends, challenges, and prospects," *Journal of Socialomics* 6(1). doi: 10.41 72/2167-0358.1000189.

Mwambari, David. 2017. "Women-led non-governmental organizations and peacebuilding in Rwanda," *African Conflict & Peacebuilding Review* 7(1), 66–79.

Nduku, Elizabeth, and John Tenamwenye. Eds. 2014. *Corruption: A Threat to Justice and Sustainable Peace.* Geneva: Globethics.net.

Ogbonna-Nwaogu, Ifeinwa M. 2008. "Civil wars in Africa: A gender perspective of the cost on women," *Journal of Social Science* 16(3), 251–258.

Okech, Awino. 2016. *Gender and Security in Africa.* Accra: African Women's Development Fund.

Siwila, Lilian C. 2015. "The role of indigenous knowledge in African women's theology of understanding motherhood and maternal health," *Alternation*, Special Edition No. 14, 61–76.

Specht, Irma. Ed. 2006. *Red Shoes: Experiences of Girl-Combatants in Liberia.* Geneva: Programme on Crisis Response and Reconstruction, International Labour Organisation.

UN Women. 2012. *Women's Participation in Peace Negotiations: Connections between Presence and Influence.* New York: UN Women. Available at: www.unwomen.org/en/what-we-do/peace-and-security/young-women-in-peace-and-security, accessed 16 January 2020.

UN Women. 2015. *Preventing Conflict, Transforming Justice, Securing the Peace: A Global Study on the Implementation of United Nations Security Council Resolution 1325.* New York: UN Women. www.peacewomen.org/sites/default/files/UNW-GLOBAL-STUDY-1325–2015%20(1).pdf, accessed 18 January 2020.

UN Women online. Available at: www.unwomen.org/en/what-we-do/peace-and-security/young-women-in-peace-and-security, accessed 18 January 2020.

UNAIDS. 2010. *Global Epidemic Update.* Geneva: UNAIDS.

UNFPA. 2014. *The Power of 1. 8 Billion Adolescents, Youth and the Transformation of the Future.* New York: UNFPA.

United Nations. 2018. "The missing peace: independent progress study on youth and peace and security," New York: United Nations. (Lead author, Graeme Simpson). Available at: www.unfpa.org/sites/default/files/resource-pdf/Progress_Study_on_Youth_Peace_Security_A-72-761_S-2018-86_ENGLISH.pdf, accessed 16 January 2020.

United Nations Department of Economic and Social Affairs. 2016. *World Youth Report: Youth Civic Engagement.* New York: United Nations. Available at www.un.org/development/desa/youth/wp-content/uploads/sites/21/2018/12/un_world_youth_report_youth_civic_engagement.pdf, accessed 18 January 2020.

Woldemichael, Selemawit B. 2013. "The vulnerability of Ethiopian rural women and girls: The case of domestic workers in Saudi Arabia and Kuwait." A project submitted in fulfilment of the requirements for the degree of Masters of Humanities and Social Science in the subject of Sociology. Uppsala: Uppsala University.

World Bank. 2011. *World Development Report 2012: Gender Equality and Development.* Washington, DC: World Bank.

World Bank. n.d. Gender Statistics Databank. Available at: http://databank.worldbank.org/data/reports. aspx? Source=Gender%20Statistics, accessed May 2016.

World Bank and United Nations. 2017. *Pathways to Peace: Inclusive Approaches to Preventing Violent Conflict. Main Messages and Emerging Policy Directions.* Washington, DC: World Bank.

Yanagizawa-Drott, David. 2012. "Propaganda and conflict: Theory and evidence from the Rwandan genocide," *CID Working Paper*, No. 257. Cambridge, MA: Harvard University Press.

5 Building sustainable peace in post-conflict settings in Africa

A case study of Liberia

Pearl Karuhanga Atuhaire

Background

This chapter examines the nature of current peacebuilding and reconstruction efforts in post-conflict Liberia. The terms peacebuilding and reconstruction will be used interchangeably. Despite the growing desire by Liberia to sustain peace through various strategies, much is still desired. In this chapter, I assess the practical implementation of these strategies, with a specific focus on their impact on the socio-economic development of Liberia in view of the Agenda 2030 on achieving sustainable peace. This chapter articulates key development and human security issues in Liberia, and the roadmap to sustainable development, with key challenges and recommendations to address these challenges. It draws insights from thematic analyses and country experiences from when the conflict started in 1989 up until the current era. Throughout, the chapter employs a gender lens to highlight women's contributions.

Introduction

Liberia is now in its reconstruction phase of development following three critical phases of crises (two civil wars, 1989–1997 and 1999–2003, and the Ebola epidemic of 2014–2015), which exacerbated the country's instability socially, economically and politically, and resulted in hundreds of thousands of lives being lost and millions displaced, with widespread traumatisation (Herbert 2014; Singh and Connolly 2014). Liberia's final peace agreement was signed in 2003, putting an end to 14 years of violent civil wars. While overt armed conflict is now relatively rare, with various peacebuilding mechanisms in place, and post-conflict brutality in the form of sexual and gender-based violence is lower than during the armed conflict, many of the root causes that led to the conflicts remain the same today.

Since 2003, Liberia has maintained a steady peaceful environment, with Liberians committed to not returning to war, as evidenced by the successful implementation of the Comprehensive Peace Agreement (CPA), which was signed in Accra, Ghana (Singh and Connolly 2014). This is combined with international support through operationalising a robust peacekeeping United

Sustainable peace in post-conflict Liberia 65

Nations Mission in Liberia (UNMIL), which provided security for the government and citizens of Liberia. The mission wound up in March 2018 after 12 consecutive years of the operation, leading to the government of Liberia assuming full security responsibilities for the state on 30 June 2017.

After the protracted war, the government of Liberia, together with the United Nations and other development partners, established the Liberia Peacebuilding Plan in response to UN Security Council Resolution 2333 (December 2016). The plan was submitted to the President of the Security Council via the Secretary General of the United Nations in April 2017. It consolidates commitments across development, security and human rights operations, and defines priority areas for mutual engagement in order to prevent a relapse into conflict, continue reform efforts, promote reconciliation, strengthen the security environment and lay the foundations for conflict-sensitive development.

Despite progress in the implementation of reforms of the justice system, the rule of law and the security sector, efforts on national peacebuilding and reconciliation continue to stall due to ineffective leadership and the lack of a coherent strategy and coordination framework. However, following the peaceful 2017 presidential and legislative elections, UNMIL finally departed Liberia in March 2018.

This chapter examines recent literature that deals with development and human security issues in Liberia and articulates the post-conflict interventions aimed at achieving sustainable peace. The chapter provides a background on Liberia's conflict situation, the conflict reconstruction process, national efforts toward peacebuilding, the current national status and the challenges faced, and also provides recommendations to address these challenges.

Conflict reconstruction processes

Since the end of the civil war, Liberia has successfully held three non-violent democratic elections, which restored a measure of confidence in the institutions of government and proved that differences can be resolved through peaceful political competition at the polls. The peaceful elections in 2017 marked the first democratic transfer of power from an elected incumbent to an elected executive since 1944, as President Ellen Johnson Sirleaf, Africa's first woman president, handed over power to H. E. George Manneh Weah at the end of her constitutional mandate. Liberia is one of the earliest test cases for the ongoing reform of the United Nations Development System and implementation of the secretary general's recommendations on peacebuilding and sustaining peace (Connolly and Mincieli 2019).

Throughout this process, the role of Liberian women has been crucial in bringing peace to Liberia and women are now a vital element of the conflict reconstruction process. Women and women's movements have played key roles in achieving and maintaining peace in Liberia, although this has not happened without challenges. During the war, women's organisations worked tirelessly to bring warring parties to the negotiating table so that the country

66 Pearl Karuhanga Atuhaire

might achieve peace. It is widely noted that women voted in great numbers in the 2005 election and now comprise a significant constituency in Liberian politics. According to Dorina and Christina (2007), their efforts reveal how well-coordinated grassroots movements can establish more inclusive peacebuilding practices. Nevertheless, in continuing to advance the participation of women, women's movements today face the challenge of transitioning from the grassroots level to a mainstream policy and advocacy group.

In addition, Liberia's transition has been supported by national and international conflict responses, including: the 2003 Accra Comprehensive Peace Accord; national reconstruction and poverty reduction strategies; and peacekeeping and development programmes from the UN, the US, and the EU (among other multilateral and bilateral donors); plus the Agenda for Transformation and the recent National Development Plan enshrined the Pro-Poor Agenda. Although Liberia has made progress in establishing measures to build peace, conflict reconstruction has not met expectations (Vinck et al. 2011). Some of these processes are discussed in the following sections.

Liberia's United Nations Peacebuilding Commission

In 2010, Liberia asked to be placed on the UN peacebuilding agenda to bolster the nation's peacebuilding and post-conflict recovery efforts. The Peacebuilding Commission (PBC) adopted the Statement of Mutual Commitments (SMC) to guide the PBC's engagement in 2010, wherein three peacebuilding priorities were agreed upon and further developed in the Liberia Peacebuilding Program (LPP), including: (1) strengthening the rule of law; (2) supporting security sector reform; and (3) promoting national reconciliation. A revised SMC was adopted in May 2015, which highlights five priority areas: (1) security sector development; (2) rule of law; (3) promoting national reconciliation; (4) promoting peaceful and inclusive 2017 elections; and (5) human rights (Singh and Connolly 2014). These priorities have since been influential to the policy and implementation levels of the peacebuilding programme in Liberia. While progress has been achieved in strengthening rule of law and the security sector reform priority areas, promoting national reconciliation has been stifled, with recommendations from key government officials requesting a coherent strategy and coordination framework. Nonetheless, the role of the PBC remains crucial to keep Liberia on the international radar.

The national strategy for achieving 20% women representation in security sector institutions has influenced the recruitment of women into the Liberia National Police (LNP), the Armed Forces of Liberia (AFL), the Bureau of Immigration and Naturalisation (BIN), and the Bureau of Corrections and Rehabilitation (BCR). As of 2018, women made up 29% of the Liberia Immigration Service (LIS), 19% of the LNP and 3% of the AFL. In addition, women held 5.88% of ministerial positions and made up 15% of the Liberian Drug Enforcement Agency (LDEA), Women also comprised 7.7% of the judiciary (21% in Corrections and 5.4% in Prosecution). The Women and Children Protection Service (WACPS) of the LNP has 100 female officers out of 190,

Sustainable peace in post-conflict Liberia 67

while in the Sexual and Gender-Based Violence (SGBV) Crimes Unit, all victim support officers are female.

Truth and Reconciliation Commission (TRC)

The CPA provided for the establishment of a Truth and Reconciliation Commission in 2006 (Singh and Connolly 2014) to address the wounds of war with significant funding from international donors. Some of the injustices were committed by public officials, such as key political and military figures from the civil war, who not only have impunity with respect to their human rights violations but also hold positions of political and economic power, especially in the counties.

In a brief produced by the Catholic Relief Services (2016) following the Catholic Bishops' Conference of Liberia on the State of Peace, Reconciliation and Conflict in Liberia, it was highlighted that most Liberians believed that the main perpetrators of wartime violence had escaped punishment and that the victims of violence were denied justice. More than 80% of the population felt that people who suffered grave injury during the war did not receive justice through the national Truth and Reconciliation Commission and half of them believed that post-war reconciliation failed to achieve its objectives, particularly at the grassroots level, where efforts were seen as piecemeal and superficial.

The TRC was mandated to essentially establish truth, through public dialogue on the nature and causes of Liberia's turbulent civil wars between 1989 and 2003 (Singh and Connolly 2014). Unfortunately, the TRC process was fraught with operational challenges, particularly staffing, the timely development of a comprehensive workplan and budget, and incoherent policy and programme planning, among other issues. Most importantly, the report was widely ignored by those in power at the time. This was coupled with weak institutional capacities that impeded the materialisation of the TRC, leading to minimal impact and, later, inconsequential implementation of recommendations. However, despite the challenges, the TRC had some significant influence in contributing to peace and reconciliation in the country. For instance, the 2009 TRC report offered the first publicly available and extensive account of human rights violations, and provided significant insights on the critical socio-economic, political and cultural factors that gave rise to and exacerbated the country's history of civil war (Singh and Connolly 2014).

According to the Final Report of the TRC of Liberia, it is highlighted that, in 2006, to ensure proper coordination and broad participation by women in the TRC process and to guarantee that women's concerns would be adequately expressed and addressed, the TRC established a gender committee comprising a wide spectrum of civil society and international partners. Members of this committee included women NGO Secretariat of Liberia, the Ministry of Gender, Open Society, Liberia Crusaders for Peace Women's Wing, Traditional Women Association of Liberia, Women on the Move and the Liberia Media Women Association.

68 *Pearl Karuhanga Atuhaire*

The United Nations Mission in Liberia

In August 2003, the UN Security Council authorised a Chapter VII mandate for the establishment of a 15,000 strong peacekeeping mission in Liberia – the United Nations Mission in Liberia (UNMIL)[1]. This was formally adopted in September 2003 under UN Resolution 1509. UNMIL replaced the previous UN Office in Liberia and subsumed the Economic Community of West African States Monitoring Group (ECOMOG) (Shilue and Fagen 2014). UNMIL's withdrawal and change of administration in 2018 provided a prime opportunity for the UN to set up a new structure to implement the secretary general's recommendations on peacebuilding and sustaining peace (Connolly and Mincieli 2019). The Executive Committee decided in July 2017 to strengthen the UN Country Team's capacities, including by reviewing the UN Development Programme's Country Office capacity, ensuring the sustainability of the Office of the High Commissioner for Human Rights and immediately establishing a Multi-Partner Trust to support transition efforts and further support by the Regional Team.[2] With relatively stable security and promising peace in Liberia, UNMIL withdrew in March 2018.

Strategic Roadmap for National Healing

In March 2013, the government's Peacebuilding Office developed a Strategic Roadmap for National Healing, Peacebuilding and Reconciliation in an attempt to fill important peacekeeping gaps (Singh and Connolly 2014). The 18-year roadmap was to foster coherent institutions and systems to support national healing and reconciliation and strengthen efforts around sustainable peace. It posited a comprehensive vision for the advancement of the nation that moves forward by taking stock of the past and achieving sustainable peace which is fundamentally informed by the process of national reconciliation[3] (Singh and Connolly 2014). Although this was a significant step towards sustainable peace, intercommunal cohesion and trust are still lagging behind. This is because the protracted conflict in Liberia distorted the fabric of community cohesion, with people now divided along ethnic, social, religious and political lines. Nonetheless, notable progress of the roadmap includes the Palva hut[4] process of addressing past wrongs, although this is an emerging initiative which is currently in its inception stages of implementation wherein the terms of references are still being developed and methodologies and procurement processes are being developed (Singh and Connolly 2014).

Current country context

Although Liberia is stable and free of no conflict, the situation is still fragile as the nation tries to transition from autocracy to a new order guaranteed by the rule of law. Following the conflict, there were mass population movements inside and outside Liberia. The mass internal displacements saw

Sustainable peace in post-conflict Liberia   69

many Liberians flee to Monrovia, the country's capital, leading to increased pressures on urban services and transformed livelihoods of the population (Shilue and Fagen 2014). However, post-conflict reconstruction has been taking place in alignment with the National Development Agenda. Today, Liberia's economic growth and development is aligned to the Pro-Poor Agenda for Peace and Development (PAPD), which was established in 2018 and is the second in a series of 5-year National Development Plans (NDPs) anticipated under the Liberia Vision 2030 framework. The PAPD follows the Agenda for Transformation (AfT) 2012–2017. It is informed by lessons learned from the implementation of the Interim Poverty Reduction Strategy 2007 (iPRS) and the Poverty Reduction Strategy (2008–2011). To make progress towards the Vision 2030 goals over the next 5 years, the strategies are built around these four PAPD pillars as follows:

1. **Power to the people:** To empower Liberians with the tools to gain control of their lives through more equitable provision of opportunities in education, health, youth development and social protection.
2. **The economy and jobs:** Economic stability and job creation through effective resource mobilisation and prudent management of economic inclusion.
3. **Sustaining the peace:**[5] Promoting a cohesive society for sustainable development.
4. **Governance and transparency:** An inclusive and accountable public sector for shared prosperity and sustainable development.

The government of Liberia acknowledges that progress in development and security has been made because of donor investments and assistance. The Human Development Index (HDI) increased by 10.6% between 2000 and 2015,[6] projecting an increase in life expectancy at birth of 14 years and mean years of schooling of 1.8 years, over the same period. The gross national income (GNI) per capita rose by 8.4% between 1990 and 2015.[7] However, despite this progress, Liberia remains in the low human development category, with absolute poverty on the rise in five of the six national statistical regions (Matshalaga et al. 2018).

Population and human security

According to the Populations Census Report of 2014, Liberia has an estimated population of 4.8 million,[8] roughly half of which is under the age of 18, with a median age of 18.7. According to the Common Country Assessment Report 2018, the government of Liberia has conducted four censuses to date, with the most recent one having been carried out in 2008. A population survey on attitudes about security, dispute resolution, and post-conflict reconstruction conducted in June 2011 in Liberia indicated that most of the insecurity is related to witchcraft, local crimes and robberies (Vinck et al. 2011). Although

70   *Pearl Karuhanga Atuhaire*

the UNMIL contributed to establishing peace in the country since its establishment in Liberia in 2003, its withdrawal in March 2018 created concerns among Liberians who believed that local security had limited capacity to maintain peace. Additionally, according to the Common Country Assessment Report, 2018, it is noted that corruption, land disputes, high levels of youth unemployment and governance and inequality issues associated with concessions are potential triggers of conflict (Matshalaga et al. 2018).

Human rights and discrimination

While the government has made efforts to address and improve human rights situations in the country, discrimination and human rights violations are still common. Progress in upholding human rights is evident with the establishment of human rights institutions such as Independent National Commission on Human Rights (INCHR) and Independent Information Commission (IIE) as well as Liberia's acceding to the regional and international human rights community and putting in motion processes to address human rights issues in the country, including prioritising CEDAW reporting.

It is reported that despite women constituting a higher proportion of the population as compared to men, development indices are negative for women (Matshalaga et al. 2018) and their participation in politics is equally low. While Liberia set a record in 2005 when the country elected the first female president in Africa, this progress did not have ripple effects in empowering more women to join in political participation. Although efforts are underway to increase women's participation in peacebuilding processes, their contribution to durable peace has not been systematically explored.

Economic context

On the 2017 global ranking of the 30 poorest countries, Liberia sat in fourth position, with a gross domestic product (GDP) per capita of US$882.9. The country's economic growth fell to almost zero in 2014, when the country was hit by the Ebola virus disease (EVD) crisis and by falling international prices for rubber and iron ore, Liberia's two key exports. Agriculture was the biggest livelihood sector before the war, involving about 75% of the population. In the post-war period, however, most of the populace now live in Monrovia. This increased the degree of socio-economic inequality between Monrovia and the rest of the country (Connolly and Mincieli 2019; Vinck et al. 2011). Conflict disrupted the traditional tribal fabric which existed before the war.

According to the PAPD, nearly 80% of the economically active population is in informal employment. About 35% of Liberian households still make their living predominantly through agricultural activities.[9] According to PAPD, it is also projected that the population in the informal employment sector will grow from nearly 1.3 million in 2018 to 1.6 million by 2023 without significant intervention in job creation. In formal sector employment, 65% of wage earners

Sustainable peace in post-conflict Liberia 71

work for private employers in the service sector (LISGIS 2016).[10] About 20% work for the government and 15% work for non-profit organisations.

Women have limited participation in the economy compared to their male counterparts. Women represent 53%, compared to 74% of men, involved in gainful employment (Matshalaga et al. 2018). With strong patriarchal social norms and entrenched, socially accepted violence against women and girls, Liberia ranks 154th out of 189 countries in the 2017 Gender Inequality Index.[11] Women are disproportionately represented in the informal sector, which is largely low paying. According to the 2013 Demographic and Health Survey, 48% of women and 71% of men are literate. The same survey indicates that female-headed households are typically poorer than male-headed households and women are most likely to be employed in sales and services (49%), followed by agriculture (42%). Although women also constitute the biggest percentage of labour in the agricultural sector, their access and ownership of land is very limited.

Despite the large proportion of the labour force in the working-age category, low labour productivity and an acute shortage of workers with the appropriate skills inhibit the potential of both the formal and informal sectors. This constrains broad-based economic growth and recovery. The 2010 labour force survey established that the formal sector employed less than 20% of the labour force. It also found only 56% of the working-age population was literate; and when disaggregated, female literacy in the labour force was 44.8%.[12] Women in Liberia have less access to education (45%), less available capital to start businesses, and less access to land and properties (29%) when compared to men (Vinck et al. 2011).

To bridge the economic gap between men and women, several initiatives aimed at enhancing the economic status of women, namely skills training and business development programmes to reduce poverty and vulnerability, have been established with the support of donors. One of such initiatives is the United Nations joint program on Gender Equality and Women's Economic Empowerment, which not only provides skills development but also grants loans to businesswomen to empower them financially and reinforce their independence. According to the 2011 evaluation report on the UN Women Liberia Country Program, positive steps towards women's economic empowerment included: the establishment of the Association of Women in Cross Border Trade (AWICBT) and enhancing organisational development, management and leadership for 65 women leaders; consultations held between Ministry of Commerce and industry and AWICBT on free movement of goods; design for warehouses developed; and recruitment of business and literacy training providers.

According to a 2019 report from the Convention of Elimination of all forms of Discrimination Against Women (CEDAW), gender-responsive budgeting has been identified as one of its 20 priority areas of the National Gender Policy to ensure gender-equitable budgetary allocations by government institutions according to the gender-specific needs of women and men, girls and boys

72 *Pearl Karuhanga Atuhaire*

and other vulnerable groups by enhancing the capacity of the concerned spending entities. In line with this priority area, an interministerial Gender-Responsive Planning and Budgeting (GRPB) Technical Working Group was created in 2016, comprising representatives from the ministries of Finance and Development Planning; Health; Gender, Children and Social Protection; and Internal Affairs as well as the Governance Commission and UN Women.

Women in peace and security

When the United Nations Security Council (UNSC) adopted Resolution 1325 on Women, Peace and Security on 31 October 2000, it reaffirmed the important role of women in the prevention and resolution of conflicts, peace negotiations, peacebuilding, peacekeeping, humanitarian response and in post-conflict reconstruction and asserts the importance of their equal participation and full involvement in all efforts for the maintenance and promotion of peace and security. The resolution urges all actors to increase the participation of women and incorporate gender perspectives in all United Nations peace and security efforts. It also calls on all parties to conflict to take special measures to protect women and girls from gender-based violence, particularly rape and other forms of sexual abuse, in situations of armed conflict. Liberia is a signatory to UNSCR 1325 and has made some progress in advancing its principles.

In their report entitled "Women's Role in Liberia's Reconstruction," Dorina and Christina (2007) argue that the Liberia National Action Plan (LNAP) was the first of its kind in a post-conflict country and continues to be example of the country's commitment to enduring peace and stability. The LNAP acknowledges women's role in reaching the country's 2003 peace agreement. Women from different regions and religious backgrounds formed a peace movement (Women of Liberia Mass Action for Peace Campaign) to demand an end to the civil war. Indeed, the impact of this movement is a practical example of women's role in achieving peace. The 2011 Nobel Peace Prize Laureates Leymah Gbowee and former Liberian president Ellen Johnson Sirleaf have always been outspoken advocates for women's inclusion in peace and security processes.

In October 2015 the CEDAW adopted the General Recommendation 30 on Women in Conflict Prevention, Conflict, and Post-Conflict Situations. The recommendation aims to ensure respect for women's human rights in all situations, not only during armed conflict but also including internal insurrections and emergencies. The recommendation, besides urging member countries to draw up action plans on Women, Peace and Security, requires that reporting on actions taken be incorporated into the periodic reporting on the implementation of CEDAW. This new reporting procedure will further promote cooperation with civil society and NGOs in the implementation of the Women, Peace and Security agenda and make them also accountable to the United Nations CEDAW Committee.

Sustainable peace in post-conflict Liberia 73

Violence against women and girls

Violence against women and girls (VAWG) in the form of sexual violence was exacerbated during the conflict period, as rape was used as a weapon of war, driven by unequal gender relations. For many Liberian women and girls, the appalling violence they experienced during wartime is still evident as physical and mental scars. Sexual and gender-based violence (SGBV) reports between 2014 and 2018 from the Ministry of Gender, Children and Social Protection (MoGCSP) indicate a general acceptance of the most common types of SGBV, identified by communities as rape, child marriage, offensive touching, wife beating, denial of resources, acid attacks as well as the more subtle and hidden forms of violence and female genital mutilation (FGM).

Progress in peacebuilding and security over the past decades has not translated into actions to eliminate VAWG and marginalised groups; rather, VAWG has contributed to destabilising the peace and security, with increasing media attention leading to demonstrations by the public. Youth, making up 63% of the population, especially have been expressing frustration at the lack of response and action from the government.[13] However, the country will not reap the benefits of this demographic dividend unless the situation of women and girls improves. To address issues of VAWG, the government has indicated a strong focus on improving the realisation of women's and girls' rights in its recently launched 5-year development plan, the Pro-Poor Agenda for Prosperity and Development (PAPD). The PAPD is aligned to the Sustainable Development Goals (SDGs), which are strongly embedded within the overall PAPD.

According to the Common Country Assessment report of 2018, women face the brunt of insecurity more than their male counterparts (Matshalaga et al. 2018). They experience this as mothers, as breadwinners in their homes, as caregivers to their children and relatives, as salespersons on streets or even markets. Women face violence at a rate of 41.2%, mainly from their intimate partners (Matshalaga et al. 2018). According to the Interagency Conflict Assessment Framework (ICAF), the pathways for increasing levels of violence are in place, as many of the grievances and root causes of the wars have not been addressed (USAID 2016).

While some researchers contend that conflict reinforces SGBV, others argue that SGBV during conflict situations is actually a continuation of the violence perpetrated prior to conflict (Sigsworth 2008). For instance, Atuhaire et al. (2018) argue that conflict–associated sexual violence reflects gender inequality and gender norms that predispose a society towards violence and should be viewed as a national and international security issue. While war is accompanied by an increase in violence, especially domestic and sexual violence, the root cause of violence against women is the inequality between men and women and the accruing power differentials that exist even in absence of conflict. Despite the relatively stable situation in the post–conflict years, human security in Liberia remains a challenge, especially for women and girls who are largely affected by sexual and gender-based violence. According to Shilue and Fagen

(2014), Liberian women, particularly those from rural areas and the displaced women in border areas, continue to experience various human rights abuses and marginalisation.

Violence that occurred during the 14 years of war continues to manifest in terms of sexual violence and domestic violence, with reports escalating each year. The root causes of the violence are identified as negative social and cultural norms, power imbalance and other contributing causes including poverty, high illiteracy rates due to poverty and weak state preventive and response mechanisms to address these challenges and to provide effective human security and justice equally to all citizens. Although Liberia established a Sexual and Gender-Based Violence Crimes Unit in 2009 and Criminal Court "E" in 2008, adjudicating rape cases is still a big challenge. Moreover, lines between the formal and informal/traditional justice[14] systems are blurred (M'Cormack 2018), as evidenced by most of the population seeking help from informal and traditional justice systems even for criminal cases.

According to a SGBV/HTP Joint Programme Report on Liberia, numerous factors are interplaying to account for the fluctuations in the number of cases reported per year. The increase in the number of cases reported is partially attributed to an increased awareness on SGBV issues at community level and service provision[15] at national and sub-national level. The sharp decreases in the number of cases reported in 2014 is attributed to the Ebola virus disease (EVD) outbreak, when health centres shifted much of their focus to the management of the EVD, with less on SGBV issues, which affected the reporting levels from communities and the lack of a functional referral services, especially in health (see Figure 5.1). County case analysis by the GBV Division of the Ministry of Gender, Children and Social Protection (MoGCSP) indicates that Montserrado County reportedly has the highest numbers of SGBV cases. This is because it includes Monrovia and is densely populated (1,118,241 people

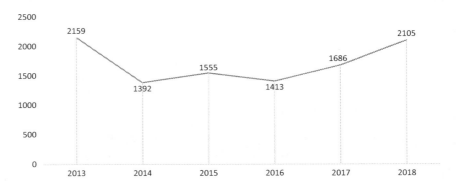

Figure 5.1 Trend of SGBV cases reported in Liberia from 2013–2018
Source: SGBV/HTP Joint Programme Report, Liberia, 2018.

according to the 2008 Population Census). Owing to the lack of decentralisation of services, large numbers of people have migrated to the city in search of better opportunities.

For its part, FGM, among other harmful practices, is widely practised and deemed acceptable in 11 out of 15 counties in Liberia. It is promoted by the Sande Society,[16] to which approximately 72% of rural women and girls belong. This leads to over 40% girls dropping out of mainstream school education after attending the Sande School and then becoming brides/wives. Social and cultural norms and practices that give rise to some of these abuses are normalised, including early sexual exposure and the practice of casual and multiple sexual relationships, especially by men in what is known as "market day marriages," practised in some communities (particularly commercial trading centres, such as border towns, fishing communities and areas with concentrated business activity). This increases the vulnerability of young girls who are always the target of these practices.

Nonetheless, the government of Liberia, in partnership with the United Nations and development partners, has initiated various programmes to combat SGBV. Other efforts include, the United Nations Development Assistance Framework (UNDAF) and its accompanying Costed Action Plan and the identified priorities for the post-Ebola recovery phase, which aim at addressing vital and urgent structural issues. It contributes to the National Development Plan, the Pro-Poor Agenda for Prosperity and Development (PAPD),[17] 2018–2023.

Legal frameworks and access to justice

While Liberia has made noteworthy progress in developing a number of legal frameworks that support the prevention of SGBV – including the Education Reform Act of 2011, which seeks to advance girls' education at all levels; Rape Law (2005), which stipulates a 10 year imprisonment if proven guilty and a life sentence in the case of statutory rape; Domestic Relations Law; Refugee Act; Human Trafficking Act; Inheritance Act; National Commission on Disability Act; Children's Law; Penal Code 14.72,74; Domestic Violence Act; Executive Order 92 on FGM; the revised National Gender Policy 2017; and National Public Health Law – a lot more is necessary to make these laws more practical.

According to the 2019 CEDAW report for Liberia, there are significant improvements related to access to justice for women and girls in recent years, particularly in institutional terms with the creation of Criminal Court E and the SGBV Units under the Ministry of Justice, which include more than 60 WACPS (Women and Children Protection Section) officers with special training to handle SGBV cases. These have been created under the umbrella of the LNP and devolved to all counties along with 11 "One-Stop Centres" being established in seven counties to provide legal, medical, protection and

76 Pearl Karuhanga Atuhaire

psychosocial services to survivors.[18] Consequently, over 860 survivors have received psycho-social protection and legal services through the referral pathway (One-Stop Centres, referral hospitals, police and the Criminal Court "E") in 2017 alone.[19]

Despite this progress, the capacity of women to access justice is still limited due to various challenges including the limited number of qualified personnel and weak institutional capacity, the under-representation of women in the justice sector, corruption, the limited knowledge women have of their legal rights and the legal process, the lack of public defenders and legal aid available, the logistical and financial constraints on travelling to police stations and courts (especially in rural areas), and the societal pressure to resolve situations in traditional ways.[20]

Recommendations

While Liberia will unquestionably benefit from the present focus on infrastructural development in its post-conflict reconstruction, there is a critical need for both government and non- government institutions to address some of the consequences of the country's massive and long-term displacement, particularly its impact on development and human security. Recommendations for this include the following.

The government of Liberia

1. There is a need for institutional strengthening through capacity building and provision of comprehensive and coordinated response services for survivors of SGBV, including psychological help with trauma healing and mental health, access to adequate medical facilities and access to justice[21] among others.
2. There is a need for the government of Liberia to build a strong body of public support and political buy-in for national reconciliation in order to achieve sustainable peace. Most wounds since the 14 years of war have never been healed. This is manifested in the various types of violence in most communities. One of the triggers of sexual violence and domestic violence is the pent-up war-related frustrations felt by perpetrators of such violence. It is important to note that a transformation of gender relations is integral to the process of reconciliation through exploring and building relationships, bringing about healing and forgiveness between warring parties (Schirch 2004). Indeed, Lederach (2003) posits that reconciliation is a multifaceted process that aims to address the issues of the past and move the country forward towards sustainable.
3. It is vital for the government to strengthen the rule of law and restore justice, security and protection services in Liberia, with a special focus on the needs of women in this sector and improving their accessibility to

the justice system. This is based on the fact that while the formal justice system has made significant progress in reforming laws and institutions, most people have lost trust in these formal systems and thus rely more on informal and traditional justice (M'Cormack 2018).

4. To incentivise women's participation and go beyond tokenism, the government needs to reinforce the quota system or take affirmative action to increase the representation of women in peacebuilding processes. Quotas are pertinent for increasing gender balance among constitutional members, arguably contributing to higher levels of women's participation. In many cases, however, women have had to overcome a perceived lack of legitimacy and often did so through subject matter expertise or by asserting political authority.

Development partners

1. In keeping with the Sustainable Development Agenda of ensuring that by 2030 no one is left behind, development partners should support the government's decentralisation efforts and ensure development is inclusive of large proportions of the population located away from the centre, especially the rural poor. With the 2018 Local Governance Act, decentralisation of resources and services will be made much easier if development partners support government in achieving its national development agenda (PAPD), also established in 2018.

2. The establishment of high-quality and affordable education and skills development that are matched to the demands of the labour market must be a focus for all those who want to assist Liberia in this post-conflict period. This means providing basic education for girls and boys to make sure they reach a level of education that enables them to move on to tertiary education, technical and vocational employment skills training, starting businesses of their own, participation in agricultural production and so on. This must involve constructive engagement with the youth to ensure inclusion of their views, ideas, peace, security and reconciliation. The support must include financial support and infrastructure to enable the youth to participate in economic development and leadership in all spheres of life including politics.

3. To address the problem of youth unemployment, gender inequality, marginalisation and exclusion, which are key drivers of fragility in Liberia, development partners should support the government in promoting employment opportunities for youth (including adolescent girls). This should involve establishing frameworks and approaches for targeting youth and women with skills development and Small Media Enterprise initiatives where these groups can benefit. Youth and women's involvement in leadership and participation in the development of policies and peace efforts is critical.

78   *Pearl Karuhanga Atuhaire*

Civil society organisations

Civil society organisations (CSOs) potentially can be a force for peace and stability. Involving CSOs and women's movements including those facing intersecting forms of violence is essential for advancing human security and development. These organisations can operate outside of the politics in peacebuilding. They also have the capacity to increase social cohesion and involve all practitioners (Atuhaire et al. 2018). These CSOs should include the groups of those facing intersecting forms of violence and inter-religious council because religion has been reported to exert a powerful influence on Liberians, as witnessed by their belief in and worship of the supernatural. According to the report by the Catholic Relief Services in 2016, more than three-quarters of respondents (76.3%) saw religion as important in their daily lives, and almost the same number (72.1%) felt that religious leaders can exert influence over their communities to promote peace. A similarly high percentage (73.7%) stated that interfaith collaboration represents a positive force for peace in the country. Inter-religious tolerance was also lauded as a traditional value of Liberia's confessional communities. Nonetheless, 65.5% of Christian respondents and 57.5% of Muslim respondents felt that religious intolerance was on the rise and, if left unchecked, could trigger violent conflict. Half of all respondents (48.8%) thought that religious identity was being used to discriminate in employment, business opportunities, or school admissions (Catholic Bishops Conference of Liberia 2016).

The private sector

Although the private sector is relatively weak in Liberia, following the conflict there has been progress, with some private sector institutions such as Firestone, Orange, Total and other concessions companies working with the government and other development partners to tackle development and human security challenges. Companies and businesses in the private sector are catalytic in enhancing human security and development if engaged within peacebuilding processes. Business communities can voluntarily decide to expatriate their financial means if the situation is deemed too risky and volatile. However, through their corporate social responsibility role and philanthropy funding, private sectors companies can support schools, health centres and community associations, thereby contributing to solving human security and development challenges in the country.

Conclusion

The process of conflict transformation in Liberia shows a disjuncture between policy and practice, with progress in the post-CPA period largely confined to the development of policies, normative frameworks and prescriptions on paper, at the expense of any considerable practical, state-sanctioned implementation.

Sustainable peace in post-conflict Liberia 79

A fundamental factor for government of Liberia to consider when addressing the challenges to peace reconstruction is the fact that the absence of war cannot merely be interpreted to mean that the country is peaceful. Indeed, while post-conflict transformation at a national level may be done through a peace agreement between warring parties, local-level problems, such as inequality, divisions, mistrust, economic deprivation, fear and violence, may persist (Atashi 2009). Therefore, peace should be measured by how secure, safe and peaceful Liberians feel. Johan Galtung (1996) refers to this as "Positive Peace." Women's security must feature prominently in the quest for peace and security in Liberia.

Transformation in the lives of people socially, economically and politically is imperative for sustainable peace to be achieved. This transformation does not require a linear approach, but rather a multidimensional approach that requires several actors for sustainable peace to be achieved. These include the government of Liberia and development partners, CSOs and the private sector, who all have key roles to play in order to address the various challenges the country is facing. The government of Liberia should provide institutional strengthening through capacity building and provision of comprehensive and coordinated response services to survivors of SGBV; build a strong body of public support and political buy-in for national reconciliation in order to achieve sustainable peace; and strengthen the rule of law and restore justice, security and protection services. On the other hand, development partners should provide quality and affordable education for all; provide incentives for youth to bridge the unemployment gap; and engage women and youth in peacebuilding initiatives.

CSOs and the private sector have a catalytic role given that they are normally non-partisan. CSOs should include the groups of those facing intersecting forms of violence and inter-religious council because religion has been reported to exert a powerful influence on Liberians, as witnessed by their belief in and worship of the supernatural. On the other hand, the private sector through their CSR role and philanthropy work in various sectors of the economy and community initiatives can drive socio-economic development leading to sustainable peace in Liberia. Prioritising women's leadership, paying attention to their security and engaging them, will remain critical as the nation moves towards positive peace and prosperity.

Notes

1 See United Nations Security Council Resolution 1497 (2003), S/RES1497, 1 August. Coalition for International Criminal Court.
2 UNDP Liberia, UNDP Mission Report: Supporting Peaceful Transitions and Sustainable Development Pathways in Liberia, September 2017.
3 The Roadmap defines reconciliation as a multidimensional process of overcoming social, political and religious cleavages; mending and transforming relationships; healing the physical and psychological wounds from the civil war, as well as confronting and addressing historical wrongs, including the root causes of conflict in Liberia.

80   *Pearl Karuhanga Atuhaire*

4   Traditional conflict resolution mechanism, mainly male dominated.

5   Sustaining Peace is defined as

> a goal and a process to build a common vision of a society, ensuring that the needs of all segments of the population are taken into account, which encompasses activities aimed at preventing the outbreak, escalation, continuation and recurrence of conflict, addressing root causes, assisting parties to conflict to end hostilities, ensuring national reconciliation, and moving towards recovery, reconstruction and development.
>
> (Source UN Security Council Resolution 2282 (27 April 2016), UN Doc. S/RES/2282; UN General Assembly Resolution 70/262, UN Doc. A/RES/70/262)

6   UNDP, Human Development Report, 2016.

7   Ibid.

8   See www.worldometers.info/world-population/liberia-population/.

9   LISGIS, Household Income and Expenditure Survey, 2016.

10   Ibid.

11   The Gender Inequality Index is a composite measure reflecting inequality between women and men in three different dimensions: reproductive health (maternal mortality ratio and adolescent birth rate), empowerment (share of parliamentary seats held by women and share of population with at least some secondary education), and labour market participation (labour force participation rate).

12   LISGIS, Liberia Labour Force Survey, 2010.

13   See www.indexmundi.com/liberia/demographics_profile.html.

14   Formal justice systems include the courts; informal/ traditional justice systems include: Palava huts, Kola nuts, trial by ordeal, community forums, which are primarily the domain of men and the Peace Huts led by women.

15   One-Stop Centres, Women and Children Protection Sections (WACPS) and GBV Observatories, among others.

16   Sande Society is a women's secret society where young women and girls are initiated into adulthood by rituals including female genital mutilation.

17   Objectives include: to build a stable resilient, and inclusive nation embracing our triple heritage and anchored on our identity as Africans; to lift an additional 1 million Liberians out of absolute poverty over the next 6 years (and reduce absolute poverty by 23% across five of the six regions) through sustained and inclusive growth driven by scaled-up investments in agriculture, in infrastructure, and in human capital development.

18   "Assessment of Existing Initial Services Available on Sexual and Gender-Based violence Cases," UN Women, Liberia, 2019; Addressing Impunity for Rape in Liberia, Office of the High Commissioner for Human Rights/United Nations Mission in Liberia, Monrovia, 2016, p. 25.

19   Joint program to prevent and respond to sexual and gender-based violence (SGBV) and harmful traditional practices (HTPS), Programme Brief, Government of Liberia (GoL)/United Nations (UN), 2016/See Article 5: Sex Roles and Stereotyping.

20   Revised National Gender Policy (2018–2022), Ministry of Gender, Children and Social Protection, 2017, Liberia, p. 39.

Sustainable peace in post-conflict Liberia 81

21 According to Singh and Connolly (2014), weak formal legal systems are a key feature of most post-conflict states. As such, a trade-off is often made in favour of broader restorative forms of justice over more retributive actions, in order to support national reconciliation and guard against a relapse into conflict.

References

Atashi, E. 2009. "Challenges to conflict transformation from the streets," in B. W. Dayton and L. Kriesberg (Eds.) *Conflict Transformation and Peacebuilding: Moving from Violence to Sustainable Peace*. London: Routledge.

Atuhaire, P. K. et al. 2018. *The Elusive Peace: Ending Violence Sexual Violence During and After Conflict*. Washington, DC: United States Institute of Peace (USIP).

Catholic Relief Services. 2016. *The State of Peace, Reconciliation and Conflict in Liberia*. Baltimore, MD: Catholic Relief Services.

Connolly, L., and Mincieli, L. 2019. *Sustaining Peace in Liberia: New Reforms, New Opportunities*. New York: International Peace Institute. Available at: www.ipinst.org/wp-content/uploads/2019/05/190529_Sustaining-Peace-in-Liberia.pdf

Dorina, B., and Christina, P. 2007. *Women's Role in Liberia's Reconstruction*. Washington, DC: United States Institute of Peace (USIP). Available at: www.usip.org/publications/2007/05/womens-role-liberias-reconstruction

Galtung, J. 1996. *Peace by Peaceful Means: Peace and Conflict, Development and Civilization*. Oslo, Norway: International Peace Research Institute.

Herbert, S. 2014. *Conflict Analysis of Liberia*. Birmingham, UK: GSDRC, University of Birmingham. Available at: www.academia.edu/11369675/Conflict_analysis_of_Liberia

Lederach, J. P. 2003. *The Little Book of Conflict Transformation*. Intercourse, PA: Good Books.

Liberia Institute of Statistics and Geo-Information Services (LISGIS). 2010. *Household Income and Expenditure Survey*. Monrovia: LISGIS.

Liberia Institute of Statistics and Geo-Information Services (LISGIS). 2016. *Household Income and Expenditure Survey*. Monrovia: LISGIS.

M'Cormack, F. 2018. "Prospects for accessing justice for sexual violence in Liberia's hybrid system," *Stability: International Journal of Security & Development* 7(1), 1–16.

Matshalaga, N. et al. 2018. *Liberia Common Country Assessment*. Harare: Primson Management Services.

Schirch, L. 2004. *Strategic Peacebuilding: A Vision and Framework for Peace with Justice*. Intercourse, PA: Good Books.

Shilue, J. S., and Fagen, P. 2014. *Liberia: Links between Peacebuilding, Conflict Prevention and Durable Solutions to Displacement* Washington, DC: Brookings Institution. Available at: www.brookings.edu/research/liberia-links-between-peacebuilding-conflict-prevention-and-durable-solutions-to-displacement/

Sigsworth, R. 2008. Gender based violence in transition (online). Johannesburg, South Africa: Centre for the Study of Violence and Reconciliation (CSVR).

Singh, P., and Connolly, L. 2014. *The Road To Reconstruction: A Case Study of Liberia's Reconciliation Roadmap*, Policy and Practice Brief. Durban, South Africa: African Centre for the Constructive Resolution of Disputes (ACCORD). Available at: www.africaportal.org/publications/the-road-to-reconciliation-a-case-study-of-liberias-reconciliation-roadmap/

UN Women. 2019. *Women in Politics*. New York: UN Women.

82 *Pearl Karuhanga Atuhaire*

UNDP. 2016. *Human Development Report: Human Development for Everyone*. New York: United Nations Development Programme. Available at; http://hdr.undp.org/sites/default/files/2016_human_development_report.pdf

USAID. 2016. *Liberia Conflict Vulnerability Assessment*. Available at: http://democracyinternational.com/media/Liberia%20Conflict%20Assessment%20Final%20 Report%20(External).pdf

Vinck, P., Pham P. N. and Kreutzer T. 2011. *Talking Peace: A Population-Based Survey on Attitudes about Security, Dispute Resolution, and Post-Conflict Reconstruction in Liberia*. Berkeley: Human Rights Center, University of California.

6 Women and peacebuilding in Madagascar

Gaby Razafindrakoto

Introduction

The development of Madagascar cannot be achieved without peace and security. Further, there can be no meaningful development in Madagascar without women's leadership and active participation. The 2018 elections, which brought the new president to power, have been commended by the international community as a great and peaceful transition to a democratic dispensation. Though the country has not been witnessing armed and open conflicts, the population lives in a state of permanent anxiety. Widespread law violations are occurring both in rural and urban areas, which constitute a serious obstacle to sustainable development and peace. Women and girls are particularly vulnerable when peace is threatened.

Since the reform of the security sector initiated in 2014, Madagascar has achieved some progress. Among other things, it has mainstreamed gender in the recruitment process of the armed forces, taking into consideration women's qualifications and specific needs, without discrimination. This is key, as security sector reform is strategic for peace, security and development (Hendricks 2011).

On the other hand, non-governmental bodies and peace associations are forming coalitions to foster peace culture and education. To what extent have all these efforts been effective? How can women bring about changes and tangible results in this area? What is their impact on the achievement of peace in the country?

This chapter focuses on three points: namely the implementation of the United Nations Security Council Resolution 1325, the reform of security sector, and the access of women to decision-making circles related to peace talks in Madagascar.

Madagascar

To put the chapter into its proper perspective, there is a need to begin by describing Madagascar. The island covers an area of 592,800 square kilometers (228,900 square miles) and is the world's 47th-largest country as well as the fourth-largest island. The country is situated in the Indian Ocean, next

84   Gaby Razafindrakoto

to La Reunion and Mauritius to the east and separated from Africa by the Mozambique Channel. Madagascar is divided into six provinces, 22 regions, 119 districts and 1,695 municipalities. With a population of 23,201,926 (50.3% of whom are women), Madagascar is ranked a low-income country (LDC), with a low socio-economic and Human Development Index (HDI) ratings.

Madagascar regained political independence and sovereignty in 1960 and since then has never engaged in any armed conflict, whether against another state or within its own borders. As such, the armed forces of Madagascar have primarily served a peacekeeping role. However, the military has occasionally intervened to restore order during periods of political unrest.

In more recent years, security issues have become the Gordian knot for the authorities. Almost everywhere on the island the population, both urban and rural, is facing not only growing insecurity, armed attacks, daylight robberies, thefts of cash crops, kidnappings and hostage-taking but also acts of violence perpetrated by this very population. A population that has become exasperated, wanting to do justice by itself, drifts into resorting to popular prosecution or revenge. In such a context, women's interpretation of security becomes important (Okech 2016; McKay 2004). Civil society, aware of this latent explosive situation, has initiated some actions related to security matters. The first ones concern the UNSC Resolution 1325.

The UNSC Resolution 1325

Despite the existence of several previous declarations, commitments and legal instruments on women, girls and agreements on armed conflict, women remain a vulnerable group in times of conflict. They are insufficiently represented and are not able to become involved in the prevention, management and resolution of issues that concern them. They are most often victims of abuse perpetrated either by members of the military or by civilians.

United Nations Security Council Resolution 1325, on Women, Peace and Security, was adopted unanimously by the UN Security Council on 31 October 2000. The resolution acknowledged the disproportionate and unique impact of armed conflict on women and girls. It calls for the adoption of a gender perspective to consider the special needs of women and girls during conflict, repatriation and resettlement, rehabilitation, reintegration and post-conflict reconstruction.

Resolution 1325 was the first formal and legal document from the Security Council that required parties in a conflict to prevent violations of women's rights, to support women's participation in peace negotiations and in post-conflict reconstruction, and to protect women and girls from sexual and gender-based violence in armed conflict. It was also the first United Nations Security Council resolution to specifically mention the unique impact of conflict on women. The resolution has since become an organising framework for the Women, Peace and Security agenda, which focuses on advancing the components of Resolution 1325. A study of the implementation of this resolution has highlighted some of the advances and challenges (UN Women 2015).

The promotion and maintenance of peace would be easier if women were involved in all these processes. The differentiated impacts of wars and conflicts on men and women must be understood. A national strategy and institutional mechanisms are required to carry out any planned actions.

Regarding UNSCR 1325 specifically, the Institute of Security Studies (ISS) workshop report on women and peacebuilding in Africa insisted, among other recommendations, on the following points:

- Simplify, translate into local languages and widely disseminate UNSCR 1325.
- Develop National Action Plans ensuring that national laws, policies and programmes promote equal participation and are in line with UN Resolution1325. The ratification, domestication and implementation of continental and international human rights instruments are among the requisites too.
- Countries have to enact laws and ensure the development of policies that promote gender equality and the empowerment of women and protect the rights of women, besides developing guidelines and training tools to enable staff to mainstream gender in peace missions shall be implemented as well.
- Equal representation of women and men at all levels of peace missions, including the decision-making structures at head office and mission areas, the review of strategies and programmes to improve the conditions of women in peace missions, including how welfare, conduct and discipline issues are handled should be in the agenda too.
- Build collaborative partnerships with women and men constituencies.
- Conduct customised and generic training and training tools.
- Establish a database of trainers and of women who can be deployed in areas of need.
- Ensure civilians are adequately trained for peacekeeping (Hendricks and Chivasa 2008. See also Hendricks 2017).

Implementation of Resolution 1325 in Madagascar

With this in mind, Madagascar's networks of Malagasy women, in partnership with the Ministry of Gender, the SADC Protocol Alliance on Gender and Development, UNDP, UNFPA, ADB, UNIFEM Southern Africa, with technical support from ISS South Africa, organised workshops to develop a National Action Plan for the implementation of Resolution 1325.

The first workshop, under the theme "Women and Peacebuilding," was held in November 2011 in Antananarivo, the capital city. The third day of the workshop was devoted to a round-table discussion among the political parties and saw the active participation of the "four mouvances," the main protagonists in the 2009 crisis. It recommended among other things, the development of a

86   *Gaby Razafindrakoto*

National Action Plan for Resolution 1325 "Gender, Peace and Security." It also addressed the international community: namely, UN Women to take up the leadership for supporting Malagasy government and civil society in this process, to provide financial and technical support for programmes on gender-based violence, and the necessary support for peacebuilding processes in Madagascar.

To political parties, it recommended promoting a culture of gender, peace and security in order to stop political violence. It equally advised them to include gender parity in all party manifestos. Further, it reiterated the need for the capacity building of women candidates within political parties to stand for elections.

As for civil society, they were to organise a national dialogue for Malagasy women in order to bridge political divides and develop a common purpose and vision for women, to conduct peace education amongst the communities, to advocate for a culture of independence in the media, and ensure gender parity in the decision-making structures of civil society organisations.

A second workshop was organised the following year, 2012, for the drafting of the plan; that second workshop invited representatives of the 22 regions of Madagascar.

The plan included the six following pillars:(1) adoption and implementation of relevant international, continental, national and regional Gender, Peace and Security related legal and policy instrument; (2) effective peacebuilding for all; (3) gender mainstreaming in the peace and security sector; (4) fighting gender-based violence (GBV), HIV and AIDS; (5) poverty eradication for sustainable development; and (6) monitoring and evaluation.

In 2015, the Fiombonan'ny Fiangonana Kristianina eto Madagasikara or FFKM (Conseil oecuménique des Églises Chrétiennes de Madagascar/the Ecumenical Council of Christian Churches in Madagascar) organised regional dialogues on national reconciliation.This was a significant development, as religious peacebuilding can be quite effective (Agensky 2018). It was noticed that, effectively, women's participation was almost non-existent. Thus, a "Women's Dialogue on Peace and Security" was convened, in partnership with the bureau of the African Union in Madagascar, to advocate and ensure the effective participation of women in all spheres of security decision making and processes of national reconciliation. Malagasy women from the 22 regions met in the capital; later, all the participants were invited to attend the National Reconciliation Conference conducted under the aegis of the FFKM at Ivato.

The National Conference resolutions provided for the establishment of a structure to finish the process. The FFKM organ put in place during the transition could be preserved, but its composition would be improved and increased.The other option was the establishment of a National Reconciliation Committee, instead of the FFKM. Participants discussed the creation of a Ministry of National Reconciliation.

The participants of the FFKM conference also wanted to regulate political practice. It would start with the monitoring of the military so that they would not yield to the call of politics and respect ethics.A body would monitor parties and see how they operated. Madagascar could have its "council of the wise" (Conseil des Sages) or presidium bringing together former presidents and heads of state. Finally, a new, less republican, institution was proposed: The House of Ampanjaka, bringing together representatives of royal dignitaries present and respected in the grassroots community.

Still in the context of national reconciliation, there were two possibilities for changing the constitution. First, the Constituent Assembly could amend the current basic text to establish a "strong presidential regime." Secondly, all types of possible regime resurfaced: presidential regime, parliamentary regime, monarchical regime, federated states, autonomous provinces and even a religious state or "*fanjakam-pisorona.*" The Constituent Assembly would therefore be called upon to propose several constitutions and the people will make their choice. It would not be a unique proposition to submit to a referendum.

But the resolutions of the National Reconciliation were not unanimously accepted and fully carried out, since they advised the suppression of some state institutions. Now, the FFKM does not miss an opportunity to ring the alarm or warn the government at any time they feel it does not meet the urgent needs of the population facing poverty.

The Government Council of 10 July 2018 made a verbal statement concerning the setting up of a restricted committee for the updating and validation of the National Action Plan on Resolution 1325 "Gender, Peace and Security" for Madagascar. For now, the National Action Plan for the implementation of the resolution is still pending, though we can say that the reform of security sector is integrating it and gender dimensions in its process.

It is to be noted that UNSC Resolution 1325 has been translated into Malagasy to facilitate a better understanding.

Overall, then, the opening remarks by Cheryl Hendricks for the 2008 workshop are still valid:

> we do not need more legal instruments; rather, we need to give our instruments teeth, ... and that we must not lose sight of the political aspects of gendered relationships – they are fundamentally about the imbalance in power and the skewed distribution of resources between men and women.
>
> (Hendricks and Chivasa 2008)

The reform of security sector

In 2014, at the request of the Malagasy government, a joint assessment mission of the security sector reform (SSR) was conducted. The report of the mission recommended the creation of a Technical Committee for the Organisation of the National Seminar on SSR: it conducted regional and national consultations to identify and analyse the needs of the populations. A national seminar on SSR and the drafting of a general policy letter of SSR endorsed by the president of the republic could be organised. The funding from the United Nations

88   Gaby Razafindrakoto

Peacebuilding Fund (PBF) for the country allowed the development of the project for support to SSR in Madagascar.

The goal of the reform is to support the security sector reform process in Madagascar, including the development of a national vision for security, the strengthening of the skills and capabilities of the Defence and Security Forces (FDS), the consolidation of the control mechanisms and the promotion of trust between security forces and vulnerable populations.

Some steps have been achieved: namely (1) the technical support and material provided for the preparation and finalisation of the strategic and operational plans of the SSR and the draft decree of the coordinating body for the implementation of the reforms; (2) the study on security needs to develop a national vision for security that will be reflected in action plans; and (3) the evaluation of the normative and procedural framework of the management and control of firearms. On 20 March 2019, a workshop to revive security sector reform and to coordinate the security strategy was held.

The *dahalo* (banditry) phenomenon requires the utmost efforts from the government (see Gardini 2019). Reforms have been carried out to modernise tools and defence techniques of the territory, the population and their belongings, as well as the securing of people's economic activities. Professionalism of security agents and proximity protection have been prioritised. Security forces must be restructured, coordinated and regulated. Besides, new zones of interventions have been targeted, hence the building and setting up of new military camps or units, especially in the "red zones" or the "Zone Rurale Prioritaire de Sécurité" (ZRPS; Security Priority Rural Zones).

For the time being the army and gendarmerie have been provided with new defence equipment, such as bullet-proof vests, weapons, vehicles and armoured cars, speedboats and aircraft (e.g. helicopters and drones). These will be allocated to law enforcement officers to enable more effective security missions to be carried out, including pacification operations and the restoration of order, throughout the island. These measures are intended to produce tangible results in a short time. Another recent security measure consists of inserting a microchip into all cattle. Initially introduced free of charge, it will allow the animals to be tracked by a geo-location and deter the cattle rustlers. From now on, as the president says, "the criminals are to feel frightened, no longer the population."

At the same time, intensive monitoring operations on the national roads will be carried out in order to fight against the trafficking of narcotics and the country's natural resources. It is also about controlling the circulation and marketing of cattle, as well as the movement of firearms. Census data are being collected on the inventory of arms in the hands of civilians. This is being done to control guns and to encourage sustainable peace.

The number of intervention units has been increased to implement community policing. Some patrols are carried out within districts or villages to restore the population's confidence in the armed forces. These often call for the collaboration of the community. Community vigil groups or *andrimasom-pokonolona* have been set up, and some of the chiefs of fokontany have been equipped with

Women and peacebuilding in Madagascar   89

mobile phones to sound early alarms. Civilians' participation is also solicited to raise the alarm or call the police if they become aware of unusual or suspicious activities.

The SPDSN, or the Permanent Secretary of Defence and National Security, has conducted workshops and consultations at regional level throughout the country to collect community inputs and suggestions related to issues of security. This will enable every citizen, including women, to express their concerns.

Recently, it has been announced that the regulation about the military service will be changed: it is voluntary and limited to males aged 18 to 25. There was a time when every citizen, men and women, was required to perform either military or civil service for a minimum of 18 months. However, this requirement is not currently enforced. Now, every young man has to undergo a medical check up to get a green card that is issued free of charge. This green card is required in some administrative processes.

As for the number of women in the armed forces, it is currently unknown because there has been a lack of released statistics. But what is clearly noticeable is the increase of female intake in the entrance examination for the armed forces, and efforts are being made to make the military infrastructure meet their needs. The instructor staff at the military academy of Antsirabe includes some women trainers too.

For history, a few names are worth mentioning in relation to the armed forces in Madagascar: that of late Denise Fisher, the first woman to be a general controller within the police; Professor Manorohanta Marie Cecile, a civilian who was minister of defence and whose appointment had been criticised by some males in the army; then, recently, Anjanirina Nadia Randriamalaza, who was the first woman in the Malagasy marines. All this can be considered as paving the way to increasing feminine presence and participation in the security sector (see Valasek 2008).

Women and peacebuilding

In terms of gender equality, Malagasy women are said to be positioned well in comparison to some of their African and world counterparts. They are entitled to several advantageous rights, such as the customary "*misintaka*," (namely, the right to leave the household temporarily in cases when they are having severe disagreements with their husbands); the right to pass on their nationality to their children; and the right to a 50:50 share of common marital property in cases of divorce (in earlier times, women had a right to only one-third).

As for the role of women in the Malagasy community, it was not negligible in the past. Though often considered as "weak furniture" in everyday life, with roles limited to household chores and child rearing, it has to be recognised that during the era of monarchy and the precolonial period, women held many significant positions. Indeed, royal marriages were arranged between kings of the Imerina and princesses of the other coastal kingdoms to circumvent open conflicts and to facilitate peaceful coexistence throughout the island. Later,

90 *Gaby Razafindrakoto*

some queens came to power, mainly in the Imerina Highlands. Among them was Ranavalona I, who ruled the country strictly and was feared. She fiercely suppressed any threat to her power, especially from foreign influence. However, surreptitiously, women's status and influence dwindled under colonisation; their powers were usurped by their prime ministers and eventually stripped by the French colonisers.

In the present day, the status of women has changed. Women have particular roles and competencies in peacebuilding and conflict resolution. They can also be efficient mediators or facilitators in instances of gender-based violence. Prevention of violence is a sector where policewomen and female gendarmes can be trained to handle the more sensitive cases. Giving support to victims of gender-based violence can bring about better outcomes if beaten or raped women and girls are given space to speak out confidently about their experiences. Women have repeatedly been told that their marital lives ought to be ones of tolerance and should not be brought out into the open. New strategies of engagement must be developed in order to enable women to be more confident to address gender-based violence.

Some peace or conflict resolution bodies have women members. For example, the CFM (Conseil for the Fampihavanana Malagasy) and the National Council for Reconciliation include six women members and the Truth and Reconciliation committee is headed by a woman.

The mediation body also includes women members and the CNIDH (Commission Nationale Indépendante des Droits de l' Homme/the National Independent Committee for Human Rights) is chaired by a woman. These institutions or bodies challenge the authorities whenever human rights are not taken into consideration or are flouted. Moreover, non-governmental organisations and religious associations that work in the struggle for peace express their concern any time political crises occur. Such was the case in 2009, when the coalition of women's associations raised their voice to condemn the bloodshed as demonstrators were killed in Ambotsirohitra. They strongly advocated dialogue and peaceful ways to solve such conflicts. Malagasy people cherish social values such as *fihavanana*, solidarity and justice and those values forge the Malagasy philosophy which people live their lives by.

Today, however, these values seem to be crumbling. Life is no longer safe, and poverty and insecurity are widespread, both in urban and rural areas. Women are frequently among the victims of the increasing rate of kidnapping or hostage taking perpetrated by the *dahalo*, the bandits that steal cattle. These criminals have changed their modus operandi and drifted into blackmailing to coerce families into paying huge ransoms for the release of their kidnapped relatives. Murders of hostages are also part of the landscape.

The artisanal manufacture of guns and other weapons is one of the reasons for the increase in criminal behaviour. The situation is made worse by members of the armed forces renting or selling weapons.

All of these factors have impelled the civil society organisations and most women's associations to seek ways of fostering peace culture and peace education. The celebration of International Peace Day with "white marches" and the 16 days of activism against gender-based violence each year are high on the agenda of these organisations. They try to win this fight against GBV by working to empower young girls, encouraging them not to abandon schooling, but to strive to achieve a better life. These are the most efficient ways to prevent sexual and gender-based violence. This struggle has been given new impetus with the First Lady's role.

The First Lady's commitment

The UNFPA appointed the First Lady, Ms Mialy Rajoelina, as their ambassador for the fight against violence towards girls and women. The First Lady is the founder of FITIA, an organisation created to support vulnerable people, to restore their dignity as well as to ensure that their human rights are respected. One of the focuses of FITIA is to provide innovative strategies for combatting sexual and gender-based violence (SGBV), including in humanitarian settings.

The First Lady's commitment, publicly voiced on Women's Day, confirms her determination to help survivors of gender-based violence, to raise awareness of the importance of education, especially for young girls, and to prevent child marriages and early unwanted pregnancy. Ms Mialy Rajoelina attended a meeting, "From Grass-roots to Leadership," in Oslo, Norway, in May 2019. The First Lady described the alarming situation in Madagascar as far as SGBV is concerned: 30% of Malagasy women have experienced at least one type of GBV and more than 55% have been victims of violence in some form or other. Sexual assaults account for 44% of the cases. Most of the time, this violence occurs within the family circle, being perpetrated either by intimate partners or close individuals. The legal age of marriage is 18, yet early and forced marriages are still increasing and still depriving young girls of the right to choose the path for their lives and to do what they want with their bodies.

Moreover, harmful traditional practices are still prevailing in some areas of the island, where women do not have a say in their own lives. They are still subversient to patriarchal authority exercised by male family members, or the clan, or the ethnic group. Any attempt to rebel may end in repudiation or expulsion from the family, clan or ethnic group. In the end, women surrender, since they often lack means of survival and cannot fend for themselves. They dare not or do not want to get involved in civic or community life, merely assuming that it is men' s roles to attend to such matters.

To end this situation, some legal and counselling centres – for example, the Centre d'Ecoute et de Conseil Juridique (CECJ) or the "*Trano Aro Zo*" (literally, Home to Protect Rights) – have been set up in some strategic areas. Gender-based violence survivors can utilise these centres for advice, psychological support or legal assistance to prosecute the perpetrators of violence. However, the attendance is still low, and sometimes these centres lack resources. Awareness-raising campaigns have to be conducted and lobbying for funding. Moreover, in some prosecutions of those who have raped under-aged girls, the

92   Gaby Razafindrakoto

case ends in compromises between the offender and the parents of the victim, thus denying the young girl her rights.

Lately, the BFP (Brigade Feminine de Proximité/Proximity Women Brigade) has been introduced in some areas to address sexual and gender-based violence. It is composed of about 40 female gendarmes. To help them fulfil their tasks properly, the First Lady has ensured these units are adequately equipped, with such things as computers, cameras and so on. Their capabilities to handle GBV cases and to support victims psychologically have been strengthened too.

Sexual and gender-based violence is a major aspect, if not in the core, of security issues: a community cannot fully develop and ensure the population's well-being without peace and safety. Women should be given their place within the community on an equal basis to any other members.

Women's access to positions of power have slightly increased in recent times. Some non-governmental organisations, such as the Electoral Institute for Sustainable Democracy in Africa (EISA), have worked to train women and prepare them for high-ranking responsibilities. EISA aimed first at strengthening the capacity of the election management body, civil society organisations and political parties to play a constructive role in the electoral process; secondly, supporting the legislature and civil society organizations and their formalised interactions; and reinforcing the capacity of political parties to be effective and internally democratic.

With civil society, they have conducted gender mainstreaming campaigns to encourage and empower women to apply for political positions. Training in areas such as the drafting of a social project, communication skills and self esteem have been conducted for capacity building.

More women are getting involved in political and public life, yet the numbers of women in decision-making circles in Madagascar are still low. Indeed, the percentage of women in political poisitions has fluctuated in recent years. Pre-election campaigns often promise the integration of women in public life, as some political parties include women in their lists of election candidates. However, this is often just to attract votes and once the parties come to power, these women are completely relegated and are not given any positions of influence.

At the time of writing, among the 1,695 local councils in the country, only 81 are headed by women (4.8%). The National Assembly previously counted 29 women among its 151 deputies (19.2%). As for the Senate, 13 seats out of 63 are held by women (20.6%). The previous government had six women members out of 22 ministers (27%) while the latest one also has six women. No woman is head of the 22 regions. The recent legislative elections received 855 candidates, with 126 being women. The new National Assembly includes 27 women, which amounts to 17.9%. The Chair of the new National Assembly is a woman and the permanent bureau of this institution counts seven women deputies. The government had earlier announced that the number of senators would be reduced from 63 to 18 and here the percentage of women is still unknown. The objective of 50:50 parity has certainly not yet been reached.

Strategies for women's empowerment

It will take more than a critical mass of women to bring about tangible changes in Malagasy women's life. Access to high political positions should be supported by actual participation of elected or appointed women. This will require the eradication of common stereotypes about women and the latent distrust towards them, which are still deeply ingrained in society. Women decision makers have to break the "glass ceiling" that often denies them top level managerial positions. They should demonstrate their strong determination to fight for real equality, not just be figureheads.

This will take time, but it has to be started and tenaciously pursued. Activists will have to work towards much greater mobilisation of young women associations. Education and empowerment of young girls are among the key initiatives and solutions. Yet it requires strong political will, systematic substantial budgeting and monitoring mechanisms from the authorities and everyone's commitment to build a culture of peace, day in and day out.

In addition, the passing and enforcement of laws related to the issue is the most effective way to achieve rule of law and social peace. The First Lady has already met the Ministry of Justice to proceed to the legislating process. Indeed, the law will put an end to the impunity of perpetrators of gender-based violence. Strong legislation will give an opportunity for the Malagasy people to change their mindset and take responsibility. Women are sure to be protected and will gain more confidence in fulfilling their roles and duties in the community. They will be more commmitted as Malagasy citizens, with men as partners in the development of the country. On the other hand, Malagasy men, traditionally considered as heads of households, political decision makers and power holders, will be enlightened on how to interact with women, their partners, in daily life, and to consider them as their equals. Parents would treat their children on an equal footing and would not deny young girls their basic rights to schooling, whatever financial hardships they may encounter. Girls can and should be encouraged to take up any career they would like, as per their own choice. But most of all, they should have high self-esteem and believe in their potential.

The way to perrenial peace and sustainable development has to be the "ever lasting commitment" of an undivided nation. The pillars that can ensure peace within the Malagasy community comprise these major structures: first, the executive bodies, from the grassroots to the top levels, that is, the Chiefs of Fokontanys (villages), the mayors and the deputies; second, the defence institutions that include the police, the gendarmeries, the military and the penitentiaries; third, the judicial organisations with the law makers and the Ministry of Justice; and, fourth, the education system, which should be made up of not just the conventional institutions or schools and the Ministry of Education, but also exploit input from civil society plus informal and traditional leaders. Indeed, the oral tradition can be used as a channel to convey peace messages and principles. The influence of traditional leaders, and the speakers or *mpikabary*, has to be emphasised, especially now that there are women speakers. Social media and community events can be platforms to start peace or conflict-resolution forums and discussions. Higher institutions should emphasise the training of students in administrative and political strategies, as well as in ethics.

Activism should be reinforced and built up as a powerful resource, to avoid the interference of, or the appeal to, the army in political crisis settlement. Women political party leaders would gain more if they show more determination to remain in the election contest arena, make their voices heard, and not be subdued without a fight. Some of the women political leaders change their position midway through an election campaign or join or support other male candidates during the process. Instead, political parties headed by women should anchor and assert their presence in the political life of the country. The recognition of women's rights plays an important role in the "building" of peace. In Madagascar, the way to actual women's participation is still full of obstacles. The hope of a "generation capable of implementing peace" would be achieved only by true and strong commitment, not through half-hearted dabbling or whimsy. Citizen education in democratic and human values has to be carried out right from primary schooling. For the time being, the Ministry of Culture and Communication is carrying out intensive media campaigns on citizen responsibility and participation in improving the shared environment and well-being. It has instituted the Tagnamaro Programme that devotes one day a month to public service.

Conclusion

The authorities must demonstrate strong political will, legislative reform and enforcement, together with violence prevention via education and capacity building, backed up by a sense of accountability in civil society for anyone involved in areas related to women's rights and activism. These are the foundations and stages required to get more women involved in peacebuilding. Peacebuilding and conflict resolution should not be men's sole preserve: it is everyone's concern. As Nancy Lindborg (2017) has argued, "Evidence indicates that women participants in peace processes are usually focused less on the spoils of the war and more on reconciliation, economic development, education and transitional justice – all critical elements of a sustained peace." By mobilising more women peacebuilders, Madagascar is making a worthwhile investment that will secure peace in the present and into the future.

References

Agensky, Jonathan C. 2018. "Religion, governance, and the 'peace–humanitarian–development nexus' in South Sudan," in C. de Coning and M., Peter (Eds.) *United Nations Peace Operations in a Changing Global Order*. Cham: Palgrave Macmillan.

Gardini, Marco. 2019. "Profiting from remoteness: the economic and political centrality of Malagasy 'red zones,'" *Social Anthropology* 27(2), 172–186.

Hendricks, Cheryl. 2011. *Gender and Security in Africa: An Overview.* Uppsala: Nordic Africa Institute.

Hendricks, Cheryl. 2017. "Progress and challenges in implementing the Women, Peace and Security agenda in the African Union's peace and security architecture," *Africa Development* 42(3), 73–98.

Hendricks, Cheryl, and Mary Chivasa. 2008. *Women and Peacebuilding in Africa workshop report: Tswane (Pretoria), 24–25 November 2008.* Pretoria: Institute of Security Studies.

Lindborg, Nancy. 2017. *The Essential Role of Women in Peacebuilding.* Washington, DC: United States Institute of Peace. Available at: www.usip.org/publications/2017/11/essential-role-women-peacebuilding.

McKay, Susan. 2004. "Women, human security and peace-building: A feminist analysis," in H. Shinoda and J. Jeong (Eds.) *Conflict and Human Security: The Search for New Approaches to Peace-Building.* Hiroshima: Institute for Peace Science: Hiroshima University.

Okech, Awino. 2016. *Gender and Security in Africa.* Accra: African Women's Development Fund.

UN Women. 2015. *Preventing Conflict, Transforming Justice, Securing the Peace: A Global Study on the Implementation of United Nations Security Council Resolution 1325.* New York: UN Women.

Valasek, Kristin. 2008. "Security sector reform and gender," in M. Bastick and K. Valasek (Eds.) *Gender and Security Sector Reform Toolkit.* Geneva: DCAF, OSCE/ODIHR, UN-INSTRAW.

7 Women as religious citizens and peacebuilding in Kenya

Loreen Maseno

Background

The influence of religious institutions in developing countries is well known. In many African settings, over the weekends there are chains of services filling hours of television and radio broadcasts (De Witte 2011: 190–191). In Kenya, there are many public manifestations of religion, with religious groups asserting a sustained and important presence in the public sphere. Religious women with religious inclinations in Kenya mobilise for different causes, including peacebuilding. Using the analytical perspective on the positions of the religious citizen (Wolterstorff 1997; Habermas 2008), this chapter demonstrates how women in Kenya as religious citizens promote peacebuilding. This chapter points to Kenyan women's peacebuilding responsibility in society as including communicating messages of peace and listening to and supporting the people affected by violence, which are a means to psychological healing (Rogers and Ideh 2008). The chapter analyses the different roles that women as religious citizens in Kenya perform in peacebuilding (Steele 2011).

Introduction

Peacebuilding as a concept encompasses not only internationally led forms of intervention, but also bottom-up and locally led approaches. It is not only restricted to post-war processes, but its methods are relevant during all phases of conflict transformation, from preventive diplomacy, peace processes and recovery. In general, peacebuilding efforts can be employed before, during, and after violent conflict occurs, by a wide range of actors in government and civil society and at various levels. Therefore, unlike peacekeeping, peacebuilding has a more ambitious goal. Peacebuilding aims to foster the political, legal, economic and social transformation of post-conflict states. On the other hand, peacekeeping has generally focused simply on containing conflicts (Duncanson 2016).

Peacebuilding strategies seek to address all three dimensions of violent conflict (behavioural, attitudinal and structural). These share a common focus on methods to mitigate tension and adversity, even as they seek to de-escalate the level of violent conflict. According to Lederach (1997:71), peacebuilding at the attitudinal level seeks to redefine violent relationships into constructive and cooperative patterns through formal or informal dialogue and reconciliation efforts. Further, he points out that transformation in any conflict must be integrated into a systemic approach with a predominant focus on relationships, which is described as "the basis of both the conflict and its long-term solution" (Lederach 1997: 26). In general, Lederach proposes a conceptual framework that includes the structure, which is concerned with the systematic elements in a protracted conflict. He also emphasises process, which includes the long-term nature of the conflict as it progresses, reconciliation, which stresses a full range of psychological dimensions central to conflict transformation, and resources.

At the structural level, peacebuilding strategies seek to reform oppressive state structures and policies and build mechanisms and "infrastructures for peace" (Unger et al. 2013). At the behavioural level, peacebuilding would encourage negotiating ceasefires and comprehensive peace accords.

Some scholars have contributed significantly to peacebuilding theory. A contribution by Sampson (1997) indicates that Adam Curle, a founding professor of the Department of Peace Studies at the University of Bradford in the UK, was appointed to the Chair in 1973. This department launched its teaching and research programmes in 1974. Curle is known to have pioneered the idea of peacebuilding from below, currently recognised as a leading mode of peacemaking amongst practitioners and academics. Sampson sums up that Curle developed a peacemaking framework that emphasised the importance of a balance of power between conflicting parties. As a Quaker conciliator, Curle envisioned and explained how peacebuilding requires restructuring relationships between the two conflicting parties, thereby empowering the weaker party, and addressing structural sources of inequality. Lederach on the other hand, focuses on transforming violent destructive conflict into constructive, peaceful relationships. Being a Mennonite conciliator who believes that by facilitating such transformations peace will be achieved, Lederach believes religious actors will act both as mediators and as advocates (Sampson 1997:277). Religious peacemakers tend to focus on building relationships and community. Religious advocacy in peacebuilding is always non-violent and will generally focus on encouraging empowerment and human rights.

Ramsbotham et al. (2007: 217) argue that the effectiveness and sustainability of peace cannot be achieved through the manipulation of peace agreements by the elite, who have vested interests. Rather, communities need to be involved from the grassroots level up. This opposing school of thought advocates for bottom–top peacebuilding, or, in the words of Lederach, "peacebuilding from below." In the above imagery the foundation and walls need to be constructed before the roof can be added. At the same time, the evolution of the thinking about the complex dynamics and processes of post-conflict peacebuilding has brought about popularity of the concept of peacebuilding from below and what Lederach calls indigenous empowerment. This form of peacebuilding

98   *Loreen Maseno*

"empower[s] people of goodwill in conflict-afflicted communities to rebuild democratic institutions" (Ramsbotham et al. 2007: 219).

The need for peacebuilding measures to take into account the community's structure while instituting long-term development frameworks and incorporating local actors, which will go a long way to preventing recurring violence. The practice of peacebuilding from below, therefore, is seen as a better alternative for practitioners and academics.

Examples of main institutional religious peacebuilders across the African continent include the Catholic Church, the Quakers, the Mennonite Church, the international, non-denominational group, Moral Re-Armament, The International Network of Engaged Buddhists, and the Nairobi Peace Initiative, which, although not itself a religious organisation, actively engages religious groups across Africa in peacebuilding. These religious peacebuilders train women, enhance their capacity and accord them space to function in their contexts.

Feminist critique of religious women in peacebuilding

There has been a common misrepresentation of women as "natural" peacemakers. This has been largely discussed among feminist scholars (Cockburn 1998; Alison 2009). Such a posture has been critiqued as being an essentialisation of all women, effectively lumping them into one category and which can be "a dangerous political force." This position works to sustain dominations, operating fixed and stereotyped dualism of "women victim, male warrior" (Cockburn 1998: 13).

Feminist literature continues to raise several interesting points against one-dimensional and simplistic accounts equating women to victims. Firstly, it points out the need to understand the role of structural violence suffered by women during the conflict.

In many cases, peacebuilding policies and conflict studies established the link between women and victimhood as their primary representation. In peacebuilding studies, women started to be visible as a monolithic and singular entity. They were depicted as sufferers of an evil and crazy violence that had no roots in any kind of structure. However, this violence has sexual underpinnings and was primarily sexual violence against women. On the other hand, it has also been claimed that, in working for peace, women challenge authorities (Sørensen, 1998). Women do not just take up positions for the sake of power, but they are agents who try to ensure that there be transformation.

Further, feminist research has emphasised that women are not just victims but agents, during and after the armed conflict. Some of these studies have focused on women's involvement in the military and in other movements that have used armed force to achieve their objectives. At the same time, studies on women and their opposition to violence have been numerous. This outlook has

Kenyan women as religious citizens   99

been particularly accentuated in relation to women as religious citizens. It is to this concept that we turn.

The religious citizen

In political theory, there has been a liberal account, elaborated most fully in the work of John Rawls and Robert Audi, who argue that the religious voice in political life in particular ways is widely understood as constraining. Summarily stated, religious arguments in the public ream have been placed into two main competing positions. The liberal position is promoted by John Rawls. Here the religious voice in political life is constrained and that fundamental political questions in a constitutional democracy should be drawn from public reasons – shared public reasons accepted by all. The revisionist position taken by Wolterstorff is what I take on board precisely because in African countries we see public manifestations of religious groups which assert a powerful presence in the public sphere. It is on this basis that De Witte has shown how, contrary to normative, secular ideals, in many African countries religion plays a constitutive role in democracy. He sidesteps the Habermasian ideal of a rational and secular public sphere, which for many years has been taken for granted (De Witte 2011: 191).

A sufficient overview of Rawls's position for our purposes is provided by Freeman (2007). Rawls's position is that fundamental political questions should be decided based on "public" reasons; that is, reasons capable of being shared by all reasonable citizens in a constitutional democracy. As such, since citizens hold diverse sets of "comprehensive moral views" about ethical, religious and philosophical questions generally, Rawls argues that in a free polity it is unreasonable to expect consensus because of religious reasons. The religious voice in a constitutional democracy should, therefore, be stifled so that other reasons are elevated for adoption. In general, Rawls proposes that citizens in a constitutional democracy, for purposes of political determination of basic constitutional questions, should sidestep reasons drawn from their (conflicting) comprehensive views such as religious orientation and instead restrict themselves to using only the set of shared, public reasons that could be accepted by all.

However, according to Nicholas Wolterstorff (1997), the religious voice in political life needs not be stifled. His challenge to Rawls is directed at this split: from the point of view of the religious citizen, the citizen one's perspective is, in a way, "detached" or "split" from their full ethical perspective as a person. On the other hand, as a person, he or she has a "comprehensive view" about the nature of reality. This metaphorical "split" between different components of a person's identity in the Rawls' proposal became problematic for Wolterstorff.

Wolterstorff advanced a revisionist position on the place of religious arguments in the public realm and argued for a much greater role of religious

100 Loreen Maseno

arguments in democracies. This he did by opposing the liberal position, which restrains the place of religion in the public sphere in particular ways. He argues (Wolterstorff 1997: 105) that the religious citizen is driven by his or her religious values and notes:

> It belongs to the religious convictions of a good many religious people in our society that they ought to base their decisions concerning fundamental issues of justice on their religious convictions. They do not view it as an option, whether to do it or not. It is their conviction that they ought to strive for wholeness, integrity, integration in their lives: that they ought to allow the Word of God, the teachings of the Torah, the command and example of Jesus, or whatever, to shape their existence as a whole, including, then, their social and political existence. Their religion is not, for them, about something other than their social and political existence.

The revisionist response by Wolterstorff would consider, for example, the fact that Kenyan women as religious citizens (as opposed to non-religious citizens) can freely express and justify their convictions in religious language. These Kenyan women as religious citizens centre their conviction on the necessity of peacebuilding, which they freely express to their membership in the hope that this information would be of use for its audience. Indeed, the basis of these qualities is drawn from what they read in the word of God and as such they are not hesitant to express these views for the nation at large.

Peacebuilding by Kenyan women religious citizens affirms the need for fairness, justice and healing/reconciliation throughout the entire process of prevention, mitigation and post-violence reconstruction (Rogers and Ideh 2008). As religious citizens, women in Kenya engage in civic education and their engagement with governance does not start and end with casting a vote. Rather, they are alert to the need for people to make right choices through civic education from the onset.

Further, as religious citizens, women in Kenya remind their members of their democratic right and responsibility to make a choice for good and upright leaders who shall represent them. This is a form of active participation in the governance of Kenya. Kenyan women, as religious citizens are driven by community defined needs in their peacebuilding efforts primarily because they are key stakeholders who desire peace for their families and communities. These are women who, as partners from the local church and other organisations, represent diversity and share common values for peace efforts.

At the same time, women as religious citizens build upon indigenous non-violent approaches to conflict transformation and reconciliation. In their pursuit of peace and for the purpose of peacebuilding, they use their transformative narratives, folklores, songs, and poems for communicative purposes. On the other hand, the emergence of female Pentecostal-Charismatic preachers in East Africa (Mhando et al. 2018) confirms the changing status of women in the region.

Negotiating Kenyan women's experience for peacebuilding

Numerous Kenyan religious women have witnessed post-election violence and terror first hand. Some of them have immediate relatives whom they have had to take in before, during and after the violence. This experience of violence, loss and pain makes some of these women take a stand to help. How can these experiences count and be taken seriously?

Over the years, a notion of "women's experience" as an alternative source of knowledge has been questioned. This is so because it is related to the claims of a female nature being one, universal and historically stable. The argument today is that there is no transpersonal nature that is constitutive of humans or women as such. In fact, there is a profound critique of the supposed universal nature of "woman." Instead, there is the claim that what we label as woman already has connotations attached to it, created by society for its female species.

However, this chapter contends that while the critique is helpful in terms of promoting analytical rigour and caution, it remains possible to analyse women's experiences collectively. Commitments and characteristic assumptions that typify theological reflection labelled feminist very often embrace appeals to women's experience. Indeed, many Kenyan religious women, having encountered violence and terror, are committed to the emancipation of women and to incorporating women's experience in their efforts and analysis. One challenge is that women's experiences have been considered either insignificant on their own or subsumed under the males' category of human experience.

Kenyan women's peacebuilding responsibilities lead to a consideration of what women's experience actually is. It has been problematised that it is not always clear whether the experience referred to in the feminist discourse is an "inner experience" or a wider notion "life or general experience." Consequently, "women's experience is both a complex and troublesome category in feminist theory; when used, it needs to be examined and explicated" (Eriksson 1995: 46). However, it is also pointed out that women's experience as the norm arose because of its privileged character. This privilege arises from claims about women's status and ontological nature, coupled with women's historical experience of oppression (Davaney 1997: 200).

Women's experiences can include women's bodily experience, women's historical experience, women's socialised experience or even women's feminist experiences (Young 1990: 60–62). Though women's experience is problematic, to eliminate it wholesale is unrealistic because both women and men experience the world as gendered beings. If we were to do away with the category women, then that negates attempts geared towards the emancipation of women. In general, there is a historical entity, women's experience (Maseno and Elia 2019). However, it is important to note that traditionally, the use of the category "women's experience" has often denied the recognition that there are other forms of oppression rather than gender. This is because the emphasis on the commonality of women's experience easily conceals racial and class differences among women. It renders

102   *Loreen Maseno*

invisible and absorbs the lives of the varieties of women in the world. In essence, there is a need for a more localised interpretation of women's experience that traces the historically particular situations of the women concerned.

In Kenya, women's experience at national level is influenced by several factors such as cultural, physical, environmental, economic and political variations. At the personal level, the variety is even more distinct where lifestyles vary according to rich and poor, single or married, with no children or with ten children, with husband present or absent, rural or urban, to mention but a few (Nasimiyu-Wasike 1989: 124). Further, many Kenyan women struggle for bare necessities. They work hard carrying heavy burdens such as firewood, fetching water from far away rivers and wells, planting, weeding, caring for children, grinding corn and preparing food. Kenyan women in rural sectors, especially those who take on the status of rural educators, tend to work long hours. Besides fulfilling the duties expected of them as women, they also do 8 hours' work in their professional fields (nursing or teaching) (Nasimiyu-Wasike 1989: 123–124).

Tracing particular situations of women in particular contexts involves storytelling. Narratives with records and accounts of these women prevail in both oral and written materials. Stories play a normative role in Africa in general and, therefore, Kenyan and African women accept stories as a source for theological and religious reflection (Oduyoye 2001: 10).

According to Carole Ageng'o (2009),

> The Kenyan elections crisis should also be viewed from a gender perspective. Such analysis is important when considering how women ultimately participated in the mediation of the conflict. Men and women's experiences during the elections – in the campaigns as well as the polling and through the crisis – are rooted in the social construction of their roles as women and men in Kenyan society. The different experiences of men and women were also influenced by the inadequacy of the existing laws and institutions, such as those governing political parties and elections, contributing to the unequal representation of women and men in the political process.

It follows, that experiences of numerous women in Kenya cannot be equated to those of men during the elections crisis in Kenya. It is only in isolating these gendered responses that the depth of the conflict can be understood. At the same time, in Kenya it has been shown how the Waki Commission reported several cases of women attempting to report rapes to the police during the election crisis. Many women at the police station were turned away or told to choose between reporting burning of their houses and property, or gang rape, but not both. These experiences in the Kenyan context continue to be a stimulus to Kenyan women as religious citizens to take a firm stand on peacebuilding.

Kenyan women's peacebuilding responsibilities

Kenyan women have not been passive during peacebuilding efforts, as they are actively involved in peace advocacy; by waging conflict non-violently in pursuit of democracy and human rights, they also take up the roles of relief workers, mediators, trauma healing counsellors and participants in development and decision-making processes (Onsanti 2014: 3). Research has shown that broader inclusion of women in formal peace processes often plays a role in increasing the credibility of the peacebuilding process and goes a long way to contributing to the sustainability of the peaceful coexistence. Further, the active involvement of women in peacebuilding and peace processes has been found to be more sustainable compared to those with no women's involvement (Potter 2008).

Kenyan women in religious groups have been very active in peacebuilding in recent decades. Sampson (1997) identifies several reasons for this increased activity. Drawing from her explanation, it is clear that Kenyan women find themselves in religions that are organised at national and international levels, and so offer existing channels for wide communication and organisation.

Secondly, these women find in religions ethical visions that can motivate believers to action. Several Kenyan women are, therefore, spurred to act in order to assist others who have been victim of post-election violence and other forms of violence. According to Muthoni Wanyeki (2010), during the post-election violence Nairobi Women's Hospital reported an upsurge in cases of sexual violence – with such cases being three times the normal intake. The cases primarily involved girls and women from the low-income areas of Nairobi. The cases of sexual violence against women were, at this point, believed to be largely opportunistic – related to the general breakdown of law and order and the upsurge of criminality of all kinds. However, reports were also received of forced circumcision of girls. A number of women from their religious persuasion and who are members of the Kenyan women's movement responded to the violence with attempts to document women's experiences and respond with increased services, as well as with advocacy to ensure that those involved in the humanitarian and relief effort did the same.

Thirdly, as seen in some cases in Kenya where the central government is in disarray, religious organisations may be the only institutions with some degree of popular credibility, trust and moral authority. Kenyan women in these religious institutions take up the space and, together with their male counterparts, start initiatives meant to enhance peacebuilding in their villages and the localities. At the same time, over many years, indigenous religious groups and their female membership continue to be long-term players who are present throughout the conflict's lifecycle, starting from colonial expansion, post-independence and to date.

Kenyan women, as religious citizens, also play a role in conflict prevention. These women are open and encourage the opening of space for mediation. Several have taken a step to bringing together actors in the conflict for

104　*Loreen Maseno*

mediation. Women's organisations have been known to have broad grassroots networks, which are often uniquely placed to detect the signs of conflict and work towards conflict prevention.

With increasing tensions and conflict the world over, it is important to consider the role of religious women in peacebuilding. According to Sampson (1997: 275), "the primary arena of church activity and faith … that of the spiritual, emotional, and relational well-being of people … lies at the heart of contemporary conflict." There are, therefore, roles that religious groups and individuals have played in conflict resolution and peacebuilding. Many of these are women who are led by religious reasons and persuasions.

Religious women deliver religious peacebuilding interventions in four main roles, as explained by Sampson (1997). The first role is that of educators. These women, as religious citizens, ensure that they build their capacity as trainers of trainers and hold the community to account when violence and conflict, which likely primarily affects women, takes place.

Another important role undertaken by religious women is that of observers. Here, these women provide a watchful, compelling physical presence that is intended to discourage violence, corruption, human rights violations, or other behaviour deemed threatening and undesirable (Sampson 1997: 286).

Third, as intermediaries, religious women in Kenya are engaged in mediation efforts at various levels. These women see that not all conflicts are useful and can be toned down through successful mediation. As intermediaries, many of these religious women in Kenya are involved in fact finding, peace-process advocacy, facilitation, conciliation and mediation, usually in some combination.

Fourth, religious women in Kenya are also advocates. Here, they work to empower the disenfranchised and to restructure relationships and unjust social hierarchies. Independent advocates are able to promote the weaker group's cause to the opposition and to the greater community. Within this cluster are also activists who champion and contribute to the course of advocacy.

Challenges faced by women religious peacebuilders

Emphasis has been often placed on the importance of women involvement in peace and reconstruction. Onsanti (2014) has shown the way women were credited as vital during the conflict in disseminating peace education and maintaining social order. The same women would highlight the plight of other women and children and help in coming up with effective ways of healing the society while fulfilling the needs of all the members of the society. However, in spite of these aforementioned achievements, women and girls are seldom consulted on, nor actively involved in, the reconstruction process during peacebuilding and their specific interests are seldom a top priority (Onsanti 2014: 27).

According to Onsanti in her study in Eldoret, Kenya, younger single women who did not participate in peacebuilding and ranged from the ages of 22–30 years. Their lack of involvement was occasioned by the fact that these particular women were single and preferred to flee the violence-prone area at the height of the conflict (Onsanti 2014: 95), which meant they were unable to play a meaningful part in peacebuilding processes.

Women in religious peacebuilding have largely been ignored in the religious arena. Most women who are trying to legitimise themselves in the religious spheres within their countries face challenges from the patriarchal communities they serve in and struggle to legitimise themselves (Mhando et al. 2018). A number of these women's religious roles in driving peacebuilding is often viewed through a male lens, thus hindering their efficacy.

Much of the work of women in peacebuilding is often overlooked, owing to the preferences of most of these women for anonymity and working away from the limelight (Marshall et al. 2011: 11–12). Often the hard work and determination of these religious women is not as appreciated as it ought to be, though there are some who consciously decide to keep a low profile and take pride in the quality of modesty.

Conclusion

Religious women are important shapers of religious narratives and motivations that support peacebuilding. Women in Kenya and in other parts of the world have been effective implementers of religious peacebuilding, particularly through interfaith or intercommunal activities (Marshall et al. 2011).

Peacebuilders seek to build bridges across conflict divides in order to restore constructive relationships and (re)build peace-conducive institutions. Kenyan religious women employ conventional methods of conflict mitigation and are best supported by multitrack approaches to conflict intervention through coordinated efforts by international, state-based, civil society and grassroots bridge-builders. As bridge builders themselves, Kenyan religious women play an important role in protracted conflicts rooted in structural asymmetry between state elites and their challengers (for example, oppressed minorities or disempowered majorities) to ensure these are effectively transformed. This chapter has demonstrated that women in Kenya as religious citizens can engage in peacebuilding successfully. Using the analytical perspective of the religious citizen, the chapter has pointed to Kenyan women's peacebuilding responsibility in society as including communicating messages of peace, rebuilding democratic spaces and supporting the people affected by violence.

References

Ageng'o, Carole. 2009. "Kenya: Peace and security imperatives for women," *Pambazuka News*. Available at: www.pambazuka.org/en/category/features/60353

Alison, Miranda. 2009. *Women and Political Violence: Female Combatants in Ethno-National Conflict*. New York: Routledge.

Cockburn, Cynthia. 1998. *The Space between Us: Negotiating Gender and National Identities in Conflict*. London: Zed.

106 *Loreen Maseno*

Davaney, Sheila. 1997. "Continuing the story, but departing the text: A historicist interpretation of feminist norms in theology," in Rebecca Chopp and Sheila Davaney (Eds.) *Horizons in Feminist Theology: Identity, Tradition, and Norms.* Minneapolis, MN: Fortress Press.

De Witte, Marleen. 2011. "Business of the spirit: Ghanaian broadcast media and the commercial exploitation of Pentecostalism." *Journal of African Media Studies* 3(2), 189–205.

Duncanson, Claire. 2016. *Gender and Peacebuilding.* Malden, MA: Polity Press.

Eriksson, Anna. 1995. *The Meaning of Gender in Theology: Problems and Possibilities.* London: Coronet Books.

Freeman, Samuel Richard. 2007. *Rawls.* The Routledge Philosophers Series. New York: Routledge.

Habermas, Jürgen. 2008. *Between Naturalism and Religion: Philosophical Essays.* Malden, MA: Polity Press.

Lederach, John Paul. 1997. *Building Peace: Sustainable Reconciliation in Divided Societies.* Washington, DC: United States Institute of Peace Press.

Marshall, Katherine, and Susan Hayward with Claudia Zambra, Esther Berger, and Sarah Jackson. 2011. *Women in Religious Peacebuilding,* USIP Peaceworks Report No. 71. Washington, DC: United States Institute of Peace Press.

Maseno, Loreen and Elia Mligo. 2019. *Women within Religions: Patriarchy, Feminism and the Role of women in Selected World Religions.* Oregon, USA: Wipf and Stock.

Mhando, Nandera, Loreen Maseno, Kupa Mtata and Mathew Senga. 2018. "Modes of legitimation by female Pentecostal-Charismatic preachers in East Africa: A comparative study in Kenya and Tanzania," *Journal of Contemporary African Studies.* doi: 10.1080/02589001.2018.1504162

Nasimiyu-Wasike, Anne. 1989. "Jesus and an African woman's experience," in Jesse Mugambi and Laurenti Magesa (Eds.) *Jesus in African Christianity.* Nairobi: Initiatives Publication.

Oduyoye, Mercy. 2001. *Introducing African Women's Theology.* Sheffield: Sheffield Academic Press.

Onsanti, Katherine. 2014. Religion, gender and peacebuilding in Africa; A case study of Kenya 2007/8. Unpublished Master's research project submitted in International Conflict Management, University of Nairobi.

Potter, Antonia. 2008. *Gender Sensitivity: Nicety or Necessity in Peace Process Management?* Geneva: Centre for Humanitarian Dialogue.

Ramsbotham, Oliver, Tom Woodhouse & Hugh Miall. 2007. *Contemporary Conflict Resolution: The Prevention, Management and Transformation of Deadly Conflict.* Cambridge: Polity Press.

Rogers, Tom B., and Julie Ideh 2008. *Pursuing Just Peace: An Overview and Case Studies for Faith-Based Peacebuilders.* Baltimore, MD: Catholic Relief Services.

Sampson, Cynthia. 1997. "Religion and peacebuilding," in I. William Zartman and J. Lewis Rasmussen (Eds.) *Peacemaking in International Conflict: Methods and Techniques.* Washington, DC: United States Institute of Peace Press, pp. 273–316.

Sørensen, Birgitte Refslund. 1998. *Women and Post-Conflict Reconstruction: Issues and Sources.* Geneva: United Nations Research Institute for Social Development (UNRISD).

Steele, David. 2011. *A Manual to Facilitate Conversations on Religious Peacebuilding and Reconciliation.* Washington, DC: United States Institute of Peace Press.

Unger, Barbara, Stina Lundström, Katrin Planta and Beatrzix Austin (Eds.). 2013. *Peace Infrastructures Assessing Concept and Practice*, Berghof Handbook Dialogue Series No. 10. Berlin: Berghof Foundation.

Wanyeki, Muthoni. 2010. "Lessons from Kenya: Women and the post-election violence," *Standpoint: Feminist Africa* 10, 91–97.

Wolterstorff, Nicholas. 1997. "The role of religion in decision and discussion of political issues," in Robert Audi and Nicholas Wolterstorff (Eds.) *Religion in the Public Square: The Place of Religious Convictions in Political Debate*. London: Rowman & Littlefield, pp. 67–120.

Young, Paula. 1990. *Feminist Theology/Christian Theology: In Search of Method*. Minneapolis, MN: Augsburg Fortress.

8 Women as agents of peace in the Midlands Province, Zimbabwe

Towards sustainable peace and development[1]

Sophia Chirongoma

Zimbabwean women have been a force in the political evolution of the country before and since its independence in 1980. They have affected and been affected by the various political conflicts which the country has witnessed. Their political activism stretches back to the important, albeit insufficiently acknowledged, role as combatants and "mothers of the revolution" in the Second Chimurenga.[2]

Background

Women have not been spared from brutal repression, beatings, rape and torture during times of war and political violence. Be that as it may, women have gone beyond their trauma, suffering and pain to look for alternatives and connections to resolve conflict. In most cases, women are left to pick up the pieces after the tsunami of violence has passed. Women's skills and social positions give them different perspectives on issues of peace and conflict, which have often been neglected. Women have demonstrated their abilities to achieve common ground in conflict situations beyond doubt, as they are more prepared than men to make sacrifices in order to find solutions. Women and women's experiences are essential in peace and reconciliation. The focus of this chapter is to illustrate the fact that in order to achieve meaningful peace, reconciliation and sustainable development, Zimbabwe needs to empower women and promote their participation in governance and political leadership. Tapping from the field research conducted in the Midlands Province of Zimbabwe, the chapter illuminates women's initiatives and contribution towards peacebuilding and self-empowerment. The chapter sustains the argument that, if empowered, women can work effectively to improve their communities. The conclusion reached in this chapter is that the empowerment of women is integral to building and maintaining peace in the community.

Introduction

Women and children suffer the most from violent conflict. They are often targeted because they are considered to be weak and vulnerable. Many times, women are left to pick up the pieces and salve bitter wounds after a war or

Zimbabwean women as agents of peace   109

violent conflict, creating pathways for forgiveness, healing and nation building. The United Nations Security Council Resolution 1325 of 2000 is an acknowledgment of women's selfless contribution towards peacebuilding processes, as well as a recognition of women's peculiar vulnerabilities to violence during armed conflict. However, marginalisation and sidelining of women has impeded their capacity to fully participate in peacebuilding and sustainable development. Although on paper the Zimbabwean pieces of legislation has provisioned for equality between men and women in terms of legal and human rights, the reality on the ground is starkly different. These vast differences are made visible by the fact that women are generally under-represented in decision-making bodies, policy formulation, and in leadership.

The situation is worse in rural communities, such as in the various parts of the Midlands Province, where patriarchy excludes women from public life. More often than not, some women not are aware of their rights, to the extent that they end up infused with oppressive patriarchal norms, which deny them a voice. The traditionally male-dominated social constructs are key impediments to women's participation in economic and political leadership, and thus limit their capacity and involvement in peacebuilding processes. Against such a backdrop, this chapter calls for a conscious effort from government, civil society and the church to recognise women's potential in peacebuilding and leadership. Drawing insights from the life experiences of women in the Midlands Province, the chapter highlights women's contributions towards peacebuilding and self-empowerment. The chapter also articulates the various challenges encountered by women in the process and it proffers possible solutions to such challenges. In the concluding section, the chapter reiterate the fact that, if given a chance, especially within a conducive environment, women can play remarkable roles in peacebuilding work, reconciliation and sustainable development. To begin, the following section discusses the roles of women in peacebuilding within traditional African societies.

Women and peacebuilding in traditional African societies

Across the different historical periods, women have always been involved in peacebuilding and conflict resolution. Recent studies have shown the contribution of African women towards this endeavour (Koen 2006; Shulika 2016; Masunungure and Mbwirire 2016; Rukuni et al. 2016; Mbwirire 2017). Peace in Zimbabwe is closely connected with social harmony, hence it is important to maintain harmonious relationships. Any *chivi* (bad deed) has the potential to disrupt this harmony, with self, with family, the whole community, with the ancestors and principally offends God (Shoko 2007). If anyone commits a *chivi*, he or she invites misfortune. Hence, most Africans share a communal responsibility to try to refrain from any actions that might provoke the ire of the spirit realm, which would expose the community to the risk of misfortunes such as droughts or some other natural calamity (Mwandayi 2011; Taringa 2014). Informed by perceptions of such an intertwined and tripartite worldview, many

110   *Sophia Chirongoma*

Zimbabweans have come to the conclusion that the current socio-political and economic crisis bedevilling the nation is being caused by collective "sins of commission or sins of omission." Such rhetoric is also being guided by the insight that Zimbabweans have not adequately dealt with past wrongdoings. Consequently, the general viewpoint is that the nation is in urgent need of social transformation to provide fertile ground for reconciliation, lasting peace and prosperity.

In most traditional African communities, women were tasked with imparting knowledge and wisdom to children. Hence, the education of children was the preserve of women. Such knowledge and wisdom was often imparted through storytelling and folklore. It is in this role that women taught the children moral values, responsibility and honesty. In particular, girls were specifically trained in their duties and responsibilities as women and mothers. The socialisation of the younger folk, particularly the appropriate grooming for girls, was the responsibility of the mother, aunts and grandmothers. Because of these close ties between a child and her female relatives, the elderly women in Africa have a lot of influence in social reconciliation, as well as building bridges towards peaceful coexistence.

The maternal role in traditional society was the framework for perpetuating society's values, identity and social behaviour. In traditional Africa, peace germinates and flourishes because of the positive influence of the mothers. Women, especially mothers, aunts and grandmothers, played critical roles in mediating peace in the family and the community as a whole. Elderly respectable women were often sent as peace mediators and they usually played a key role in crisis management and conflict transformation, especially in potentially explosive situations. In the event of worsening hostilities, elderly women would go on their knees or threaten to expose their naked bodies. This would signify a curse and, because of the aggrieved parties' respect for the elderly woman, no matter how heated the conflict, her intercession would result in the cessation of hostilities and peace being established.

In contemporary times, elderly women's role as mediators for peace and reconciliation is still respected and acknowledged. In cases when children are fighting, especially owing to petty sibling rivalry, and it has come to blows, the mother will often step between the two in a bid to separate them. Whenever that happens, the children quickly have to put their differences aside because they realise that if they continue fighting they might hurt their mother. Thus, out of their respect for the mother, they will have to find other peaceful means of resolving the conflict. The same method is also used in the event of spousal violence; if the mother positions herself between a fighting couple, this will be the cue for them to find alternative means for settling their dispute. In this light, women have played and continue to play a formidable role in inculcating and maintaining peace in their homes and in the community.

Among the Shona in Zimbabwe, if a member of the family committed murder, the cultural mode of reparation for the spirit of the murdered person was through the *kuripa ngozi* ritual, a process whereby the family of the offender offers a young virgin girl to the family of the victim. This was considered as a peace offering to propitiate and avenge the spirit of the murdered victim (Gelfand 1962). The young woman given as a peace offering would be expected to bear a child who would replace the dead victim, after this she could return to her people. If any man within the offended family develops a bond with her and expresses the desire to keep her as a wife, then the two families would perform the necessary marriage rituals (Bourdillon, 1976). In Zimbabwe, as in other African countries, the marriage bond between offending parties was used to heal the wounds, cement an agreement and stabilise the situation. The marriage itself constituted an inviolable alliance between the parties. However, this clearly compromises the autonomy of the girl child. Peace was achieved at the expense of the liberty of the girl.

In many African societies, older women were often used as peace envoys. Women, especially the older women, were not perceived as threats by warring parties. They could travel without harm in conflict situations. It was these elderly women who facilitated contact and communication between the parties in conflict. For instance, in the traditional Zulu culture, in the midst of social discontent and conflict, it was the women who would appeal to the Queen Mother, iNdlovukazi, to plead with her son (the King) for an end to hostilities.

While African women have played, and continue to play, a formidable role in mediating for peace, unfortunately because their work is usually done behind the scenes as advisers, most of their influential roles rarely receive the credit and recognition they deserve. This chapter sets out to unveil the layers of shrouds covering the unsung heroes of Africa so that we can celebrate African women's contribution towards peacebuilding and sustainable development. Using the lived realities of Zimbabwean women in the Midlands Province, the key argument of this chapter is that there can never be peace and conflict resolution without a meaningful contribution by women. Women represent an untapped resource in peacebuilding. Women are survivors and they are protectors, while they have been socialised to play a leading role in peacebuilding. It is unfortunate that women's strategic roles in peacebuilding remain unacknowledged by African political leaders. As noted above, African women have an indispensable role in negotiating and mediating for reconciliation. The next section of the chapter reiterates the need for creating a conducive environment for reconciliation in Zimbabwe.

A call to reconciliation

The history of Zimbabwe has been mired by violent legacies and delays in reconciliation. The culture of violence dates from the colonial period to the present. Zimbabwe as a nation has not dealt decisively with its history of violence from 1886 (militant resistance to colonialism) to the time of writing. Most Zimbabweans believe that peace and reconciliation are potential remedies to socio-political and economic problems. Even the church leadership has

112 *Sophia Chirongoma*

called for reconciliation. The following excerpt (ZCBC, EFZ and ZCC 2006) reflects the clarion call made by several ecumenical bodies in Zimbabwe:

> The events in Zimbabwe today show that reconciliation was not fully achieved. We were as a nation never taken through a process where the truth was told about the pain experienced during the years of the struggle for liberation and oppression by the colonial regime. The nation needs to end the years of conflict in a formal way by ritual of truth telling and forgiveness. Even in our African cultures, conflict was never resolved by simply believing people will be back to normal. It involved some ritual ceremonies that would reconcile the warring families or factions through forgiveness.

The general consensus among Zimbabweans is that the national leadership cannot continue on their trajectory without facing the festering wounds manifesting in the form of a polarised nation caused by its violent past. The coming of the new dispensation (after the November 2017 ousting of Robert Mugabe) has brought with it renewed calls to address issues such as the Gukurahundi massacres of the 1980s where tens of thousands of civilians were killed in the Matabeleland and Midlands provinces. The failure to deal with the past will continue to haunt Zimbabwe (ZCBC, 2009). Zimbabwe needs a sustainable peace and reconciliation framework to deal with all the major unresolved issues. The government is complicit, it has to acknowledge past wrongs and take responsibility by addressing past violations. There is need for truth telling, public apology, reparations and prosecution of perpetrators. Without the necessary institutional reforms, the National Peace and Reconciliation Commission (NPRC) remains but a toothless bulldog. Clearly, women cannot effectively exercise their skills in mediating for reconciliation if the culture of violence remains unaddressed. Below we present a brief chronological exploration of the contexts in which various episodes of violence have evolved in Zimbabwe to help us to contextualise the current status quo.

Legacies of violence in Zimbabwe

In order to understand where we are and where we need to go, it is pertinent to examine the history of the country to understand the legacies of violence that have had an impact on Zimbabwe. In precolonial times, the Ndebele raids on Shona groups negatively affected long-term Ndebele–Shona relations. This is mainly because, from one generation to another, the Shona have passed down stories about the raids, which involved seizure of cattle, food, and young men and women by the Ndebele. These acts promoted feelings of hatred, contempt, suspicion and a desire for revenge. This rivalry and animosity continued during the liberation struggle and provided a pathway for the Gukurahundi atrocities. In addition to these historical tragedies, the irreconcilable Ndebele–Shona tensions and hatred manifest themselves in violence during sports competitions

Zimbabwean women as agents of peace   113

or any other platforms where there are cultural and political interactions between the two ethnic groups. Ndlovu-Gatsheni and Benyera (2015: 18) aptly capture it as follows:

> Shona-speaking people continue to harbour a grievance against the descendants of the pre-colonial Ndebele-speaking people. Ndebele raids continue to be counted as a historic grievance. Even the Fifth Brigade atrocities were justified in some quarters as vengeance for what the Ndebele did in the 19th century. But such an approach to conflict resolution creates unending cycles of perpetrators and victims, and possess the potential to seriously hinder every effort at nation building.

The colonial system's divide and rule strategies further polarised the African communities. These wounds of the past have been carried into the present through memories. Yesterday's victims have become today's perpetrators of violence. Hence, there is an urgent need to deal with issues of the past.

Colonialism left deep scars and trauma in the African psyche. The white minority systematically taught Africans to hate themselves and all things African. They proceeded on the myopic premise that the African is like an animal that only understands brute force. Hence, violence was consistently inflicted on the African to bring about conformity. Africans were treated as slaves and as beasts of burden. They were systematically dispossessed of their land and wealth, leading to the impoverishment of blacks (Chirongoma, 2008). The racial tensions were worsened by the disenfranchisement of the black people as they lost their land and property, which was systematically stolen through legislation such as the Land Appointment Act of 1931 and the Land Husbandry Act of 1959. Many blacks saw the land reform as payback time for the injustices inflicted during the colonial times (Chirongoma 2012).

During the liberation struggle, atrocities were committed by both the Rhodesian government (Chung 2006) and by the liberation movements. Many innocent people were beaten, tortured, raped and even murdered during the liberation struggle at the hands of the Selous Scouts and the guerrillas, especially those perceived to be guerrillas or "sell-outs." Zimbabwe's independence was born out of this violent conflict. The blanket amnesty proclaimed by Prime Minister Robert Mugabe did little to heal the wounds of war. It was believed that people would forget the past and start afresh. Unfortunately, the victims soon became the perpetrators of violence. The violence of the Gukurahundi massacres in 1982–1987 in Matabeleland and the Midlands regions led to the deaths of more than 20,000 people (CCJP/LRF 1997).

To this day, many are still bearing the scars of torture, assault, kidnapping and rape. The unrelenting pursuit of political power has been demonstrated before, during and after national elections. The cycles of electoral violence spanning from 1979 to 1980, worsening in 2001, 2002 and 2005, and then rising to unprecedented levels in 2008 remain indelibly etched in the hearts of many Zimbabweans. These high degrees of violence became even more

114 *Sophia Chirongoma*

severe especially during the presidential election re-run. The violence that took place after the "harmonised" elections of 29 March 2008 left deep scars and a trail of destruction. The Catholic Commission for Justice and Peace noted the "country-wide reports of systematic violence in the form of assaults, murders, abductions, intimidation, and wanton destruction of property against innocent civilians whose alleged crime is to have voted 'wrongly'" (CCJP 2008: 1). The Catholic Church in particular has sought to expose human rights violations in Zimbabwe (Chimhanda and Dube 2011).

Other major unresolved human rights abuses and concerns which continue to cause many Zimbabweans to demand justice and restitution include the government-initiated chaotic land reform programme, which dispossessed about 3,900 commercial farmers and destroyed the livelihoods of 224,000 farm workers. Furthermore, Operation Murambatsvina of 2005, which resulted in the wanton destruction of property and livelihoods (Chirongoma 2009), as well as the forcible removals of the Tugwi-Mukosi communities, where some people were beaten and arrested for demanding recompense, all remain major obstructions to achieving lasting peace and reconciliation in Zimbabwe (Heal Zimbabwe Trust 2018). In addition, the abrupt and chaotic displacements of the Marange community after the discovery and consequent exploitation of the Chiadzwa diamonds; the displacement of the people around Chisumbanje to make way for the ethanol project; as well as the forced removals of people from Matabeleland because of the ARDA project extension have all continued to inflame the already aggrieved communities. All of these government-orchestrated programs – which leave the displaced communities worse off while also denying them benefits from the projects – create major barriers to achieving lasting peace and prosperity. What is even worse is the harsh reality that the government has reneged on its promises to these displaced communities, whose livelihoods have been badly affected. The people of Zimbabwe will continue to be angry until meaningful measures are taken to offer justice to the victims. Against the backdrop of such a volatile environment, the hopes and aspirations for reconciliation, lasting peace and prosperity will remain a distant dream.

The current socio-economic, political and humanitarian crisis confronting the nation of Zimbabwe is a product of the history of impunity and arrogance of the political leadership. Instead of taking practical steps towards addressing the root causes of the problems, the political leadership unfortunately continues to hide under various amnesties such as Amnesty Ordinance 3 of 1979, Amnesty (General Pardon) Ordinance 12 of 1980, and the Clemency Order of 2000. According to the Heal Zimbabwe Trust (2018: 52), the 1980 Reconciliation (Forgive and Forget), the Unity Accord of 1987, and the Global Political Agreement of 2009 did a lot to protect the perpetrators of heinous crimes:

> This is one of the reasons why reconciliation attempts have so far failed because of impunity. The result of failure of several reconciliation processes

can generally be attributed to the non-transition of the ruling government and political regime, ZANU PF.

What is even more heartbreaking is the harsh realisation that there is no sincere effort on the part of government to embark on an effective programme of national healing and reconciliation. This process can only become effective if all Zimbabweans share in the common vision of "the Zimbabwe we want," for themselves and their children, and begin to reconstruct their broken economy and national pride so as to begin healing the festering wounds (ZCBC, EFZ and ZCC 2006). The violence continued after the 2018 elections (Motlante 2018). After chronicling the history of violence whilst noting how this culture of violence has become a stumbling block in achieving sustainable peace and development in Zimbabwe, we will now turn to discuss the role of women in waging peace, not war, using the case study of the initiatives by women in the Midlands Province.

Women in peacebuilding in the Midlands Province

Zimbabweans from all walks of life will attest to the need for national healing as a matter of urgency. Women have an essential role to play in peace work and development. Women in the Midlands Province, especially the rural communities, have been involved in peacebuilding. Women in rural communities have transformational power and potential to help keep families together and call for an end to conflict.

Women in the Midlands Province are playing crucial roles in peacebuilding processes, especially at the grassroots levels. Through various activities, they mediate conflict situations, conduct sustained dialogues for peaceful coexistence within their context, and engage in sustainable livelihoods and development projects with activities such as childcare, building roads and clinics, market gardening, rearing chicken and livestock, and attending adult literacy classes. Most of these development programmes are being coordinated by non-governmental organisations (NGOs) such as AFRICOM, CARE, Heifer International and World Vision. According to some of the NGO officials who participated in this study, the philosophy behind mainstreaming these projects in the rural communities and encouraging women to participate is undergirded by the realisation of the fact that as long as women are not economically empowered, their voices and their initiatives towards building peaceful communities will remain muffled. Women who are actively participating in the various income-generating projects and sustainable livelihoods projects coordinated by these NGOs testified to how much economic empowerment had not only enhanced their social status in the community but they also added that they have become so focused on these projects such that they do not find time to waste by engaging in politically motivated squabbles. Hence, the motivation of becoming economically empowered has also indirectly contributed towards women's capacities to foster peace and development in their communities.

116   Sophia Chirongoma

Women, especially the elderly, have been actively involved in mediation of conflict situations at various levels. In Zimbabwe, and in the Midlands Province in particular, it is apparent that women play a pivotal role in giving counsel as well as mediating for peace between wrangling parties, both within the family structures and in the community. The elderly women are referred to as *chipanga mazano* (one who counsels), especially when there is a misunderstanding. The mediation role is especially given to the oldest woman in the family, who has the responsibility of maintaining harmony within the family and the community at large. It is against such a background that whenever an individual behaves in an inappropriate and often irrationally violent manner, the Shona people often respond by making the following comment, "*wakazvagwa chembere dzainda kudoro*" (you did not receive wise counsel because you were born during the time when all the elderly women were busy consuming beer; hence, they neglected to guide you properly). This is informed by the understanding that if an individual had received proper counsel during their childhood, such values should mould them to become a civil and law-abiding member of the community. Such an individual would therefore become a harbinger of peace.

Women in the Midlands Province also play an especially crucial role in maintaining peace and resolving conflict. In light of the fact that in the past few years, the Midlands Province has been in the spotlight of politically charged violence between supporters of the ruling party (ZANU PF) and the main opposition party (MDC), several study participants made reference to numerous incidents where women have been the cornerstone of restraining their husbands, children or family members from engaging in politically motivated violence or shedding the blood of people who choose to belong to a different party. Some of the rural communities in Mberengwa benefited from programmes coordinated by the Ecumenical Church Leaders Forum of Zimbabwe (ECLFZ) as well as training on conflict prevention, management, resolution, and transformation (CPMRT). Most of the peer educators who were trained by the ECLFZ are women and they have continued to utilise their knowledge and skills to establish peaceful coexistence.

Since the Midlands Province is located in a geographical zone that is rich in mineral wealth, another major cause of violence and instability within this province involves illegal mining activities. Such illegal mining operations have become widespread in Gokwe, Mberengwa, Shurugwi, Silobela and Zvishavane; these are also the various parts of the province where most of the field research for this study was conducted. According to the study participants, the violence often erupts mainly because – under the influence of either drugs and alcohol, or out of sheer greed, as well as sporadic squabbes over mining claims – some illegal miners end up attacking and assaulting each other. Such an explosive environment of violence does not always remain confined to the mining areas and it often filters into their family circles whereby some family members tend to take sides. In response to such outbreaks of family rifts and warring camps, women from such families have also become the pillars of mediation between the parties in conflict within their communities. Several study participants mentioned incidents where the intervention of women has resulted in restoring peace and unity among the squabbling parties.

Another aspect where women have been actively contributing towards building bridges for peaceful coexistence originates from the challenges caused by the unfair and unequal distribution of the proceeds from the sale of cotton produce in Gokwe. Since the production of cotton is labour intensive, during the season of growing and harvesting cotton, all family members, whether old or young, male or female, channel all their energies into the cotton fields. Unfortunately, because of the highly patriarchal structures that remain deeply entrenched within the community, after selling the products and collecting the proceeds from the family's hard labour, some elderly male family heads selfishly spend the money recklessly, while neglecting the family's essential needs. Reports of such incidents emerged from the majority of the study participants in various parts of Gokwe. They noted how such behaviour from male family heads often causes family conflict whereby some of the children who were pinning their hopes on having their educational needs paid for by the money from cotton sales often turn violent towards their fathers. As such, women have been at the forefront in mediating for reconciliation and peace within the family.

Because of their role as mothers and their caring nature, women are better placed in devising ways of peaceful coexistence for the parties in conflict. Since Zimbabwe is predominantly a Christian country, the churches have also become a formidable force for inculcating peace. The majority of women in the Midlands are members of *Ruwadzano* (church women's organisations). It is through participation in the weekly *Ruwadzano* meetings and activities that women share biblical insights as well as offering each other support on how to address conflict in their homes and in their communities. Participation in the *Ruwadzano* activities also provides a platform for women to share ideas and skills aimed at attaining and maintaining sustainable livelihoods (Young Women's Christian Association 2010). Peace is closely tied to sustainable livelihoods.

Most peace programmes in rural communities promoted by the NGOs and churches have targeted improving the lives of women as the bedrock for developing their communities. They have also come to the realisation that there can never be meaningful peace and development without socio-economic empowerment. Many of the women who participated in this study were involved in income-generating projects, such as market gardening projects, cross-border trading and rearing chickens to support their families. They also noted that ever since they became financially empowered, there has been less or no conflict in their homes. They reasoned that eliminating economic deficits in their homes enhanced peace and harmony between them and their spouses. Whilst acknowledging that women are an essential cog in the wheel of peacebuilding and sustainable development in Zimbabwe, it is also important for us to be attentive to numerous factors that inhibit women's peacebuilding and development initiatives. It is to an exploration of these obstructing factors that we now turn.

118 *Sophia Chirongoma*

Challenges faced by women peacebuilders in the Midlands Province of Zimbabwe

Women peacebuilders in the Midlands Province face enormous challenges. They feel that their participation in building and sustaining peace is not fully recognised due to the patriarchal nature of their communities. Most of the study participants reiterated the fact that in some rural communities, women are discouraged from running for political positions, especially the married women. Several male study participants said that they feared that if their wives run for political office, they would become "loose or prostitutes." Hence, some men discouraged women from taking up leadership positions in a bid to protect them from the perceived moral lapse connected with political involvement. However, many men and women appreciated the contribution of women councillors, members of parliament and senators compared to the men. Female leaders were considered as fair and just in their dealings with the community and a lot more progressive. However, most male study participants registered their reluctance to have either their daughters or wives engage in politics.

In many cases, male study participants echoed the view that they would rather encourage their wives or women in their community to take up income-generating projects rather than to participate in politics. Furthermore, most of the men expressed their abhorrence towards married women who either engage in cross-border trading or those who work as "*makorokoza*" (gold panners), arguing that such livelihoods threaten the stability of marital bliss. The majority of male study participants in rural communities in the Midlands Province averred that they would prefer their wives and daughters to be confined to household chores such as cooking, housework and taking care of children rather than engaging in other livelihood strategies which might keep them far away from home over prolonged periods.

Based on the views expressed by most of the study participants, empowered women pose a real threat for many men, especially in the rural communities. Most of the successful and economically independent women were single mothers and widows who did not have to contend with restrictions or confinements. However, they were often viewed with judgemental eyes and were often accused of being morally loose. With such rigid societal values, the integral role of women towards attaining sustainable peace and development in their communities faces a major barrier.

Women in the Midlands Province have suffered from politically motivated violence during the Gukurahundi carnage, as well as before, during and after elections. Several female study participants, especially in rural communities, revealed that they had experienced property destruction, displacement, rape and torture, especially during and after elections. Other studies have confirmed women's susceptibility to violence in Zimbabwe (Nhengu 2011). Some of the rape and sexual abuse against women was used as a tool to exact revenge for participating in politics or as a punishment for a spouse or a brother who is well known for supporting a different political party from the perpetrators of the violence. The sexual abuse cases often go unreported in rural communities and most of the women are traumatised for life. In some cases, women who fell pregnant or contracted HIV during these ordeals face the threat of divorce, societal stigma and discrimination. This is because some of their spouses will not be willing to accept a wife who has either been sexually abused, contracted HIV or got impregnated by another man, even if they know that the women were defenceless victims of violence and abuse. Clearly, women are susceptible to various forms of abuse and violations, especially in situations of political violence. Nevertheless, the life experiences of women who participated in this study are a clear testimony to the fact that women are able to rise from the dust, picking up the pieces and moving on with their lives.

Another ubiquitous challenge hindering women from flourishing in their peacebuilding and development initiatives in the Midlands Province is gender-based violence, which threatens their safety as well as diminishing their dignity and sense of self-worth. Gender-based violence (GBV) is a challenge especially in rural communities, where under-age girls are commonly forced into child marriages, even when the law forbids it. Many women continue to endure abuse either from their family members or their sexual partners. According to the statistics availed by the UNDP Zimbabwe Human Development Report (2017), Midlands Province has the highest incidences of GBV. The findings that have emerged from the present study also affirm these statistics. Consequently, much work is still required to stop GBV, not only in the Midlands Province, but in the whole country and the rest of the global community. Gender-based violence is a major breeding ground for other forms of violence, posing a threat to sustainable peace and development.

The exclusion of women from key leadership and decision-making fora also mitigates against their active participation in instilling values that foster sustainable peace and development. Since there were very few or absolutely no women holding key positions of economic and political leadership within most of the communities where this study was conducted, most of the young women who participated in this study lamented the fact that they did not have female mentors or role models to look up to. Hence, many found refuge in early marriages and some of them were even resorting to entering into polygamous relationships out of desperation to get married. There is therefore an urgent need to challenge these entrenched patriarchal paradigms if women's efforts to actively participate in socio-economic and political fora are to be realised. In order for women to fully participate in peacebuilding and sustainable development, they have to be empowered through dissemination of information through radio and television. Such information should focus on educational, employment and business opportunities tailored towards uplifting the lives of women and girls, especially in rural communities. Below we turn to exploring various avenues that can be pursued towards attaining sustainable peace and development in Zimbabwe, focusing particularly on enhancing women's participation.

Enhancing women's participation

The government of Zimbabwe needs to adopt a clear National Action Plan to guide the National Peace and Reconciliation Commission (NPRC) as regards the implementation of the United Nations Security Council Resolution 1325 of 2000. Women's role and positive initiatives need to be part of the national vision. Women have been severely affected by violence and conflict (UN Women 2013). In order to effectively empower women in all sectors of life, including their visionary leadership in peacebuilding and sustainable development, the government of Zimbabwe should focus more on supporting income-generating projects. Once women have been economically empowered, their dignity and self-esteem will be boosted and there is a high likelihood that they will be able to openly express their views in public. This will eventually inspire more women to take up key leadership and decision-making positions where they can influence policies on peacebuilding and sustainable development. Promoting gender equality and women's participation at all levels of leadership and governance is one of the major steps towards opening doors for women to transform their communities towards sustainable peace and development.

There is also need for the government of Zimbabwe to adopt a multisectoral approach towards achieving sustainable peace and development. In light of this, collaborating with and creating synergies with churches and the civil society in educating and training women, especially in rural communities where access to information is limited, on human rights, gender-based violence, CPMRT and peacebuilding initiatives will go a long way. Further, the work of the NPRC should be people driven, with no imposition by politicians.

Most of the study participants in the Midlands Province shared the view that peace will not prevail in Zimbabwe until the government has decisively dealt with perpetrators of violence, especially the violence perpetrated against women. The contention by the study participants is that the government should not be too quick to grant amnesty. They reiterated the view that amnesty should be received on merit depending on the circumstances. Another crucial issue that emerged from study participants is the need to provide safe space for the victims or survivors of various episodes of violence, somewhere to tell their stories without fear of reprisals. Most of the female study participants felt that this space is essential if peace is to be achieved. As such, women in the Midlands Province reiterated the need to be able to name their pain and their numerous frustrations. This suggestion or request rather was made in light of the fact that the people in the Midlands Province have long been on the receiving end of various kinds of violence and human rights abuses, as already noted above. Other study participants also felt that the media and security sector were biased. Hence, they proposed reforms in these key sectors to allow for national healing and reconciliation. It is, therefore, apparent that in order to promote and enhance women's participation in peacebuilding and sustainable development, the government needs to take into account women's specific concerns.

Conclusion

Women constitute more than half of the Zimbabwean population. Many women have been directly or indirectly affected by violence and conflict. Due to the patriarchal nature of the Zimbabwean culture, most women have been socialised to accept a subordinate position as normative. There is, therefore, a pertinent need to empower women to speak out on their experiences of violence and conflict. This chapter has restated the integral role of women in attaining sustainable peace and development in Zimbabwe. Taking cognisance of the influential role of the churches, especially how the church influences women in Zimbabwe, any successful endeavours on nation building, reconciliation and the national healing process should involve the church as an important or leading stakeholder. As we draw towards concluding this discussion, it seems befitting to echo the following observations made by the Heal Zimbabwe Trust in their baseline survey (2018:10):

> Zimbabwe has a volatile socio-economic and political environment characterized by polarization, political discord, economic decline and rising costs of living, authoritarianism and institutional decay. These factors pose challenges to peace and reconciliation processes in the country by shifting people's interests and priorities, multiplying layers of victims and perpetrators, blurring the distinction between a perpetrator and a victim and acting as the state's justification for ignoring past injustices.

The findings emerging from the field research in the Midlands Province which form the basis of this chapter resonate with the pertinent issues raised in the above excerpt. Clearly, Zimbabwe has experienced different kinds of conflict from the precolonial period to the time of writing, ranging from the impact of colonialism, the violence of the liberation struggle, Gukurahundi, Operation Murambatsvina, the chaotic land reform program, political violence before, during and after political elections and the prevailing humanitarian crisis. There is therefore an urgent need to deal with the past injustices and violence before the country can forge ahead. As illustrated above, the gallant women of Zimbabwe are helping to deal with the painful past as mothers, mediators and counsellors. Women have been able to transcend their own pain and make sacrifices for their families and communities. Thus, any processes aimed at national healing should include women. Women have suffered the most in times of politically orchestrated violence. They have been made to sing aggressive songs that fan violence, and were subjected to sexual violence as a way to humiliate or dominate them. Unlike men, women do not usually run away in the face of violent conflict or war; rather, they remain behind to take care of the children, the sick and elderly. We therefore need to acknowledge the role of women as peacebuilders and to empower them to participate in economic and political leadership.

122 Sophia Chirongoma

Notes

1 The data collection for this paper was made possible by utilising the funds from the Special Research Grant awarded to the author by the Research and Postgraduate Office at Midlands State University to conduct field research on the topic "Young Christian Women as Agents of Peace in the Midlands Province, Zimbabwe."
2 Zimbabwean women have been a force in the political evolution of the country before and since its independence in 1980. They have affected and been affected by the various political conflicts which the country has witnessed. Their political activism stretches back to the important, albeit insufficiently acknowledged, role as combatants and "mothers of the revolution" in the Second Chimurenga (UN Women 2013: ix).

References

Bourdillon, Michael. F. C. *The Shona Peoples: An Ethnography of the Contemporary Shona, with Special Reference to Their Religion.* Gweru: Mambo Press, 1976.

CCJP (Catholic Commission for Justice and Peace). 2008. "Grave concern over post 29 March 2008 political situation in Zimbabwe." Available at: http://archive.kubatana. net/html/archive/relig/080430ccjpz.asp?sector=HR&year=2008&range_start=931

CCJP/LRF (Catholic Commission for Justice and Peace/Legal Resources Foundation). *Breaking the Silence, Building True Peace: A Report on the Disturbances in Matabeleland and Midlands 1980 to 1988.* Harare: CCJP, 1997.

Chimhanda, Francisca Hildegardis and Aleta Dube. "Post-election violence in Zimbabwe (2008–2010): The agency of the Roman Catholic Church in national healing and democracy," *Missionalia* 39(3), 2011, 268–285.

Chirongoma, Sophia. "A historical exploration on church and state in Zimbabwe: The role of the Catholic Church for the independence of Zimbabwe," in Katharina Kunter and Jens Holger Schjorring (Eds.) *Changing Relationships between Churches in Europe and Africa: The Internationalization of Christianity and Politics in the 20th Century.* Wiesbaden: Harrassowitz Verlag, 2008.

Chirongoma, Sophia. "Operation Murambatsvina (Operation Restore Order): Its Impact and implications in the era of HIV and AIDS in contemporary Zimbabwe," in Nontando Hadebe and Ezra Chitando (Eds.) *Compassionate Circles: African Women Theologians Facing HIV.* Geneva: World Council of Churches Publications, 2009.

Chirongoma, Sophia. "In search of a sanctuary: Zimbabwean migrants in South Africa," in Joel Carpenter (Ed.) *Walking Together: Christian Thinking and Public Life in South Africa.* Phoenix: ACU Press, 2012.

Chung, Fay. *Re-Living the Second Chimurenga: Memories from the Liberation Struggle in Zimbabwe.* Oxford: African Books Collective, 2006.

Gelfand, Michael. *Shona Religion.* Cape Town: Juta, 1962.

Heal Zimbabwe Trust. *A Baseline Study Report on the peace and reconciliation process in Zimbabwe.* Harare. Heal Zimbabwe Trust, 2018.

Koen, Karin. "Claiming space reconfiguring women's roles in post-conflict situations," Institute for Security Studies, Occasional Paper 121, 2006.

Masunungure, Current, and Mbwirire, John. "Women's participation in resolving church conflicts: A case of the Salvation Army, Bindura Citadel, Zimbabwe," *Greener Journal of Social Sciences* 6(2), 2016. doi: http://doi.org/10.15580/GJSS.2016.2.012616022

Mbwirire, John. Peacebuilding and Conflict Transformation: A Study of Traditional Institutions of Conflict Transformation in Zimbabwe. Unpublished PhD thesis, Zimbabwe Open University, 2017.

Motlante, Kgalema. *Report of the Commission of Inquiry into the 1st of August 2018 Post-Election Violence in Zimbabwe.* Harare: Zimbabwe Government, 2018.

Mwandayi, Canisius. *Death and After-life Rituals in the Eyes of the Shona: Dialogue with Shona Customs in the Quest for Authentic Inculturation.* Bamberg: University of Bamberg Press, 2011.

Nhengu, Dudziro. *Women and Political Violence: An Update.* Harare: Research and Advocacy Unit, 2011.

Ndlovu-Gatsheni, Sabelo J., and Evaristo Benyera. 2015. "Towards a framework for resolving the justice and reconciliation question in Zimbabwe," *African Journal on Conflict Resolution* 15(2), 9–33.

Rukuni, Tinashe, Shanyisa, Wilkister, Madhuku, Johnson, Musingafi, Maxwell. "Enhancing women participation in peacebuilding and decision making process in Zimbabwean rural communities," *Information and Knowledge Management* 6(9), 2016, 56–60.

Shoko, Tabona. *Karanga indigenous religion in Zimbabwe: Health and well-being* Farnham: Ashgate Publishing, 2007.

Shulika, Lukong Stella. "Women and peacebuilding: From historical to contemporary African perspectives," *Ubuntu: Journal of Conflict and Social Transformation* 5(1), 2016, 7–31.

Taringa, Nisbert Taisekwa. *Towards an African-Christian Environmental Ethic.* Bamberg: University of Bamberg Press, 2014.

UNDP Zimbabwe Human Development Report. *Climate Change and Human Development: Towards Building a Climate Resilient Nation,* 2017. Available at: http://hdr.undp.org/sites/default/files/reports/2842/undp_zw_2017zhdr_full.pdf

UN Women Zimbabwe. *Zimbabwean Women in Conflict Transformation and Peacebuilding Past Experience and Future Opportunities.* Harare: UN and Government of Zimbabwe, 2013.

Young Women's Christian Association. *Peacebuilding and Conflict Management Initiatives.* Harare: YWCA, 2010.

ZCBC (Zimbabwe Catholic Bishops Conference). "National Healing and Reconciliation God can heal the wounds of the afflicted". Harare: ZCBC Africa Synod House, 2009.

ZCBC (Zimbabwe Catholic Bishops' Conference), EFZ (Evangelical Fellowship of Zimbabwe) and Zimbabwe Council of Churches (ZCC). "The Zimbabwe We Want: Towards a national vision for Zimbabwe: A discussion document," 15 September. Harare: ZCBC, 2006.

9 Women with disabilities, peacebuilding and development in Adamawa State, Nigeria

Jessie Fubara-Manuel and Justina Mike Ngwobia

Introduction

Women with disabilities are not just victims of conflict; often they are survivors and creative actors in peacebuilding, yet they are usually neglected and the onerous challenges they face are often given little attention in developing peace and security strategies. This is not unconnected to the fact that they are hardly ever included in the decision-making processes and implementation mechanisms for peaceful and positive post-conflict rehabilitation in their communities. Nigeria has adopted and domesticated the United Nations Security Council Resolution (UNSCR) 1325 and other subsequent resolutions – 1820, 1888, 1889, 1960, 2106, 2122 and 2242 – which form the Women, Peace and Security agenda. However, Nigeria's National Development Plan for implementation does not include the concerns of disability. This is even though inclusion, participation and involvement of persons with disabilities has been acknowledged as "an important component" of securing and maintaining community peacebuilding (Gartrell and Soldatic 2016).

This chapter draws on the ongoing peacebuilding efforts of the Justice, Peace and Reconciliation Movement (JPRM) in Nigeria. Within the past decade, the JPRM has been working in partnership with disabled persons' organisations in four states within the north-eastern region of Nigeria, namely, Adamawa, Plateau, Kaduna and Taraba. The design of the project considers the perspectives of women with disabilities, as well as other potential beneficiaries in the concerned communities. The intervention also seeks to contribute to strengthening and building the capacity of civil society organisations and government authorities on disability and inclusive development (DID). This chapter concentrates on its disability-inclusive intervention in Gombi, a community in Adamawa State and the voices of women with disabilities form the basis of this discussion. Data were collected through participant observation of the experiences of women with disabilities as they negotiate the spaces of post-conflict rehabilitation, as well as interviews conducted with 15 young women. All interviewees had physical disabilities affecting their mobility, seven were mothers of young children and all had suffered one form of abuse or another. The language of communication was mostly Hausa and Pidgin English, which necessitated translation of conversations for the purposes of this work.

The JPRM was established in 1999 as a response to the social and economic crisis that devastated the lives of the people in the northern part of Nigeria. It began to address issues around humanitarian intervention to respond to the emergency. It sought to provide a forum where issues of economics, social justice, peace promotion, public and community health matters, education, Christian–Muslim relations, women's empowerment and community conflict management strategies could be discussed and collectively acted upon. In recognition of the vulnerabilities of persons with disabilities, it adopted a more inclusive approach that led to the collaboration with disabled peoples' organisations, as well as working with individual persons with disability to address disability-specific needs.

This chapter investigates the place of development in peacebuilding and draws attention to the challenges of post-conflict management and integration for women with disabilities. In doing so, it highlights the voices of the women, their experiences in accessing safety, their vulnerability to sexual violence and the challenges of motherhood in post-conflict settings. Embedded in these narratives are the issues that should be considered in formulating frameworks and strategies for peacebuilding and development. We argue that most government and humanitarian aid agencies are guilty of excluding women with disabilities. As such, until there is an intentional inclusion of women with disabilities, issues of women, peace and security may never benefit from an adequately gendered approach.

The Gombi community and conflict

The Boko Haram insurgency and conflict since 2009 in the north-eastern part of Nigeria has led to many fatalities in addition to loss of property and livelihoods. This also resulted in millions of people being displaced from their homes, especially women and children. These women and girls were found in different camps and communities within the north-eastern states such as Gombi in Adamawa State. According to reports gathered from the field, women with disabilities were greatly affected by these crises.

From observations of the conflicts in Nigeria, the experience of women, girls and persons with disability depend largely on the nature of conflict, the security situation and the way in which humanitarian interventions are handled in such communities. In addition to the Boko Haram conflict, other conflicts afflicting Adamawa State are farmer–herder clashes over land and water resources along with inter-ethnic/communal and inter-religious conflicts. These conflicts, among others, have had a devastating effect on women and girls, especially those with disabilities, as they are often sexually abused and lack adequate access to humanitarian aid. It was also observed that some became disabled during the conflicts.

The most challenging aspect surrounding the post-conflict intervention is that humanitarian actors in Nigeria have often neglected the issue of women with disabilities when providing lifesaving assistance, thus further increasing

126 *Jessie Fubara-Manuel et al.*

their vulnerability. One woman with disability spoke resignedly that she sees "life as a struggle for survival and I have decided to face it, despite the ordeal." This resonates with Julie Arostegui's (2013) observation of the resilience of women who have lived through horrific situations, including sexual violence, domestic violence, human trafficking and other issues.

The JPRM hopes that engaging with humanitarian actors, communities and government on the need to mainstream persons with disabilities and other vulnerable groups in recovery phases of conflict will enhance resilience and maximise aid effectiveness. It would also support the capacity of national service delivery systems to address the needs of vulnerable groups among internally displaced persons (with a focus on persons with disabilities) and promote reintegration. Experience from the field indicates that when aid provision includes women with disabilities, it has often benefited other vulnerable groups such as the poor, the aged, and the very young.

The dimension of disability-inclusion adopted by the JPRM in setting up water, health and sanitation facilities, as well as in advocating with other organisations to mainstream disability, will contribute to build resilience within the disability movement. It would enhance disability self-advocating for inclusion in community development, as well as in humanitarian interventions. Representatives of persons with disabilities are recognised in the JPRM response strategies as interlocutors to development in peacebuilding and they proactively contribute to ensure that development and humanitarian interventions reach all the targeted vulnerable groups, including persons with all types of disabilities.

Peacebuilding and development: Two interrelated processes

In making the connection between peace and development, we build on Jennifer Balls's research in Uganda, in which she proposes the term "development peacebuilding" (Ball 2019: 209). Using this term, Ball acknowledges the critical importance of development to either contribute to or undermine the cultivation of cultures of peace. The JPRM can relate to the stories of the women that Ball refers to who, although they do not regard themselves as "self-defined peacebuilders," engage in peacebuilding efforts borne out of their "experiences and realities of the women's lives, often in response to their struggle for survival—both individually and for their families and communities" (Ball 2019: 210).

Development for these women is about survival for themselves and possibly for their family. It is about providing the basic needs in very challenging circumstances of conflict or post-conflict conditions. It is about seeking, receiving and distributing sustainable aid by identifying sources of aid and ensuring it reaches all concerned. These demands on developmental concerns are not based on one's disability status. As such, women with disabilities are likely to devote more energy to accessing involvement with and receiving aid. But they do this, as does every other African woman, with a biased conditioning of the female gender to domestic concerns of providing for the family.

Women with disabilities are not exempt from the responsibility of feeding the family that most African communities put on the woman. Much of African culture and religion creates the notion that attending to the basic needs of the family falls on the woman. She is the home-maker and the home-keeper.

Chimamanda Ngozi Adichie (2017: 6) notes that in some parts of Igboland, Nigeria, economic activities such as trading were the exclusive activity of the women before the colonial period. Proverbs 31:10–31 has been a very popular passage that has often been misinterpreted to portray the woman as the "virtuous woman" whose job is to provide for her family while denying her the strength illustrated by the woman in that passage. This is also part of what Adichie (n.d.) refers to as the danger of a "single story," where a story told with only one prejudiced perspective becomes the acceptable norm. Women with disabilities take seriously the responsibility to provide for themselves, their immediate families and, where possible, for the community. However, due to the social disenabling factors, there is a tendency to view the woman with disability as one without capacity to contribute meaningfully to peacebuilding.

Women with disabilities in Gombi express commitment to ensuring peaceful transition from conflict to communal peace towards wholeness and harmony. This desire to "improve their quality of life through post-conflict development strategies" is both challenging and motivating for other women in the community (Gartrell and Soldatic 2016). The JPRM's interaction with persons with disability have continued to be met by welcome acceptance by the women to disprove the stereotype that disability means inability. A changing slogan within the Nigerian disability community is from "ability in disability" to "productivity in disability." This portends an inherent drive to add value to their space of being in a way that demonstrates the gifts and resources that women with disabilities bring to development and peacebuilding.

It has been argued that feminists articulate peacebuilding as the inclusion of meeting basic human needs and the central role of women in this regard (Ball 2019: 209). For women with disabilities in Gombi, this feminist understanding is apt and peacebuilding should essentially incorporate development. This must be understood against the background of sound progress within the Women, Peace and Security agenda internally and locally.

International and local frameworks for Women, Peace and Security

In the past three decades, many scholars have written from personal experiences, empirical studies and secondary sources about the acute vulnerability of women and children in violent conflicts, as well as their roles in peacebuilding during and after the conflicts. In October 2000, the United Nations Security Council passed a landmark resolution to draw attention to this reality and to call on member states to acknowledge the plight of the female gender in conflict and to include women in peace processes. This was United Nations Security Council Resolution 1325, or UNSCR 1325, adopted by the Security Council

128   *Jessie Fubara-Manuel et al.*

at its 4,213th meeting on 31 October 2000. UNSCR 1325 was the culmination of the 1995 Fourth World Conference on Women, which produced the Beijing Declaration and Platform, with indicators that highlighted the impact of women in peacemaking and peacebuilding ("What Is UNSCR 1325?" n.d.). UNSCR 1325 provided an "internationally recognised legal framework for promoting gender equality in peace and security, ensuring the participation of women in all peace-making processes, and protecting women against violence in conflict and post-conflict situations" (Arostegui 2013: 537). It is anchored on four basic pillars of participation (increased participation of women in peace and security processes), protection (protection from gender-based violence), prevention (prevention of all forms of violence) and relief and recovery (gendered lens in design of settlements and economic empowerment).

Whilst UNSCR 1325 was the first official act of advocacy by the United Nations for the active inclusion and participation of women in peace and security matters, the United Nations has adopted seven other gendered conflict-related resolutions between 2008 and 2015. These are UNSCR 1820 (2008), UNSCR 1888 (2009), UNSCR 1889 (2009), UNSCR 1960 (2010), UNSCR 2106 (2013), UNSCR 2122 (2013) and UNSCR 2242 (2015). These subsequent resolutions buttress the need for the elimination of gender-based violence, re-emphasised tracked participation of women at all levels of peace and security and the final resolution in 2015 marked the 15th anniversary of Resolution 1325 by reaffirming its commitment to all the resolutions listed above. Yet, and in spite of UN Security Council Resolution 1325 appealing for the rights and responsibilities of women in peacebuilding, women are still often ignored in peace and peace-related development response. The precarious position of women and children has been echoed in recent writings by Ball (2019) and Issifu (2015) amongst others.

In August 2013, 13 years after the adoption of UNSCR 1325, Nigeria domesticated the resolution with the preparation and launch of the first National Action Plan (NAP) for the implementation of UNSCR 1325 and related resolutions, addressing the place of women in peace and security ("National Action Plan: Nigeria" 2014). This effort was supported by the Nigerian Stability and Reconciliation Programme as well as UN Women. Based on the four pillars of UNSCR 1325, Nigeria opted for five pillars which it called the 5Ps of engagement, which are Prevention, Participation, Protection, Promotion and Prosecution. A cursory look at the NAP indicates that while relief and recovery is not a major subhead, it specifically seeks response to socioeconomic empowerment of women. Also, it makes prosecution of violators through specially established courts a separate item. Following observed gaps in the first NAP, especially its failure to address issues of insurgencies and extremism, Nigeria launched a revised NAP in May 2017. The second NAP incorporated provisions of resolutions adopted by the UNSCR between 2008 and 2015 calling on states within the Nigerian Federation to adopt the NAP for appropriate implementation.

Women with disabilities and peacebuilding 129

Although UN Women has applauded Nigeria's efforts in producing the first and second NAPs as useful tools for galvanising action and helping to awaken many stakeholders and promote system-wide approaches for mainstreaming gender into human security concerns (Iroegbu 2018), the NAPS have failed to address issues of disability. The word "disability" does not appear in the NAPs, probably because it does not appear in UNSCR 1325. Thus, UNSCR 1325 itself overlooked the peculiar identity of women with disabilities in relation to peace and security. The detailed framework, implementation plan and progress indicators provided in the NAPs do not include women with disabilities, the aged or those with chronic illnesses. It assumes that all women and girls to be reached with the framework are persons without disabilities or disabling conditions. The closest provision under "Protection" in the framework that could be used to link to issues of disability is the "provision of adequate and accessible humanitarian services" and in this case, we may be stretching the boundaries of the word "accessible" to include accessibility for those with disabilities. Also, while some states of the Federation have heeded the call to adopt the NAP, Adamawa State, the state of our engagement, is yet to appropriate the provisions of the NAP (Marshall and Hayward 2015).

This lack of inclusion of disability concerns is not surprising to our research participants. According to one study participant:

> We are not taken into consideration in any area of life, be it education, shelter, water, sanitation, health, economy, social welfare, politics, job opportunities, and humanitarian response services, including security. What offence have I committed here on earth? Is my offence the fact that I found myself in a disability situation? Is it why the society has neglected me and look at me as if I am not a complete human person?

Often, the exclusion of women in peacebuilding is seen as a result of long-established and deeply entrenched patriarchal structures and ideologies in many African countries (Ahonsi 2010). Women with disabilities in the Gombi community confirm this as true to their reality. As one said:

> In the area of meetings, women are not really involved. Mostly men and community leaders … on few occasions the women leader was included. Decisions are usually taken without women, and the situation is even worse for women with disabilities.

It would, however, appear that the exclusion of women with disabilities is the result of neglect by men and women involved in peacebuilding and post-conflict peace process. Nigeria's two NAPs were championed by the Federal Ministry of Women Affairs and Social Development, in collaboration and support from Women in Peace and Security, as well as other women-led civil society organisations. Consequently, it could be argued that disability exclusion

130 *Jessie Fubara-Manuel et al.*

is a societal menace. As said earlier, it is evidence of the negligence of society and an outcome of both men and women's indifference to issues of disability.

Nigeria, as a nation, is yet to take disability discourse as a matter of state importance (Haruna 2017). Disability activists with legal backgrounds are attempting to embed disability rights into the non-discriminatory clause of the Nigerian Constitution. This is because the Constitution does not treat disability as a "discrete status" (Umeh 2016). The Nigerian government only passed the Disability Act (Discrimination against Persons with Disabilities (Prohibition) Act) into law in January 2019 after almost 18 years of relentless advocacy by disability rights groups and activists. This is even though Nigeria is signatory to the Convention on Rights of Persons with Disabilities (CRPD), which lays on the state an obligation for the protection of persons with disabilities. The Disability Act prohibits discrimination based on disability and imposes sanctions, including fines and prison sentences, on those who contravene it. The law will also establish a National Commission for Persons with Disabilities, responsible for ensuring that people with disabilities have access to housing, education, health care and employment opportunities.

The World Health Organization (WHO) provides an estimate that 15% of the global population are persons with disabilities and that 80% of that percentage live in "resource limited countries" of sub-Saharan Africa (WHO n.d.). Consequently, using the 15% estimate of disabled populations, Nigeria, with a recent population of over 190 million, would have about 28 million persons living with various types of disabilities. It can be hoped that the National Commission for Persons with Disabilities will see to the actionability of the international and local frameworks on Women, Peace and Security towards more informed gendered development peacebuilding in Nigeria. It is only then that, possibly, women and women with disabilities will be recognised as visible partners and agents in peacebuilding processes.

Implications of women with disabilities in peacebuilding and development

Inclusion must transcend the numbers game and transition into more active participation that takes seriously the resources of women rather than merely the gift of gender. At the confirmation of ministers for the government, the senate confirmed women nominees on account of their being women. This was paternalistic and not respectful of the experience that earned those women the nomination to be ministers of the Federal Republic of Nigeria. Christopher Isike and Ufo Okeke Uzodike (2011) write about the lack of translation of the effect of women in politics to good governance due to culturally impeding circumstances. This, in part, may be due to the "placement" instead of election of women into political platforms as "symbols" of gender consciousness instead of active presence to be reckoned with in decision-making spaces (Högberg 2019). However, involvement in mainline political activities, such as seeking public office, has not been the only way in which women have been effective

Women with disabilities and peacebuilding   131

in peacebuilding. While Isike and Uzodike's study included the Niger Delta, a mention of the peacebuilding efforts of Kalabari women in Abonnema in the conflict of 2008 would have highlighted a different method of political involvement. The women in Abonnema, under the leadership of the Amayanabo ta (the king's wife), rallied the women not only to prayers but also to prevail on their husbands and sons to desist from acts of violence.[1] This represents an indigenous response to a male-dominated conflict situation where women came together, became activists for communal peace and began what has continued to be a unifying front for the community. While it may be difficult to conceive of any positive outcome of conflict for women, Arostegui's (2013) argument that the trauma of the conflict experience also provides an opportunity for women to come together with a common agenda rings true here.

Women with disabilities should not only be thought of as victims of war but also as stakeholders in development and peacebuilding. This sentiment was expressed by the UN Women Technical Consultant on the peace situation in Nigeria, namely that "there is a growing recognition that women in conflict situations must be viewed not only as victims but also as powerful agents for peace and security in their communities" (Iroegbu 2018). However, how this recognition is measured and how practical it is in the lives of the women would constitute the topic of research for another paper. This is because the role of agent is yet to be extended to women with disabilities, as their movement to the camps is not often guaranteed. Most internally displaced persons camps in Nigeria are ad hoc settlements that are created by displaced persons who have run for safety and gather at the nearest site that offers protection from harm. Sometimes these camps are recognised and taken care of by government and/or civil society organisations such as the JPRM. However, how survivors arrive at the camps and the fate of those left behind, who are often persons with disabilities, the aged and the weak, is often not considered by the government.

The necessity for inclusion of a gendered disability approach to developmental peacebuilding was further underscored in the Gombi community. In interacting with persons with disabilities at the camp on questions of how they got to the camp and how they fared with the developmental aspects at the camp, such as provision of basic sanitary facilities and food, stories carry similar tones. One woman asserted:

> When the Boko Haram insurgents invaded my community in 2015, it was terrible for me. People all ran away and left me with my child in the village at the mercy of God. There were also few other women with disabilities and the elderly in the same situation who were not able to flee for their lives. I could not run because of the lame situation with my legs. God was so kind that I managed to survive the various attacks in my community named Dzangula, in Gombi, until we were rescued. On that fateful day, two of the elderly people were shot to death in front of my very own eyes. The trauma we went through cannot be overemphasised.

132 *Jessie Fubara-Manuel et al.*

Another told how she was rescued by being taken in a wheelbarrow to the camp. She said she felt like a commodity, some property that needed to be "carried" or left behind. On arrival at the camp, no sanitary arrangements were made for persons with disabilities. Mothers with disabilities found it much harder to take care of their infants. Meanwhile, as observed, most resettlement camp coordinators are male, without a clue as to the needs of women, especially women with disabilities. Life in resettlement camps in Nigeria is hard, but much harder for women with disabilities owing to the absence of facilities or direct access to resources and humanitarian aid. The women with disabilities interviewed expressed their dissatisfaction with not being involved in the process of developmental peacebuilding towards effective post-conflict rehabilitation strategies. Speaking particularly with regard to protection of water, health and sanitation facilities, a research participant said:

> The issues of good water, sanitation and medicare are other areas we are suffering too much. Nothing is provided in such a way that we can easily access them. The hospitals are built very far away, with no facility considering us. The medical personnel do not know much about how to care for us, they also end up making us vulnerable and marginalised. The structures here are difficult to access, there are high beds, high stairs, amongst others. These things even make our children hard to care for the way we should as mothers. The toilets are also built without considering us and we usually end up managing the bush or helping ourselves with containers within our houses, which hygienically is not right. Access to water is also a challenge to us and we find it difficult to have a meaningful life.

This is despite the clear expected outcome in the NAP for the participation of women in disarmament, demobilisation and reintegration (DDR) processes, especially in mainstreaming gender in peacebuilding, promotion of equality and the provision of such things as separate gender-based camps for men and women. Many camps are overcrowded and women are often vulnerable to various kinds of violence, especially sexual and gender-based violence. Whilst it has been argued that wartime rape is often not an intentional strategy of war (Cohen et al. 2013), the fact remains that women's bodies have become battlefields and rape used as a weapon of war (Arostegui 2013) in many conflict situations. Sexual violence is committed by both civilians and armed forces, which means women and sometimes men continue to suffer all forms of dehumanising sexual abuse throughout conflicts and into post-conflict periods.

Women with disabilities are more susceptible to rape and sexual assault due to their impairments whether sexual violence against women (SVAW) is an intentional strategy of war or not. Babatunde Ahonsi (2010) notes that the persistence of SVAW during post-conflict transitions tends to increase the risk of HIV infections among young women, relative to the phase of armed conflict He attributes this to "men's highly exploitative, transactional and cross-generational multiple sexual activities" (Ahonsi 2010: 2). While Ahonsi's assertions merit

Women with disabilities and peacebuilding   133

further investigation, it is worth noting that women with disabilities are further disadvantaged in negotiating safer sex and suffer the double stigma of gender and disability. One research participant puts it this way:

> There are lots of reported cases of sexual and gender-based violence in our community before, during and after the violent conflict. The insurgents took advantage of women and raped some of our women, they also forced some of our girls into child marriage and abducted some. It was a bad situation. Women with disability are not left out in this problem and many of us [women with disabilities] have unwanted pregnancies as a result of rape cases. We have been traumatised highly as result of this issue of rape. It is very bad, but what can we do?

Another hinted that women with disabilities, whether raped during or after conflict, could suffer as a result of faulty cultural beliefs within the Gombi community.

> It is believed that mentally challenged women can bring good fortune to men if they are raped by the men. Yes, other women also suffer even without disability but ours is a worst-case scenario.

The framework proposed in the NAP to protect women and girls from sexual violence appears more political and not within the capacity of the affected to engage with. Most perpetrators of sexual violence in conflict situations are men who are not likely to be aware of or able to respond to legal and anti-sexual violence campaigns. It is still debatable what women can do to prevent sexual violence without the cooperation of the male perpetrators. There is a vital need to change male dominance through positive masculinities that allow men to regard women as their equals (Chitando and Chirongoma 2012).

One of the objectives of the NAP was to promote the fact that "women's role in sustaining the community, providing basic needs, advocating for basic needs, needs to be recognised and acknowledged as peacebuilding endeavours" ("Nigeria launches National Action Plan on Women, Peace, Security" 2017). It would make a difference if disability concerns are recognised and noted as an objective of the NAP for future implementation.

Conclusion

The vulnerability of women with disabilities in Nigeria is seen in how they continue to suffer post-conflict neglect, abuse and discrimination. This appears to be made worse by the lack of will-power to implement existing legal frameworks. Furthermore, the National Action Plans that speak directly to gender, peace and security do not expressly acknowledge and protect the rights of women with disabilities. On the other hand, issues of development have not been properly enshrined as matters essential to peacebuilding. As such, international and local

134 Jessie Fubara-Manuel et al.

peace-related conventions and resolutions are not translated into actions that adequately transform the lives of women with disabilities in the post-conflict area of Gombi in Adamawa State. Yet women with disabilities in Gombi are survivors of conflict and are contributing to the rebuilding of the community by their resilience and courage. The peculiarity of the internal conflicts in Nigeria have also left many victims and internally displaced persons off the radar of humanitarian agencies. As the JPRM continues its collaboration with disability peoples' organisations and other vulnerable groups in Adamawa State, disability concerns will be mainstreamed to ensure inclusion of disability perspectives in the provision of basic needs, opportunities as actors of peacebuilding and motivational survivors of conflict. The Nigerian government's active involvement in a gendered disability approach to developmental peacebuilding will strengthen the efforts of civil society organisations towards inclusion of the voices of women with disabilities in post-conflict situations in Nigeria.

Note

1 Jessie Fubara-Manuel is Kalabari by marriage and witnessed the activities of the women together with her mother in-law. The prayer rallies began by the women in 2008 is now a monthly community prayer meeting popularly called *Ama Teke* (the community prays).

References

Adichie, Chimamanda Ngozi. 2017. *Dear Ijeawele, or: A Feminist Manifesto in Fifteen Suggestions.* Lagos, Nigeria: Farafina.
Adichie, Chimamanda Ngozi. n.d. "The danger of a single story," *TED Talks,* Available at: www.ted.com/talks/chimamanda_adichie_the_danger_of_a_single_story?language=en, accessed 2 August 2019.
Ahonsi, Babatunde. 2010. *Towards More Informed Responses to Gender Violence and HIV/AIDS in Post-Conflict West African Settings.* Uppsala, Sweden: Nordic Africa Institute.
Arostegui, Julie. 2013. "Gender, conflict, and peace-building: How conflict can catalyse positive change for women," *Gender & Development* 21(3), 533–549. doi: 10.1080/13552074.2013.846624
Ball, Jennifer. 2019. *Women, Development and Peacebuilding in Africa: Stories from Uganda.* Cham: Springer International Publishing.
Chitando, Ezra, Sophie Chirongoma. 2012. eds. *Redemptive Masculinities: Men, HIV, and Religion.* EHAIA Series. Geneva, Switzerland: World Council of Churches Publications.
Cohen, Dara K., Amelia H. Green and Elizabeth J. Wood. 2013. *Wartime Sexual Violence: Misconceptions, Implications, and Ways Forward.* Special Report. Washington, DC: United States Institute of Peace Press.
Gartrell, Alexandra, and Karen Soldatic. 2016. "Rural women with disabilities in post-conflict zones: The forgotten sisters of Australia's disability-inclusive development," *Third World Thematics (TWT)* 1(3), 370–381. doi: 10.1080/23802014.2016.1262749
Haruna, Mohammed Awaisu. 2017. "The problems of living with disability in Nigeria," *Journal of Law, Policy and Globalization* 65, 103–113.

Högberg, Sara. 2019. "Women and peacebuilding in Rwanda and Sierra Leone: A comparative study of the impacts of United Nations Resolution 1325." Bachelor Thesis, Södertörn University, Stockholm. Available at: http://sh.diva-portal.org/smash/get/diva2:1320861/FULLTEXT01.pdf

Iroegbu, Senator. 2018. "Nigeria: Govt urged to implement UN Resolution on Women Security." *AllAfrica.Com*, 22 February. Available at: https://allafrica.com/stories/201802220061.html

Isike, Christopher, and Ufo Uzodike. 2011. "A statistical analysis of women's perceptions on politics and peace building in KwaZulu-Natal (South Africa) and Niger Delta (Nigeria)." *Africa Insight* 41(1). doi: 10.4314/ai.v41i1.68374

Issifu, Abdul Karim. 2015. "The role of African women in post-conflict peacebuilding: The Case of Rwanda (Report)," *Journal of Pan African Studies* 8(9), 63–78.

Marshall, Katherine, and Susan Hayward (Eds.). 2015. *Women, Religion, and Peacebuilding: Illuminating the Unseen.* Washington, DC: United States Institute of Peace Press.

"National Action Plan: Nigeria." 2014. Women's International League for Peace and Freedom, 22 December. Available at: www.peacewomen.org/nap-nigeria

"Nigeria launches National Action Plan on Women, Peace, Security," 2017. *Premium Times Nigeria*, 10 May. Available at: www.premiumtimesng.com/news/more-news/230917-nigeria-launches-national-action-plan-women-peace-security.html

Umeh, Ngozi Chuma. 2016. "Reading disability into the non-discrimination clause of the Nigerian Constitution, Section A: Articles: Chapter 3," *African Disability Rights Yearbook* 4. Pretoria: Pretoria University Law Press, 53–76.

"*What Is UNSCR 1325?*" n.d. Washington, DC: United States Institute of Peace Press. Available at: www.usip.org/gender_peacebuilding/about_UNSCR_1325, accessed 5 August 2019.

WHO. n.d. *World Report on Disability*. Geneva, Switzerland: World Health Organization. Available at: www.who.int/disabilities/world_report/2011/report/en/, accessed 10 February 2019.

10 Peacebuilding through health work

Opportunities and challenges for women community health volunteers in Kenya

Roseanne Njiru

Background

Health and peace are inseparably linked. Yet, globally, discussions on the place of health workers in peacebuilding have been largely absent. This chapter explores how community-centred primary health work might increase the peacebuilding agency of women community health volunteers (CHVs), and the constraints to this agency, in two informal settlements in Kenya's capital city, Nairobi. It draws on qualitative data from 23 women CHVs from Mathare and Kibera, two informal settlements in Nairobi. Merging the scholarship on "women and peacebuilding" and "health as a bridge for peace," overall, data suggest that being a woman CHV provides enhanced opportunities to engage in peacebuilding. The study highlights how women CHVs understand peace and ways of making sense as peacebuilders through their health provision activities, and how the unique nature of the health care system boosts their capacity to engage in peacebuilding activities. It also explores how women construct informal health–peace work as women's activities, and the challenges to their health–peacebuilding work. The chapter, thus, argues for policy initiatives that recognise the health–peace nexus in order to develop multisectoral, multilevel peacebuilding approaches that acknowledge and incorporate the peacebuilding agency of CHVs.

Introduction

There is international recognition that women are instrumental in peacebuilding processes. Moreover, many studies have made visible the centrality of women's agency in peacebuilding, peacemaking and post-conflict reconstruction activities (Adeogun and Muthuki 2018; Itto 2006; Manchanda 2005; Ochen 2017; Okrah 2003). However, women remain largely absent from formal peacebuilding structures. Given women's relative lack of presence in the formal political realm of many conflict-torn nations, grassroots efforts are often one of the main outlets of women's peace activism. Much of the literature has focused on the peacebuilding efforts of "local" women and grassroots organisations in post-conflict zones in Africa (Adeogun and Muthuki 2018; Manchanda 2005;

Justino et al. 2018). In this chapter, I seek to build on this body of work by exploring the specific case of the peacebuilding agency of women community health volunteers (CHVs) in two urban informal settlements (Mathare and Kibera) in Kenya's capital, Nairobi. I employ a health–peace nexus framework to examine how these women engage in complex everyday health and peace work in poor communities that experience election-related conflicts and other forms of everyday violence.

Women in Kenya have been integrally involved in peacebuilding, developing early warning systems, dispute resolution, seeking solutions to resource degradation, working to end violence against women and children, justice, human rights, and calling for greater inclusion in peacebuilding processes from community, national, and international levels (Karimi 2018; Mueller-Hirth 2019). Indeed, the existing national infrastructure for peace – now internationally recognised – is modelled on an innovative local-level, women-led peacebuilding initiative in Wajir in north-eastern Kenya (Oseremen 2018). Moreover, Kenya has several grassroots women's peacebuilding activities that operate outside the formal/normative peace-structures (Karimi 2018).

Scholarship and policy making on women and peacebuilding has been propelled by international normative frameworks. Notably, the adoption of the United Nations Security Council Resolution 1325 on Women, Peace and Security in October 2000 was a turning point, as it stresses the centrality of gender in international peace and security processes. The resolution calls for recognition of the importance of women's participation and leadership in conflict prevention, conflict resolution, peacekeeping, and peacebuilding at all decision-making levels (Cohn et al. 2004; Karimi 2018; O'Rourke 2014; Pratt and Richter-Devroe 2011). While the UN framework has, on the one hand, received praise for calling for the substantive participation of women in peace and security, it has also attracted criticism for its liberal peacebuilding agenda, universalisation and top-down approaches (Karimi 2018; Mac Ginty 2014; Pratt and Richter-Devroe 2011). Karimi (2018) also notes that 1325 was initially designed to apply to women in post-conflict settings, thus making it difficult to actualise the provisions for peacebuilding in non-conflict countries.

Much of women and peacebuilding scholarship today examines local agency: the bottom-up or everyday processes, experiences, and methods that groups and individuals use to build peace in divided communities (Mac Ginty 2014). Mac Ginty's concept of "local turn" is a critique of the universalism and standardisation of the liberal peace paradigm that has characterised international peacebuilding and statebuilding efforts since the Second World War. The local turn in peacebuilding counters the top-down processes, formal institutions and peace "professionals" to recognise the agency of communal level (local) peacebuilders and their social practices that constitute everyday peace (Mac Ginty 2014). While much of the scholarly interest in women and peace has emphasised women's peacebuilding activities in post-conflict situations, the experiences and realities of local peacebuilders, especially in contexts of ongoing or cyclical violence, are not well captured. This chapter explores the everyday peacebuilding activities of CHVs in Mathare and Kibera, which are prone to different forms of violence, ranging from political, ethnic, religious, resource scarcity, gender violence and cycles of violent revenge. The goal of the chapter is to highlight how being part of the health care system, even though marginally, may increase CHVs peacebuilding agency.

CHVs in Kenya are part of the community health workers (CHWs) recognised under the national strategy for community health (CHS) for their contribution in enhancing access to health care, especially in high-burden, low-income communities (Ministry of Health 2014). Community health workers became prominent with the Alma Ata Declaration in 1978 that recognised primary health care as the key element for improving community health (World Health Organization 1978). The World Health Organization (WHO) (2007) defines CHWs as members of the community, selected by and answerable to the community they work for, and supported by the health system, but with shorter training than professional health workers. Typically, in Kenya CHVs receive a 10-day training on basic competencies such as health promotion practices, life-saving skills, leadership skills, and communication and counselling skills (Ministry of Health 2014). CHVs partner with government and a range of non-governmental organisations (NGOs) engaged in health and development programming, often receiving small stipends from these organisations. Largely, their work remains voluntary and at the periphery of health systems. The women CHVs I interviewed play multiple roles: as residents of informal settlements, they are victims of (structural) violence and at the same time agents of health and peace. It is, thus, important to understand how this multiplicity of roles shapes their peacebuilding agency. In arguing that health work provides opportunities for peacebuilding in the settlements, I explore women's constructions and ways of making sense as peacebuilders and ask these questions: How do the women health workers understand peace and link their health work to peacebuilding? How does being a CHV increase the women's peacebuilding agency? How is their health–peace work a gendered responsibility? Finally, in what ways is women's peacebuilding agency constrained?

This chapter then engages with two literatures: scholarship on local women and peace, on the one hand, and the health–peace nexus discourse on the other. In the following sections, I locate this work within the wider "health as a bridge for peace" framework. I then discuss how women CHVs conceptualise peace and how they link their everyday health work to peacebuilding. Following this, I examine how health–peace work is a gendered responsibility and then how the features of health care, including legitimacy, neutrality and accessibility, increase women's peacebuilding agency. Finally, I discuss how the women's peace work is hampered by institutional, economic and social obstacles which prevent the realisation of their potential. Overall, the chapter argues that local women CHVs are valuable resources for peacebuilding and there is a need to recognise and include their insights in Kenya's peace architecture.

Health–peace nexus: The peace through health framework

The link between peace, development and health is a direct one, as conflicts and violence can directly impact health or cause a disruption in the social and economic systems, leading to decline in a population's well-being. Thus, peace and health mutually reinforce each other, and development cannot take place without good health. Health as a peacebuilding tool emerged as part of the WHO's approach to provision of post-conflict health assistance (Rushton and McInnes 2006). In 1998, the WHO adopted "Health as a Bridge for Peace (HBP)" as a policy framework on the premise that the role of health providers in the preservation and promotion of peace is significant for the attainment of "Health for All" (Christensen and Anbrasi 2015; Gutlove 2008; WHO 2014). "Peace through health" (PtH) is now a major theoretical framework for examining the contributions of health care in peacebuilding (Buhmann 2005). This framework pushes health care providers to go beyond their health provision role to support peacebuilding efforts in the communities in which they work. Health professionals, including health agencies such as the Red Cross, care for those wounded in war and other conflicts, and deal with both the immediate and long-term consequences of conflicts (D'Errico et al. 2010; Vass 2001).

There are numerous local, regional and international efforts towards post-conflict reconstruction to consolidate peace and rebuild countries that have experienced protracted conflict in Africa. However, much of this attention focuses on political processes such as reconciliation, democratisation, governance, security and economic development (Njiru and Purkayastha 2015). Whereas these are essential elements in post-conflict development, discussions on the place of health care systems and health workers in peacebuilding have largely been absent. Yet, the unique nature of the health sector and its mandated position within conflict situations is such that it holds not only the opportunity but also a responsibility to make positive interventions.

Some scholars and agencies have pointed out this health–peace connection (e.g. Arya 2004; Christensen and Anbrasi 2015; D'Errico et al. 2010; Grove and Zwi 2008; MacQueen and SantaBarbara 2004; Negin 2007; Rushton and McInnes 2006; WHO 2014). For example, D'Errico et al. (2010:146) point out that, "if war, by definition, is a public health problem, it follows that part of the solution lies in the hands of public health practitioners." MacQueen and Santa-Barbara (2004) note that current thinking in peace and conflict studies support a multilevel, multisector peacemaking and peacebuilding approach in which health workers play a fundamental role that pushes their health work beyond curative health care.

While there are convincing theoretical arguments about the peacebuilding potential of the health sector, only a few case studies exist to provide the PtH framework with an empirical grounding and broader evidence base. Some case studies outside Africa exist from the WHO's implementation of the Health as a Bridge to Peace (HBP) concept in Haiti and Eastern Slovenia, but largely remain unevaluated (Rodney 2013). Other examples include post-war Croatia

140   *Roseanne Njiru*

and Nepal (Tsai 2009; Rodney 2013) which show health as a transformative political issue and a cornerstone of successful peacebuilding. In Africa, recent studies signify the potential contribution of health to peacebuilding. For instance, in Burundi, Christensen and Anbrasi (2015) found that health provision mitigated local tensions brought about by land pressure and the marginalisation of repatriated refugees, thus promoting social cohesion through a local clinic's integrated model which facilitated community interaction. In Eastern Congo, D'Errico et al. (2010) found that the legitimacy and permanence of a non-governmental health agency were central to its potential to build peace in warring communities. This emerging evidence shows the importance of more case studies that examine the health–peace connection in Africa in order to build stronger evidence base for theory, policy and practice.

Methods and data

This chapter explores women CHVs' lived experience with health and peace work. It is part of a larger ethnographic study that explores how health care systems, both private and public, contribute to peacebuilding in urban informal settlements in Nairobi. Data for this chapter are drawn from 23 in-depth interviews conducted with women CHVs in Kibera and Mathare, two large informal settlements in Kenya's capital city. The research was carried out between July and September 2018.

As a resident of Nairobi, I consciously and reflectively chose Kibera and Mathare, considering the long and complex history of conflict and violence deeply embedded in colonial practices of the city's settlement and other chronic structural problems in Kenya. These settlements experience a range of violence, including political, ethnic, religious, resource-related, gender violence, and cycles of violent revenge. Moreover, both Mathare and Kibera are marked as "hotspots" for political violence, and, indeed, ethnicised political violence has been significant in the two settlements during presidential elections. These communities carry legacies of violence from election conflicts which often provide ground for ongoing political and ethnic cleavages, as well as social fragmentation.

Aside from political violence, it is also essential to be aware and consider other forms of everyday violence that are often blurred by an overemphasis on (ethnicised) political violence, and which structure the lives of the settlements' residents. Residents of Mathare and Kibera face numerous health challenges mainly due to poverty, congestion, poor sanitation and hygiene, and inadequate health care. With only a few public health clinics, most health care provision is supported by non-governmental organisations. To further support health provision, government and NGOs engage the services of community health workers, including volunteers, whom they train on giving basic health and medical care to community members, health education, and linking residents to health care systems. The community health workers also educate providers and stakeholders within health care systems about community health needs.

Participants ranged from 25 to 41 years of age, with secondary to tertiary levels of education, and were of different ethnic and linguistic backgrounds. In both sites, initial participants were recruited through personal networks and subsequently snowball and purposive sampling techniques were used to make new contacts. The broader study from which this chapter draws had a broad range of questions covering issues such as how public and private health workers conceptualise peace and link their roles and activities to peacebuilding; how different health care programmes facilitate community interactions and affect the social fabric; what commonalities and possibilities exist for cooperation between the different roles and activities of the health workers and how they might be harnessed to promote peace; and factors that constrain health workers' activities and how they affect peacebuilding. Given that extensive data were generated, this chapter focuses on women CHVs' conceptualisation of peace and their lived experiences of health–peace work. Questions that this theme asked included: What does peace mean to you? How do you link health work to peace and peacebuilding? How does being part of the health care system facilitate/enable peacebuilding activities? How does health provision promote social cohesion? Interviews lasted from 1 to 2 hours and were audio-recorded (where possible) with permission from participants. The names of the participants have been changed to maintain confidentiality. Interviews were conducted in both Swahili and English.

Data analysis

I transcribed and translated all recorded interviews and then analysed the data manually. First, I read the transcripts in depth immediately after each transcription to gain a deeper understanding of broad ideas without coding. Second, after all the data were available, I read them all again for coding, highlighting participants' definitions of peace and closely examining how CHVs linked health provision to peace in the settlements, other types of peacebuilding activities that CHVs performed beyond their mandated health work, what opportunities being part of the health care system offered for peacebuilding, how they constructed informal peacebuilding as women's work, and the challenges experienced in their health–peace activities. Following this process of coding, I began a careful examination and review of the codes, classifying them into broader themes and identifying supporting excerpts for use in the presentation of the data. Interpretation of the themes involved a reflective process of locating them within broader "women and peacebuilding" and the "health as a bridge for peace" discourses.

Findings

Though CHVs are situated at the margins of the health system, with very little support from the state or private health systems, they play important health roles in the community. Moreover, this research finds that the women CHVs

142 *Roseanne Njiru*

performed local peacebuilding activities that went beyond their core mandate of health provision. Analysis of the data revealed four broad themes: (1) CHWs understandings of peace and the health–peace nexus, (2) health care system features that increase peacebuilding agency, (3) health–peace work as a gendered responsibility, and (4) obstacles that hamper and limit women's peacebuilding agency.

Understanding of peace and the health–peace nexus

Women CHVs were asked what peace meant to them. They had myriad responses that related peace to concepts of human rights, tolerance, mutual understanding, respect, freedom, and non-violence, among others. Moreover, all women associated peace with "need" and "right" intricately tied to the capacities of urban informal settlements' residents to afford basic necessities and services for survival. The following excerpts represent their views on the peace concept.

> Peace is when you learn to accept and respect other people around you who are different from you by their ethnicity, religion, beliefs, opinions and characteristics. The word peace to me means mutual understanding and the ability to have an open mind and to be respectful of differences ... I also think that peace is freedom, the freedom to be free from fear of anyone because you know they respect you and your choices and the way you think and behave because you are a human being like them.
>
> (Nancy, Mathare)

> Peace means that people can live without the fear of losing their life, family, or friends because of things like violence. It is living in harmony and collaboration to change our lives for the better. Look at the situation in the "slum": if we have no peace, when shall we ever be able to work together to change our lives and the lives of our children? We shall always be fighting each other, stealing from each other and making everyone live in fear because we are always suspicious of the other person. This cannot be a life of peace.
>
> (Maureen, Kibera)

> When, for example, I tell you that I have no peace, it is to mean that I do not have a job that can feed me, pay my rent or take care of my children. When you look at the situation in the "slums," people are poor, many youths are jobless, services are poor, there is poor health ... these conditions mean that people will fight each other, hate each other and we cannot have peace.
>
> (Jane, Kibera)

These quotes make it clear what the links are between citizenship rights, human dignity, and peace in the settlements. We spent a significant amount of

Peacebuilding through health work in Kenya   143

time discussing electoral violence that the two communities have experienced in the past, particularly in the 2007 and 2017 presidential elections. Generally, elections in Kenya take an ethnic dimension and both Mathare and Kibera have in the past borne the brunt of ethnicised political violence that resulted in devastating effects on residents' lives, livelihoods, ethnic divisions and a fractured social fabric. In light of this, most women pointed out the need to improve services in the communities in order to reduce feelings of ethnic animosity that breed various forms of everyday violence that become magnified during elections. Some women drew on such experiences of election violence to postulate peace as:

> It means forgiveness and being able to say "now let us move on despite our individual or ethnic differences." It is being be able to know that such differences of political opinion will continue but that we should not fight about them because after all we are the ones left suffering long after the elections are gone … so respecting everyone. It also means the ability to know that it is not the politics and politicians that really make us fight, but because of the situation we live in, poverty … This is what makes us see the differences in ethnicity and opinions.
>
> (Lucy, Mathare)

Importantly, as the excerpts above suggest, the health workers felt that peace and community health were two sides of the same coin: that there can be no peace without good health and no good health if there is no peace in the communities. Their responses drew on broader discourses of economic prosperity, human rights and social development to show how these created contexts of non-peace and bad health in the settlements. For example, poverty, marginalisation, ethnic identity and social exclusion were directly linked to violent conflict, a major determinant of health. Participants noted that many health concerns in the two sites, such as assaults and murder, were directly associated with poverty and often took an ethnic dimension. For instance, a youth gang from one ethnic group may attack and rob members of an "other" ethnic group, as was clearly narrated in the two sites.

Interviews also focused on how the women CHVs linked their community health work to peace and peacebuilding. Health interventions and the roles that the CHVs played were essential factors in building peace. There was consensus that, in deeply ethnicised and politically charged settlements such as Mathare and Kibera, health work was an important pathway to building peace, as Mary from Mathare pointed out:

> This community is divided into different zones and each zone is dominated by people from a specific ethnic community. There are everyday tensions, particularly between the Kikuyu and Luo, and this increases during the election period when it breaks out into violence. As a health worker, I am a first responder, and I do home visits across all these zones. When I visit

144   *Roseanne Njiru*

the sick or go into communities to talk about hygiene, nutrition and sanitation, I talk to people from all ethnic divides about the need to live well with others as neighbours and I remind them of the way violence affects our health in the community.

Similar sentiments were expressed in Kibera where CHVs talked about their daily activities of health provision and how these were intertwined with peace. Kibera, like Mathare, is divided into ethnic zones, each dominated by a different community, and ethnic identities mostly consolidate during election periods, erupting into violence:

> How can we talk about health without talking about peace? During elections people die, get injured, women are raped. We continue to live with the health consequences of violence long after elections pass. As a health volunteer, I have seen the full effects of election violence. I see my work as an opportunity to preach peace and I use every opportunity I have when doing home visits or going into schools to talk about the need for better inter-ethnic relations. I tell people none of the politicians will come to visit you or care about your health after the elections.
>
> (Ruth, Kibera)

Apart from "preaching peace" while performing their mandated health activities, women played other roles in peacebuilding. For example, because local community members knew that health workers had better access to the local administration, they reported cases of violence to them and expected the health workers to report these cases to police and the local administration, as the following excerpt suggests.

> Sometimes you visit a sick person and then they begin to tell you about how their clothes were stolen from the clothes-line outside, or how someone in the family was assaulted. You cannot just tell them that you visited only the sick person in the house and not to hear other stories. You realise they are telling you because they know you can do something about it. So you have to act, in this case by helping to report such matters to the chief or police.
>
> (Violin, Kibera)

While some residents saw health workers as legitimate and influential links to community security administration, others treated them as arbiters in family disputes.

> You can walk into a community or house to visit a sick family member and they also tell you about a fight or misunderstanding between a husband and wife or parent(s) and children. Apart from doing your health responsibilities,

Peacebuilding through health work in Kenya 145

you have to listen and try to resolve the issues; if you cannot solve then you refer them to the chief to talk to them and resolve their issue.

(Sarah, Mathare)

Thus, simultaneously with their core mandate of basic health provision, women health workers found themselves in situations where they settled disputes and reconciled families and communities. To their advantage, many health workers had received some basic training on guidance and counselling and were able to employ these skills when faced with cases such as marital and family disputes or children who were engaged in substance abuse.

This section has highlighted how women CHVs conceptualised peace and some peacebuilding activities that they performed concurrently with their health work. Another important theme that emerged in our interviews was related to aspects of the health care system that increased the agency of women in peacebuilding work. The following section discusses a few of these aspects.

Features of the health care system and women community health volunteers' peacebuilding agency

Though CHVs occupy a peripheral position in the health care system, being part of the system boosted the women CHVs' power and place in their communities. As women CHVs noted, their position within the health care system provided opportunities that enabled them to perform their health–peace work in the settlements. In interview discussions, participants pointed out concepts related to the nature and principles that guide health care provision including selflessness (altruism), treating everyone equally (neutrality), and the legitimate status gained from being a health care worker, which allowed them to access different social groups in the settlements. These features of health care are intertwined but I discuss them separately to make them clear.

Selflessness/altruism

Altruism is a necessary component of the medical profession that emphasises the performance of unselfish acts beneficial to others. Health care is one means by which society institutionalises feelings of care and compassion. Its association with humane, superordinate goals that transcend human differences make it a natural agent of the extension of altruism (Santa-Barbara and MacQueen 2004). For health workers, acts of altruism might include free treatment to poor individuals, working outside of contracted hours, and a genuine willingness to engage in health care provision. There was general agreement that the trainings received from government and NGOs on community health emphasised altruism as a professional obligation of the health practice and participants employed discourses of selflessness in health provision that motivated their health and peacebuilding activities. However, beyond this systemic responsibility, it is

146 *Roseanne Njiru*

important to note that CHVs had joined the health care system as volunteers and thus altruism and selflessness defined their everyday activities.

There was consensus among most participants that their decision to join the health care system as volunteers was largely motivated by their lived experiences of poverty, poor health and violence while growing up in the settlements. They had witnessed the challenges and burdens that marginalisation and exclusion of informal settlements placed particularly on women and mothers, who bore the heaviest responsibility of caring for their families and community. Health and violence were greatly intertwined and training on community health also meant enhanced capacity to contribute to peace. These experiences and concern for the well-being of their community constituted, for the most part, reasons why the women CHVs felt the need to serve their community, as the quote below suggests:

> I was born and grew up in Kibera. At a personal level, I have experienced poverty, violence, lack of proper health care. I was lucky that my family found someone to support my education. I always knew that I wanted to contribute to my community and help to improve our living conditions. When I got the opportunity to train as a health volunteer, I went because I understand what that means for people living in "slums."
>
> (Janet, Kibera)

While identification with community marginalisation had led to their acts of selflessness, participants pointed out that their now being part of the health care system meant they had to be conscious and practice even more their selfless acts. However, this was not without challenges such as financial constraints (as I will discuss later) that were crucial to their being able to give voluntary services to their communities.

Neutrality

Generally, the health sector and health workers are obligated to treat people of all social categories impartially. Closely related to altruistic acts, neutrality entails refusing to accept hate-based identities. Many CHVs drew on this characteristic of health provision and spoke about the need to practice non-discrimination in their work. Discussions on the need for neutrality primarily centred around potential risks of inflaming ethnic tensions that could lead to a break down in trust among members of different ethnic groups if they perceived that CHVs favoured members of a certain ethnic group. For the CHVs, it was thus important to be conscious of how their health activities built rather than broke social cohesion. As suggested, being part of the health care system constantly reminded them of the importance of their health work as a bridge for peace.

> Health provision knows no ethnic boundaries. My life is about helping people. When I visit people of different ethnic groups in the community or

Peacebuilding through health work in Kenya 147

in their houses, I talk about "us," not "them." When I conduct health education, I have to talk about peace and being good neighbours ... I cannot afford to divide people. I always have to remember that if I treat people differently because of their ethnic group, or even because they are men or women, then I may increase feelings of hatred amongst these groups and this may build up to violence. I am here for the health and peace of the community, not for any specific group of people.

(Lucy, Mathare)

As the excerpt suggests, not only did the formal health sector require health professionals to provide services impartially, it was also clear that CHVs in already divided communities had to be extra careful about their work. This is because if members of one ethnic group perceived the health workers to be favouring another ethnic group, then this posed the risk of dividing the community further. This is not to say that this did not happen; I heard of some cases where health workers had been alleged to favour members of their own ethnic group in home visitations and referrals to hospital. Such feelings of ethnic bias in gaining access to health care services may mean the loss of an opportunity to create a sense of cohesion, belonging and inclusivity among community members.

Legitimacy

While altruism and neutrality make reference to the culture of health professionals, legitimacy refers to the society within which health care is embedded. Generally, health professionals are accorded high legitimacy by society and this allows them to exert considerable influence in communities where they work and more widely when they choose to do so (MacQueen and Santa-Barbara 2000). CHVs' acts of humanitarianism, selflessness and neutrality accorded them a high level of legitimacy and acceptability which allowed them to conduct peace activities that went beyond their health provision mandate. Their acceptability in the community boosted their work because they were able to easily access different social groups (ethnic, gender, age) for their health–peace activities, and thus enjoyed some level of influence on community behaviour, as one health worker, Karen, in Kibera suggested:

We are respected. People know we are volunteers and appreciate the kind of work we do and the services we provide to the community. Many people cannot do this. As a result, we interact easily with everyone, regardless of their ethnic or political opinions and identification. This is what enables us to reach members of different groups; they know we provide important services and they trust us to try the best we can to help. This level of trust makes it easier to talk about the need for peace to everyone and we can influence peacebuilding.

148 *Roseanne Njiru*

In Mathare, Rahab provided an exemplary case about how her practice of self-lessness, fairness and impartiality legitimated her position as a health worker and saved her during the 2017 election violence. This broadened her opportunities to talk to people about ending violence.

> Health work has no tribalism … like now you see, during the 2017 elections communities here were divided. The Luos and Kikuyus did not see each other eye to eye. But for me, as a CHW, and I am Kikuyu, no one touched me. Everyone here knows me and the work that I do. They were like "*usiguze* Rahab" [do not touch/harm Rahab]. Because no one came after me, I was able to talk to people from the two sides about the need to end violence and to make them see how violence was affecting us and our health. Almost every day, we [health workers] were busy because cases of assault were numerous.
>
> (Rahab, Mathare)

In-depth interviews revealed how the women CHVs engaged in settling disputes and reconciling family members within households that they visited for health care reasons. Because they enjoyed a considerable level of legitimacy and were easily accessible to communities, some residents disclosed personal details to them about family and community violence. In Mathare, a CHV talked about how a woman whose young daughter was sexually violated by a male family member had called her on the phone to seek assistance. She convinced the mother to report the incident to the police. At the time of the study, the health worker had been attending court as a witness in the sexual violence case, using her own resources because there was no support from the government or any non-governmental body. In Kibera, another CHV had helped two young men who had been involved in gang violence to leave the gang and they were, at the time of the study, receiving training in community health by a non-governmental organisation.

Taken together, the three interrelated aspects of the health care system discussed above advanced the CHVs' knowledge on community life and vio-lence, which may be significant for local peacebuilding efforts. Further, their daily experiences and struggles as they performed their duties enabled them to clearly articulate different perspectives of community life and peacebuilding. Discussions on health–peace activities of the women CHVs strongly revealed that these acts were gendered. The following section discusses this gendered responsibility of health and peace work.

Community health–peace work as a gendered responsibility

Participants perceived community health work as an informal activity because it involved people who are not trained as medical professionals such as doctors and nurses. As an informal activity concerned with caring for the sick and ensuring community well-being, health work was associated primarily with

Peacebuilding through health work in Kenya 149

women's roles. Prevailing gender norms prescribe that women perform the bulk of care work, such as looking after older members of the family, caring for the sick, and preparing food. In interviews, CHVs frequently drew on images of women and womanhood and on cultural norms to construct their health work as relating to their identities as women and the socially prescribed reproductive roles of women. Within this socio-cultural context, where there was an almost clear-cut division of labour, it was mostly women who engaged in the health–peace work. Because their "informal" health work was intricately tied to peace, women also perceived informal peacebuilding activities as women's responsibility and talked about similar community perceptions of women's health and peace work.

> You know the work of taking care of sick persons is traditionally done by women. A lot of our work involves home-based care and home visits to sick and elderly people. These are activities for women; most men cannot do this.
>
> (Joyce, Mathare)

> It is during our health activities that we mostly talked about or assist in resolving violence in families and communities. So, our peacebuilding work is very informal and cannot be separated from our duties as health volunteers and as women who are concerned with the wellness of our families and community. As women, we take the responsibility to talk about peace to everyone we can because we know what it means to be poor and to live with or in fear of violence.
>
> (Hannah, Kibera)

In constructing health–peace work as women's work, CHVs talk at length about the burden women experience during violent conflicts such as political violence and the everyday violence in the form of sexual and physical assaults, petty theft, conflicts between landlords/ladies and tenants. Women and children are the main victims/survivors of violence and bear the heaviest burden of taking care of sick family members. As both victims/survivors and burden-bearers, women saw peacebuilding as one of their major responsibilities. Therefore, as the interviews suggested, it was primarily women who spoke up early before violence erupted. Women also performed informal mediation activities, talking to people about the need to stop stealing and assaulting their neighbours.

Many participants also pointed out that the everyday activities of women enabled them to build horizontal relationships within the community. Women's productive and gendered activities, such as walking children to school, church activities, caring for the sick, going to work, to markets and to women's informal group meetings (commonly referred to as *chama*[1]), were important for networking. These social networks created spaces to talk about community problems and the need to build cohesive relationships. Particularly, in churches and in the *chamas*, CHVs and other women spoke about violence, prayed for

150   *Roseanne Njiru*

peace in the community, and discussed ways in which they could reduce cases of violence, live harmoniously and improve community well-being. Women took these actions as their responsibility in communities where they felt that the formal peacebuilding structures and the enforcement of law were largely not working for them. Asked about the women's social networks that the CHVs were part of and whether the CHVs used these platforms for peace work, some, like Mary in Mathare, noted:

> When we meet at the *chama* to contribute money or visit one of our members, the conversations we have include community problems. As a CHV, I have the opportunity to talk about health and to link discussions of community problems and violence to health issues. We talk about the need for peace in Mathare and what we can do to keep ourselves and the children safe.

While it appeared that the major responsibility for health provision and peacebuilding lay with women, this is not to suggest that women are naturally better health providers and peacebuilders than men: existing literature has already warned us against employing essentialised conceptions of womanhood and traditional gender frames (Mueller-Hirth 2019). However, as Mueller-Hirth (2019) also found in her research on women and peacebuilding in Kenya, women were able to exert considerable agency as mothers and to transform social relations in communities.

The women CHVs contrasted their health–peace activities with those of men. To begin with, there were fewer male CHVs compared to women. This was associated with the nature of the work that, as discussed above, mostly involved women's traditional care work. Moreover, participants noted that men were more likely to join the health system for financial reasons. Indeed, the largest number of CHVs that had left the service to look for other gainful employment were men. In addition, participants noted that men were more likely to be engaged in formal peacebuilding processes because those gave them some level of power (leadership). For instance, in the community peace meetings that I attended, it was men who constituted security committees of the chief-led peacebuilding committees that are part of Kenya's peace infrastructure. Women headed committees on aspects such as education and sanitation. This, as the section below elaborates, constitutes one of the challenges in peacebuilding in the two communities.

Constraints and limits to community health volunteers' peacebuilding agency

As the findings above have highlighted, women CHVs' health work was greatly intertwined with peacebuilding in the settlements. Discussions on the women's activities often pointed out the challenges they faced which constrained their peacebuilding agency. Key among these included inadequate financial support,

Peacebuilding through health work in Kenya   151

lack of adequate training on peace, women's exclusion from peace structures, and ethnicity. Here, I discuss each of these constraints briefly.

Inadequate financial support

Health–peace work is not without financial costs. While CHVs voluntarily gave their service and time to community work, and did not expect much remuneration, they were faced with a lot of financial difficulties that hampered their work. Many CHVs talked about helping sick persons with food and transport to health facilities when they made home visits, yet the CHVs themselves were also struggling to survive. At the time of this research, a CHV in Mathare was helping a family deal with a sexual abuse case:

> Like, the other day, a young girl was sexually assaulted by her uncle. The matter was reported to me and I helped the family through the process of reporting it to the police and getting treatment. Now the matter is in court, and I have to go to the court for hearing as a witness at my own expense. Nobody pays us for this.
>
> (Irene, Mathare)

To participants, the lack of funding for their activities was a major reason why many CHVs had dropped out of service work, even when they had purposed to give their time voluntarily. Those who remained worked in very strenuous conditions and had reduced the number of activities they could perform if they were not well supported; with extra support, they could increase their visits to families and hold community education forums.

Training on health–peace nexus

Women CHVs worked within a health–peace framework, articulating how their health activities were linked to peacebuilding in their communities. They also spoke extensively about how being in health care increased their ability to engage in peacebuilding. However, they noted that their training on community health work made no reference to peace. Yet, as the CHVs noted, in communities that are constantly experiencing conflicts and violence, health and peace work cannot be disentangled. As one CHV in Kibera pointed out "you cannot make a home visit to find a woman had been beaten up by her husband and not do something about it because it is not your work." Some argued that training on peacebuilding could improve both their health and peace activities.

Exclusion from formal peace structures

Study findings have shown that women CHVs were greatly and variously involved in peacebuilding efforts at the local level. However, they were largely absent from formal community peacebuilding structures that were led by the

152 *Roseanne Njiru*

chiefs. Women spoke about the persistent cultural norms that exclude women from leadership positions and thus limited their capacity to exert more influence in peacebuilding. As I have noted above, in the chief-led security meetings that I attended, none of the people who spoke about security in the settlement was a woman nor was there a woman in the security committee. Women were part of committees concerned with education, hygiene and sanitation. Yet, as this research has shown, the CHVs' lived experiences in the settlements, coupled with their informal peace activities, meant that they had adequate knowledge of conflicts and violence and could articulate perspectives of community life and peacebuilding that might even challenge the dominant perspectives on security in the settlements.

Ethnicity

Many women spoke about the challenges of working in ethnically charged contexts. They were conscious and reflective of how their activities might produce ethnic tensions. Some noted how they had been accused of favouring members of their own ethnic group, for example, if community members saw them making more visits to members of their group. Such perceptions of biases in community health work may create feelings of ethnic discrimination in provision of services, such as referrals to hospitals, and had the consequence of solidifying ethnic identities and using them to attack members of other groups. This was a difficult balance for the women CHVs.

Discussion

This research examined how community-centred primary health work increases the peacebuilding agency of women community health volunteers in two poor communities in Nairobi – Mathare and Kibera. Overall, the data suggest that being a woman CHV provides opportunities to engage in peacebuilding, but peacebuilding is at the same time hampered by the social and cultural context in which the CHVs work. Mac Ginty's (2014) notion of "local turn" in peacebuilding was particularly useful in highlighting the bottom-up, informal peacebuilding activities of women CHVs that counter the liberal top-down formal peace structures. The "peace though health framework" (Christensen and Anbrasi 2015; WHO 2014) helps to show how the women's health activities were connected to peace, and how a health care system enhances peacebuilding agency.

This research explored women CHVs' constructions of peace and ways of making sense as peacebuilders through their health provision activities. For the participants, peace meant mutual understanding, respect, freedoms and the right to have life's basic necessities. Peacebuilding is thus a process of acknowledging these aspects and building relationships in communities that are crucial to realising peace. These findings resonate with other studies such as McKay and de la Rey's (2001) study on women's meanings of peacebuilding in post-apartheid

Peacebuilding through health work in Kenya   153

South Africa, which found that women understood peacebuilding and peace-making as a process and recognised their active involvement in these processes. Moreover, my participants made strong links between peace and health, often talking about how in the course of health provision, they found themselves in situations where they settled disputes and reconciled families and communities.

Findings also indicate that being part of the formal health care system – even though marginally – increased the women's peacebuilding agency. Participants were conscious of the characteristics of the formal health care system (in this research, altruism, neutrality and legitimacy) and often pointed out that health provision knew no boundaries. These aspects of health care made them more acceptable to different groups of people in their communities and this enhanced the CHVs' health–peace activities. Santa-Barbara and MacQueen (2004) have argued that health care is an institutionalised expression of human altruism and that health care provides opportunities and strengths of health workers in the promotion of peace. In the Democratic Republic of Congo, D'Errico et al. (2010) have shown how a health NGO's neutrality was essential for establishing the health facility while also implementing other activities such as the gender and justice project facility and advocating on behalf of survivors of sexual violence, in addition to their core mandate of health provision. In the present study, the neutrality of CHVs increased the levels of trust that community members had in them, enabling people to confide in the CHVs and speak out about violence in the community. Moreover, being able to access diverse groups of people implied that the CHVs were able to learn about the disparate needs of these groups, understand the link between resource scarcity and violence, and thus provide accounts of the systemic violence in the communities.

As other studies (for example, de la Rey and McKay 2006) have found, women in general bear the heaviest burden of peacebuilding, thus revealing the gendered nature of peacebuilding. In this study, CHVs employed images of women and womanhood to construct their health–peace work as a woman's responsibility, largely informed by the cultural norms that confine women to the domain of reproductive roles. They viewed their approach (informal) to peacebuilding as different from that of men. While women CHVs were able to build informal relationships through everyday women's caring tasks in the community, men mostly worked from a top-down approach in formal structures that gave them a sense of leadership and power. The men's approach to peacebuilding is equally informed by traditional norms that construct men as "effective" leaders.

Equally, this study was concerned with the barriers to CHVs' peacebuilding agency. CHVs pointed out four major aspects that limit their health–peacebuilding capacities: monetary constraints, training on health–peace link, exclusion from formal community peace-building structures, and ethnicity. In particular, women CHVs' exclusion from formal peace-building efforts was a major hindrance to achieving peace in the community. Their restriction beyond the local level was informed by persistent gender norms that restrict women's participation in political decision-making processes, as in many parts

154   *Roseanne Njiru*

of the world (Justino et al. 2018). Being excluded from formal peace structures meant a lost opportunity to tap into the CHVs' knowledge of violence and struggles of community residents. If they were included, their knowledge of and experiences with violence would be useful to local and national peacebuilding and development efforts.

As research elsewhere has shown, inclusion of women in decision-making levels of peacebuilding can complement and make more successful grassroots peacebuilding efforts. Their inclusion in formal peace processes would sustain the efforts made at grassroots level and increase gender equity (Adeogun and Muthuki 2018). However, as Heidi Hudson (2009) has argued, such inclusion must recognise women's agency in peacebuilding and not just be an "add on" to the formal peace structures.

Conclusion

Health and peace are inextricably linked. Yet, discussions on the place of health workers in peacebuilding have largely been absent. This study has shown that community-centred primary health care women volunteers are essential to peacebuilding, and that the unique nature of the health sector is such that it holds a crucial opportunity to make positive interventions in peacebuilding. The study provides more empirical evidence about the peacebuilding potential of the health sector. Therefore, for policy initiatives on peacebuilding and development, there is a need to recognise the intricate health–peace link and how health initiatives can be leveraged for peacebuilding, particularly in marginalised violence-prone communities, and fund the health–peace model holistically in these communities.

The chapter has discussed how women CHVs construct peace and see their health work as part of the peacebuilding process, thereby making links between health and peace. It has explored how certain features of the health care system (altruism, neutrality and legitimacy) increase the peacebuilding agency of women. It has analysed the gendered nature of peacebuilding and discussed the challenges and constraints to peacebuilding. For the Kenyan government, this suggests that for successful peacebuilding and social transformation in communities, the infrastructures for peace must recognise the importance of an integrated – multilevel, multisector – peacebuilding approach, which involves both bottom-up and top-down processes. Particularly, the informal peacebuilding activities and agency of women CHVs should be identified, recognised and incorporated into the peace architecture.

As the study has highlighted, women CHVs perform essential informal roles in communities and participatory approaches to peacebuilding demand the recognition and involvement of women in both formal and informal peacebuilding processes. Meaningful participation and contribution to peacebuilding means addressing the challenges that limit the agency of women in peacebuilding. For instance, institutions training CHVs in violence-prone communities might incorporate training on the health–peace nexus. Also, by recognising that

Peacebuilding through health work in Kenya 155

community health work goes beyond the formal mandate, institutions might find it necessary to provide more support to health volunteers and thus further facilitate their work.

Note

1 *Chama* is the Swahili word for merry-go-round and is used in reference to a common phenomenon among women in Kenya, in which, typically, women save some money through the groups and then hand over lump sums to fellow members, one after the other.

References

Adeogun, J. T., and Muthuki, M. J. 2018. "Feminist perspectives on peacebuilding: The case of women's organisations in South Sudan," *Agenda* 32(2), 83–92. doi: 10.1080/10130950.2018.1450572

Arya, N. 2004. "Peace through health I: Development and use of a working model," *Medicine, Conflict and Survival* 20(3), 242–257. doi:10.1080/1362369042000248839

Buhmann, B. 2005. "The role of health professionals in preventing and mediating conflict," *Medicine, Conflict and Survival* 21(4), 299–311.

Christensen, C., and Anbrasi, E. 2015. "Peacebuilding and reconciliation dividends of integrated health services delivery in post-conflict Burundi: Qualitative assessments of providers and community members," *Medicine, Conflict and Survival* 31(1), 33–56.

Cohn, C., Kinsella, H., and Gibbings, S. 2004. "Women, Peace and Security: Resolution 1325," *International Feminist Journal of Politics* 6(1), 130–140. doi: 10.1080/1461674032000165969

D'Errico, N., Wake, C., and Wake, R. 2010. "Healing Africa? Reflections on the peacebuilding role of a health-based non-governmental organisation operating in eastern Democratic Republic of Congo," *Medicine, Conflict and Survival* 26(2), 145–159.

de la Rey, C., and McKay, S. 2006. "Peacebuilding as a gendered process," *Journal of Social Issues* 62(1), 141–153.

Grove, N. J. and Zwi, A. B. 2008. "Beyond the log frame: A new tool for examining health and peacebuilding initiatives," *Development in Practice* 18(1), 66–81. doi: 10.1080/09614520701778850

Gutlove, P. 2008. "The World Health Organization: Health as a bridge for peace," In N. Arya and J. Santa-Barbara (Eds.) *Peace through Health: How Health Professionals Can Work for a Less Violent World.* New York: Kumarian Press, pp. 225–227.

Hudson, H. 2009. "Peacebuilding through a gender lens and the challenges of implementation in Rwanda and Côte d'Ivoire," *Security Studies* 18(2), 287–318.

Itto, A. 2006. "Guest at the table? The role of women in the peace process," In M. Simmons and P. Dixon (Eds.) *Peace by Piece: Addressing Sudan's Conflicts, Accord,* Issue 18, 56–59. Available at: www.c-r. org/accord/sudan/guests-table-role-womenpeace-processes, accessed 20 July 2019.

Justino, P., Mitchell, R., and Müller, C. 2018. "Women and peacebuilding: Local perspectives on opportunities and barriers," *Development and Change* 49(4), 911–929. doi: 10.1111/dech.1239

156 *Roseanne Njiru*

Karimi, V. 2018. "Securing our lives: Women at the forefront of the peace and security discourse in Kenya," Social Science Research Council, African Peacebuilding Network Working Papers, No. 20. Available at: www.ssrc.org/publications/view/securing-our-lives-women-at-the-forefront-of-the-peace-and-security-discourse-in-kenya/, accessed 24 June 2019.

Mac Ginty, R. 2014. "Everyday peace: Bottom-up and local agency in conflict-affected societies," *Security Dialogue* 45(6), 548–564. doi: 10.1177/0967010614550899

MacQueen, G., and Santa-Barbara, J. 2000. "Peacebuilding through health initiatives," *British Medical Journal* 32, 293–296.

Manchanda, R. 2005. "Women's agency in peacebuilding: Gender relations in post-conflict reconstruction," *Economic and Political Weekly* 40(44/45), 4737–4745.

McKay, S., and de la Rey, C. 2001. "Women's meanings of peacebuilding in post-apartheid South Africa," *Peace and Conflict: Journal of Peace Psychology* 7(3), 227–242.

Ministry of Health, Republic of Kenya. 2014. *Strategy for Community Health 2014–2019*. Available at: http://guidelines.health.go.ke/#/category/12/90/meta, accessed 2 March 2019.

Mueller-Hirth, N. 2019. "Women's experiences of peacebuilding in violence-affected communities in Kenya," *Third World Quarterly* 40(1), 163–179. doi: 10.1080/01436597.2018.1509701

Negin, J. 2007. "The central role of health in building peaceful post-conflict societies," *Journal of Peace, Conflict & Development* 10, 1–22.

Njiru, R., and Purkayastha, B. 2015. *Voices of Internally Displaced Persons in Kenya: A Human Rights Perspective*. London and Kolkata: FrontPage Publications.

Ochen, E. A. 2017. "Women and liberal peacebuilding in post-conflict northern Uganda: Community social work agenda revisited?" *African Sociological Review* 21(2), 15–35.

Okrah, K.A. 2003. "Toward global conflict resolution: Lessons from the Akan Traditional Judicial System," *Journal of Social Studies Research*. Available at: www.findarticles.com/p/articles/mi_qa3823/is_200310/ai_nq304242, accessed 27 April 2019.

O'Rourke, C. 2014. "'Walk[ing] the halls of power'? Understanding women's participation in international peace and security," *Melbourne Journal of International Law* 15 (1), 1–27.

Oseremen, F. I. 2018. "Infrastructures for peace: African experience and lesson," *Journal of African Conflicts and Peace Studies* 4(1), 1–18. doi: 10.5038/2325-484X.4.1.1094

Pratt, N., and Richter-Devroe, S. 2011. "Critically examining UNSCR 1325 on Women, Peace and Security," *International Feminist Journal of Politics* 13(4), 489–503. doi: 10.1080/14616742.2011.611658

Rodney, N. C. 2013. *A Biocultural Study of Intergenerational Health, Illness and the Politics of Aid in the Democratic Republic of Congo from 2009–2012*. Unpublished PhD Dissertation, University of Florida.

Rushton, S., and McInnes, C. 2006. "The UK, health and peace-building: The mysterious disappearance of health as a bridge for peace," *Medicine, Conflict and Survival* 22(2), 94–109.

Santa-Barbara, J., and MacQueen, G. 2004. "Peace through health: Key concepts," *Lancet* 364(9431), 384–386.

Tsai, T. 2009. "Public health and peacebuilding in Nepal," *The Lancet* 374(9689), 551–516.

Vass, A. 2001. "Peace through health: This new movement needs evidence, not just ideology," *British Medical Journal* 323, 1020.

World Health Organization (WHO). 1978. *Alma Ata Declaration*. Geneva: World Health Organization. Available at: www.who.int/publications/almaata_ declaration_en.pdf, accessed 3 June 2018.

World Health Organization (WHO). 2007. "Community health workers: What do we know about them?" Policy Brief. Geneva: World Health Organization. Available at: www.who.int/hrh/documents/community_health_workers.pdf, accessed 3 June 2018.

World Health Organization (WHO). 2014. *Health Action in Crisis: Health as a Bridge for Peace (HBP)*. Geneva: World Health Organization. Available at: www.who.int/hac/techguidance/hbp/en/, accessed 3 December 2018.

11 Women, artisanal mining and peacebuilding in Africa

Maame Esi Eshun

Introduction

Artisanal and small-scale mining (ASM) is an important source of income and livelihood for millions of Africans. The sector is estimated to create about 8 million direct jobs, which in turn support over 45 million Africans.[1] It is labelled as a poverty-driven activity because of its ability to provide mostly impoverished people with a source of direct employment and create additional jobs, especially in rural areas where there are few alternative livelihoods. The sector, however, has mostly been associated with negative social, economic, political, and environmental consequences. The informal, unregulated nature of much of the ASM activities makes it vulnerable to illegal dealings and an easy victim of organised crime, paramilitary operations, widespread corruption and violence, especially in highly valued minerals like gold, coltan, tin, tungsten (collectively known as conflict minerals), and diamonds. In many cases, ASM has indirectly incited political violence. Rebel groups have used revenues and profits from conflict minerals to finance political violence in countries such as the Democratic Republic of Congo (DRC), the Central African Republic, Sierra Leone and South Sudan, among others.

ASM is also associated with women who, in an attempt to reap the riches of the earth to make a living, take employment in dangerous mining conditions, often fraught with violence and conflicts. In conflict regions, women artisanal miners (WAMs) are exposed to danger, not only because they operate amid conflict but also because most armed groups use the minerals mined as a source of financing for the conflict. In Africa, women make up 40–50% of the ASM workforce, compared to the world average of 30% (Hinton et al. 2003: 1). These women are often involved in specific and multiple tasks throughout the ASM sector. They undertake a variety of activities ranging from digging, rock crushing, grinding, panning, washing and sieving, with the use of rudimentary tools and methods. Women are also predominantly responsible for carrying water from various sources to the mine sites. In some concentrated ASM environments, women become labourers and supply businesses around the mining sites, including in the sex trade (Perks 2011: 182). This, however, must not lead to simplistic conclusions whereby one associates WAMs with sex work.

Hruschka and Echavarria (2011: 13) noted that the mining activities undertaken by women are traditionally considered as female domains. This provides them with limited opportunities of direct access to mineral resources, management of mine sites, and consequently limiting their income opportunities. In addition, discussions rarely surface regarding women's productive roles in the sector and the gendered impacts of the industry arising from conflicts. An increased vulnerability to sexual exploitation, lack of access to land, and wage discrimination against women are typical of ASM communities. Findings by the Environmental Law Institute (2014: 6) showed that most women in African mines often work longer hours than men but earn, on average, about four times less than men.

Women also bear the brunt of the environmental and social risks associated with mining through the loss of productive agricultural land, marginalisation, and an increase in health risks, including HIV/AIDS. Women are disadvantaged in employment and training opportunities in mining; they are short-changed in the payment of compensation and royalties; and they are not involved during consultations along the mining value chain (AMDC 2015: 2). In the DRC for instance, although women constitute a significant portion (50%) of the ASM labour force, they are sidelined in decision making and often considered the least important in ASM programmes (Perks 2011: 185). These treatments meted out to women in ASM are mainly a reflection of existing gender inequalities deeply rooted in traditional and cultural norms. Thus, as widespread cultural beliefs prevent women from extensively exploring their potential in mining, most statistics do not even include women as artisanal miners at all (Hruschka and Echavarria 2011: 5).

Failure to address these challenges and to allow women to fully explore the opportunities available to them in ASM risks perpetuating inequalities and deepening grievances linked to natural resource rights, and access and control, which have proven to be powerful catalysts for violence. Accordingly, there are calls by the African Union (2009: 32) to initiate the empowerment of women miners by integrating gender equity in mining policies, laws and regulations to uplift women in mining. This is an important step in tackling mineral-related conflicts, as these have a negative impact on the success of peacebuilding initiatives.[2] Ensuring women have better access to, and control of, natural resources can improve the chances of sustainable peace and recovery in war-torn countries. This is because these women can identify with the resource and are heavily involved in the management of mineral resources from a livelihood perspective. Moreover, many women are dependent on these resources for the livelihood and well-being of their families. Their inclusion, therefore, broadens the peacebuilding conversations that take place because they have the knowledge to discuss these nuances. Such comprehensiveness addresses societal needs – rather than favouring one warring party – and this increases the chances of community buy-in. This, therefore, becomes a major step towards addressing the root causes of the problem, and is vital for creating sustainable peace.

Methodology

This chapter is based on a comprehensive desk study and literature review on the significant role of women in ASM towards peacebuilding. The growing interest from policy makers and experts in the field of gender, natural resource governance, and peacebuilding, especially in conflict-affected areas, has led to growing numbers of reports produced by researchers, scholars, and peace advocates that contain the valuable empirical evidence from which this chapter draws. Countries reviewed include nations in post-conflict and conflict conditions such as the DRC, Central African Republic, Sierra Leone, Sudan, Burundi, and Liberia. However, this list is not exhaustive. These countries are selected because their history of conflicts is deeply enmeshed in mineral resource extraction.

Although the category of women is diverse, this chapter makes links to literature relating to WAMs in Africa, especially in conflict and post-conflict settings. The chapter also draws together dispersed literature across issues relating to women in mining, as well as the role of women in peacebuilding. This is done in order to signpost key areas relating specifically to WAMs to strengthen the chapter's discussions, recommendations and conclusions.

What artisanal mining means to women

In recent years, the incidence of conflicts with direct links to ASM is on the increase – about five times the level it was a decade ago. Recent natural resource conflicts in the DRC, Central African Republic and Somalia, among other conflict-ravaged African countries, have largely been fuelled by ASM. In addition, conflict diamonds mined in rebel-held areas and artisanal mines in the Central African Republic, Liberia and Cote d'Ivoire are being smuggled into neighbouring countries and reaching the international diamond market. These current developments suggest an increased likelihood of conflict reoccurrence in those countries (Berman et al. 2017: 1568). Therefore, there are several reasons to focus on WAMs. First, according to Hayes and Perks (2012: 530), WAMs are doubly at risk – both as residents and informal workers in ASM communities – of the constant threat from military and rebel groups. In addition to children, they become the main victims of conflicts (fuelled by minerals), as evidenced in the past. It is also important to note that, for many African countries in conflict and post-conflict climates, like the DRC, Sudan, and the Central African Republic, women's participation in ASM has been linked to displacement from past conflicts and wars. This resulted in damage to farmlands and crops, consequently limiting livelihood opportunities. As one woman from the DRC recounts (Grown 2015: 1),

> Before the war, the fields produced ... Now we make money by growing in the fields of others and carrying things from the mines. What has changed life now is that the fields no longer produce and our husbands are no longer working.

Women, artisanal mining and peacebuilding   161

Thus where agriculture used to be the dominant economic activity, but is no longer viable, women are compelled to engage in ASM.

Women, especially in the rural areas, are the primary providers of food and water at the household and community levels. To provide such basic necessities, women are highly dependent on natural resources, especially ASM, to support the family with the proceeds. Studies have shown that money generated by WAMs contributes directly to education and medical expenses. In the Garoua Boulai district in East Cameroon for instance, WAMs reported that they offered a proportion of their mining proceeds to their husbands every September (when school usually reopens) to support in the provision of school needs (Bakia 2014). Thus, where support from their male partners is limited, women are left to shoulder the responsibilities of caring for their households, including providing the basic necessities of life and paying their children's school fees. The International Labour Organization (ILO 2007: 3) reinforces the point that though some women may be self-employed in panning their own section of a river bank; their objective is usually perceived as family help to support the income of their male counterparts.

For many women, ASM becomes an important part of their livelihoods and drives local economies. The mining proceeds are seen as a substantial supplement to the family budget, as women have a "better control of family revenues and spending, and are more likely to spend on family maintenance" (Hentschel et al. 2003: 30). However, the fact remains that ASM will "continue for at least as long as poverty makes it necessary" (Hentschel et al. 2003: 1), but it can be "a resilient livelihood choice for people who are vulnerable or looking for economic diversity in their livelihoods" (Buxton 2013: v). It is, therefore, essential to maximise any gains that the sector brings to avoid the financially motivated conflicts that often arise from mineral extraction.

In spite of the sector's utility – most importantly, in the participation of women at some stages along the mining value chain or process – unregulated ASM should be discouraged or eradicated, particularly in situations where women are exposed to chemical and toxic substances that pose health risks to them and their children (either born or unborn). WAMs should be enlightened to recognise the health and safety issues in the sector, including the impact on their children. Furthermore, community-based natural resource management programmes need to make development a priority. These can be developed and intensified through the provision of environmentally sustainable economic practices and local capacity building for WAMs. In building capacity, WAMs need to be trained on technical know-how and best practices in the sector to encourage their engagement, and allow them to compete effectively in the sector.

The case of formalising artisanal mining activities

Artisanal mining can generate peace dividends at the local and national level, and contribute to the economic growth that supports the underlying

162 *Maame Esi Eshun*

socio-economic conditions needed for peace (Bailey et al. 2015: 2). To harness these dividends, however, governments have a key role to play. The unregulated and informal nature of ASM activities must be brought into the legal domain and formalised through well-enforced legislative control. When ASM gets formalised, it is a win-win for all.

Formalisation would benefit all artisanal miners, and women miners in particular, if done effectively. The laws, policies, and reforms that govern a formalised ASM sector should be gender-sensitive, take into account the needs and interests of women, and recognise their vulnerabilities in the sector. Empirical studies have shown that ASM, if well-regulated and developed, can help women gain a foothold in new and challenging economic activities, especially in settings where they are marginalised (Labonne 2009: 117). According to Collins and Lawson (2014: 17), women miners become eligible for small grants and credits when their mining activities are technically supported and formalised. This encourages the formation of women's associations and cooperatives, which facilitates capacity building through technical know-how.

Formalising all ASM activities will improve the allocation of land and mineral rights. Ensuring fairer access to natural resource rights will enable greater participation of women in the sector and address the interpersonal and community conflicts that arise over the use of natural resources. Regulating ASM activities will, therefore, ensure the sector continues to be a viable economic opportunity for women (as well as men). Ultimately, it will help mitigate the sector's negative impacts and association with conflict and abuse, thereby ensuring greater equity and increased security for women.

Recent interventions in promoting the participation of women artisanal miners in peacebuilding

Existing literature shows that there have been several initiatives targeted at empowering women in peacebuilding processes. However, it is particularly important to identify what is missing in the current initiatives in order to define key areas that should target WAMs and their role in peacebuilding for further research and policy focus.

For women in general, spearheading the initiatives at the global level is the UN Security Council Resolution 1325 (adopted in 2000) on Women, Peace and Security. The resolution affirms the potential of women in playing an active role in conflict resolution and state rebuilding throughout the peace process. Many women's organisations (at both the regional and national levels) have embraced Resolution 1325 by invoking it in their action plans and strategies to gain more support and to make the impact of women's contributions more profound. The African Union Special Envoy on Women, Peace and Security is the primary women's group in Africa that foregrounds this principle. The Special Envoy has been active in promoting women empowerment in conflict and post-conflict African countries, with a results framework launched in 2019 to gauge women's role in peace and security. Much progress has also

Women, artisanal mining and peacebuilding   163

been made in terms of developing National Action Plans as a guide to the implementation of Resolution 1325 and the development of gender policies at the national and sub-regional levels to increase the number of women participating in peacebuilding processes. In 2008 and 2009, the first National Action Plans were introduced in conflict-affected Uganda, Cote d'Ivoire, Rwanda and Liberia. As of May 2019, about 24 African countries had finalised their National Action Plans on the implementation of Resolution 1325. In addition to these developments, a gender strategy was developed in 2014 which included the establishment of the UN Entity for Gender Equality and the Empowerment of Women (UN Women). They were tasked with the effective monitoring and implementation of Resolution 1325, and to rearticulate the objectives of continued gender mainstreaming within peacekeeping operations.

UN Women recognised that when engaged in the mining sector, women most often assumed roles in the ASM sector. Hence, to improve gender equality and promote women's participation in peacebuilding in the sector, the Extractive Industries Initiative was developed. At the country level, UN Women have been active in promoting the participation of women in the ASM sector, especially in eastern and southern Africa. In Malawi, UN Women drafted an extractive industry strategy to promote women's entrepreneurship in ASM. A comprehensive mapping of the barriers and opportunities for women engagement in mining have been developed in Tanzania. UN Women Tanzania has also contributed to the integration of gender equality in the development of corporate social responsibility policies and guidelines for the extractive industry sector. Similarly, UN Women Zimbabwe has also engaged stakeholders in providing policy recommendations on the creation of conducive legal and policy environments to enhance women's participation in ASM in Zimbabwe.

The need for greater support for the equal participation of rural women in natural resource management in the context of peacebuilding was the focus of the United Nations' 56th Session of the Commission on the Status of Women, convened in New York in March 2012. The highlight of the forum was how rural women are vital actors who bring peace and stability through their local knowledge about natural resources and the crucial role they play in managing them. In a joint project on Women, Natural Resources and Peace, UN Environment, in partnership with UN Women and the UN Development Program, are working to strengthen and increase women's decision-making role in resolving conflicts over natural resource management.

Peacebuilding and regulatory initiatives on conflict minerals – such as the Kimberly Process, OECD Due Diligence Guidance, the Dodd–Frank Act, the International Conference on the Great Lakes Region, and the UN Certification Schemes, among others – have also focused on curbing the illegal resource exploitation, trade and human rights abuses associated with conflict minerals. The regulatory initiatives have, however, provided limited provisions or guidance related to the role of WAMs in peacebuilding and conflict-free mining. Although these initiatives have largely promoted conflict-free mining, especially in the Great Lakes region, they should be continually strengthened

164 *Maame Esi Eshun*

with programmes that promote and encourage women's participation in conflict-free mining. They should also aid and prompt African governments on the urgency of formalisation of the ASM sector to validate more conflict-free mining, which will minimise the extent of violence and ill-treatment meted out to women in the sector.

Factors hindering the participation of women artisanal miners in peacebuilding

In the quest for a stable, peaceful and equitable society, the inclusion of women – and in this case WAMs – in peace processes is critical. Their inclusion in peace processes, however, has been negligible or slow at best. Generally, those who make efforts to participate in peacebuilding are threatened, slandered, ridiculed or ignored.[3] Although the factors that hinder women in peacebuilding are well documented in existing literature, this section now discusses four main impediments directly tied to WAMs.

Patriarchal societies

In many African societies, traditional cultural norms and practices, which often consider women as subordinate to men, are deeply entrenched. Thus, when women show interest in participating in local peace processes, they are seen by men as violating culture and tradition, which places them at the margins of public decision making (Amedzrator 2014: 14). This often dissipates their interest in taking part in peace processes. In Sudan one woman points out that:

> women are not allowed to sit in the same spaces as men when they are undertaking the *Judiya* [an indigenous conflict resolution mechanism] for cultural reasons. Even at meetings permissible for women to attend, when we try to make a point or express our opinions, we can be silenced by the men attending. We have important thoughts about how to help end disagreements and bring peace, but our views are not always heard.[4]

Orina (2014: 48) writes that in Burundi, for instance, typical characteristics of a "real man" are to be the one in leadership (control), to hit your wife if she speaks when standing up while you are seated, to never take your wife's opinions seriously, and to be dominant in the domain of decision making. The outcome of these attitudes is that WAMs may devalue their own role as peacebuilders and, despite their achievements, may not necessarily recognise the important role they play in building peace. Even in cases where women are mine owners, they are faced with gender bias (Collins and Lawson 2014: 42) and have difficulty in obtaining finance from banks, who may require their husbands' consent before obtaining a permit. Moreover, the customary line of reasoning is that WAMs are

Women, artisanal mining and peacebuilding 165

not eligible to contribute to the elimination of the negative impacts associated with mining activities. This further justifies why they are frequently left out of consultative, participation and leadership opportunities in natural resource governance, and peacemaking processes.

Lack of (or limited) education

Low literacy rates and the lack of technical skills among WAMs constitute an obstacle to their participation in peacebuilding and economic development (Mai and James 2015: 9). This undermines their participation in peacebuilding and local development processes. Many women also lack the capacity to voice their opinions and have influence. In communities where women feel they have the ability to influence peace outcomes and decisions, they often lack the knowledge on the procedures and strategies that will enable them act in an organised and informed manner. These shortfalls have been reinforced by some women involved in the mining sector. In field research undertaken by Mbugua (2015: 16) in Turkana County, Kenya, women miners were pleading for training on how to successfully capitalise on natural resource management to contribute to peacebuilding. According to Mbugua (2015: 36), these women noticed that although many organisations adhere to the constitutional provision to include a third of them in decision making, their low technical capacity hinders their effectiveness in influencing decision-making processes.

Lack of political will

Generally, although there has been gathering momentum to improve women's inclusion and positions at the peacemaking table, the inertia of integrating women's perspectives in peacemaking negotiations continues to undermine such efforts. Most post-conflict African countries have in place all the necessary legal, policy and institutional frameworks to ensure the increased participation of women in national issues. However, most of these countries lack the political will to implement these policy strategies (Mai and James 2015: 9). Governments' lack of commitment to enforcing existing legal, policy and regulatory frameworks in women's empowerment means these women miners cannot participate effectively in security, governance and related issues.

A USAID (2004: 7) study conducted in the DRC indicated that in most ASM communities, the core networks consist of a political and military elite (with some occupying key positions in government). Hence, who to consider in decision making is highly sensitive to military and political decisions. Moreover, the benefits and revenues generated in exploiting mineral resources deters people from mobilising for change and inclusion of women miners in peace processes. The lack of political will, coupled with the limited appreciation of the benefits of women's inclusion in peacemaking, hinders the advancement of women miners in all areas of decision making and peacebuilding.

Lack of access to resources – land

In many post-conflict African countries, women's land rights have become enshrined in new constitutions and land reforms that do not necessarily ensure equitable and feasible outcomes in terms of equitable access and control of resources. Even where women's land rights are catered for in national statutes and policies, ignorance of such rights, worsened by lack of education and poverty, makes it difficult for women to enjoy them. In South Sudan for instance, although the constitution and the Land Act (2009) make clear women's rights and entitlement to land, women are still denied access (Sigsgaard 2016: 10). In addition, most customary laws relating to land tenure systems are organised along the lines of patriarchy where male heads of households and sons constitute the exclusive locus of land holding, and women cannot own or inherit land partly because they are seen as part of the wealth of the community (Kameri-Mbote 2006: 11). In such situations, by customary law, women do not inherit their husband's mineral and land deeds. In cases where women exercise most control on land, it is over use rather than control and ownership. For women miners to effectively engage in societal peacebuilding, then their participation in local land issues – land management and land dispute resolution – is basic, as it enhances their participation in community-level decision making.

Opportunities for the engagement of women artisanal miners in peacebuilding

The United Nations (UNEP 2013: 15) notes that peacebuilding interventions often fail to recognise the challenges faced by women in their use of natural resources and therefore fail to capitalise on related opportunities. Women have often played numerous roles in promoting peace at the household and community level, as well as at the organisational level, where they have acted as heads or members of peace advocacy groups. These unique positions of women can be capitalised on to promote their roles and interests in peacebuilding efforts.

Redressing the power of women: The role of women coalition groups and local women's organisers

Local/community women's groups and organisations have strong interconnections with the realities on the ground in relation to the management of mineral resources; hence they are important sources of information for peacebuilding. In Sierra Leone, for instance, although women were not officially integrated into the peacebuilding process, they mobilised through the formation of women's groups, which are still working to increase women's representation in peace and decision making. Similarly, in Liberia, the women in Weasua, under the sponsorship of the UN Peacebuilding Fund, have formed

Women, artisanal mining and peacebuilding 167

peace groups, where each member is trained on the procedure of how to intervene in conflicts and make peace. These women further divide themselves into smaller groups and each group is charged with the responsibility to go out, find and resolve conflicts.[5]

Therefore, within an official network organisation, such as a "Women's Mining Association," women can become better equipped with information (through shared knowledge) and can pool resources. Moreover, strong women's coalitions can make significant strides in advancing women's issues in the political arena, thereby mainstreaming gender in public and private sector initiatives. Through such collective actions, women's associations can reach out to government, civil society and private sector organisations to seek institutional support and to project the voices of WAMs. They can also act as agents of social change and catalysts for the promotion of peace in ASM communities. Women's coalition groups in Africa, such as MARWOPNET in West Africa and SADC Women in Mining Trust in southern Africa, have an established presence and mediation experience in post-conflict countries in addressing the needs of women miners. The Tanzanian and Zambian Women Miner's Associations have also largely focused on the key issues facing women in the mining sector. These women's coalitions are using their influence, in addition to advocating for women's inclusion in political processes, to prioritise women's rights and access to natural resource management. This women-support-to-women strategy can create synergies where women work together to push themselves to the peace-making table. The support from fellow women can also stimulate the interest of other women who have become lazy in their efforts to promote peace, while creating platforms for competent women to engage in peace talks. Women's networks, especially in mining, have also proven useful in advocacy to improve the working conditions for women and connecting them to knowledge sharing of resources. Connecting and strengthening the linkages of women to lobby on behalf of their interests enhances their chances of making an impact, accessing information and accessing finance and other resources from credit and funding agencies.

Despite the considerable opportunities, many women's groups contend with great challenges in their continued survival while trying to achieve their objectives. These challenges are in the areas of chronic underfunding, lack of further training in management, leadership and lobbying skills, marginalisation and stigmatisation by government and non-governmental institutions (Pankhurst 2000: 17). WAMs may also exclude themselves from women's groups or cooperatives because of their inability to pay membership fees. Hence there is need for sustainable external support to these groups. UN Women have stressed how women's organisations must receive the political and financial support needed to engage in violence prevention, mediation and diplomacy, and investing in gender equality as part of the 2030 Agenda for Sustainable Development. Thus, it is the role of both local and international bodies to help strengthen women's groups towards their organisational needs and the ultimate objective of promoting peace.

Pathways: Changing social norms and the perceptions of the traditional gender roles

Social and economic equality is a prerequisite for women to fully benefit from ASM and have an impact on peacebuilding. Therefore, for WAMs to make a meaningful contribution to peacebuilding, it is essential that the underlying power structures that influence gender norms are transformed, not only in the public realm but also in the private spaces of the homes where gender is most intimate and women face the most direct obstacles to equality (Orina 2014: 48).

Zuckerman and Greenberg (2005: 2) note that during post-conflict reconstruction, it is possible to build new institutions and social structures and establish new norms and rules that are tailored towards the needs and interests of women. For instance, in Burundi, Nepal and Uganda, male leadership programmes that addressed men's masculinity resulted in a change in individual behaviours, which included reducing levels of violence against women (Strachan and Haidar 2015: 18). As gender roles are socially and culturally defined, education and a rethink must also be induced to facilitate a change in the norms. This means that mobilising the support of men is crucial. Involving men and boys as "change agents" will help them to understand the causes and consequences of their behavior in promoting change. But such support should start from the household level. In Burundi, Orina (2014: 68) stated that husbands conceived of their wives' (women's) participation in leadership positions and public life as a new and important component of the value women bring to the household. Thus, engaging men and soliciting their support brings flexibility and easy acceptance of the equitably gendered power structure. Tailoring this phenomenon to the mining sector should involve raising awareness about gender equality with miners, throughout the mining communities, and embed such awareness in the younger generation. Integrated interventions are necessary because focusing on women alone could provoke violent backlashes from men, which could make women more insecure than before. Therefore, this strategy is to position the gender argument within the broader peacebuilding framework to achieve sustainable peace.

Engendering policies and development plans with the involvement of WAMs

The Peacebuilding Commission of UN Women urges countries to strengthen the integration of gender perspectives in all policy and strategic engagements, which can be used as to leverage advocacy for gender equality, peacebuilding and funding. Therefore, mining development policies and plans should consider the different impact on men and women, and factor in experiences and ideas of WAMs when producing planning documents, guidelines and policies. WAMs should be welcomed and made to work with local governments to develop community development programmes and services that are tailored to benefiting all equally. Governments, policy makers and peace advocates should

Women, artisanal mining and peacebuilding 169

harness ideas from women in multidisciplinary environments to gain a holistic view of cross-sectional ideas for transformative and peace development.

Education and training

Access to education and training is critical to the quality of WAMs' representation and participation in peacebuilding. In enhancing the involvement of WAMs in peacebuilding, they should be trained and properly mentored to appreciate the importance of their involvement in peace processes. The essence is to acquire skills relevant in engaging effectively in mediation and communication, along with leadership and negotiation, to build familiarisation with conflict resolution mechanisms at both the communal and national levels. In Mbugua's (2015: 28) research in Turkana County, Kenya, WAMs stated that their increased access to education and training has overall improved the status of women. As a result, there has been a successful peacebuilding process in the county on account of the involvement of grassroots women in natural resource management. The role of local women's groups and organisations is significant in education and training. In Liberia, for instance, women's peacebuilding participation included activities such as education and skills training, communal farming and group micro-loans that encouraged women to collaborate to improve their quality of life (Fortune 2008: 10).

Economic empowerment

Sustainable peace goes beyond gender equality. It requires empowering mostly the victims of conflict, in this case women and children, to rediscover themselves and help in rebuilding, to become productive members of society and to prevent violence in the future. Therefore, ensuring effective inclusion of WAMs in peacebuilding also means providing the necessary conditions and empowerment structures to ensure their physical, economic and social security. Studies have shown that, generally, empowering women with the right tools is perhaps the greatest untapped potential to spur economic prosperity (Waisath et al. 2014: 7). A 2015 McKinsey & Company report revealed that as much as US\$12 trillion could be added to global annual GDP by 2025 if women participated equally in economic activities.

For WAMs, these empowerment tools should involve opportunities to diversify their economic activities through the creation of forward, lateral and backward linkages within the mining sector. This will ensure women are fully integrated into the mining value chain. It is also important to encourage value chain activities between the mining sector and other productive sectors like agriculture (which compete for similar inputs with ASM). For instance, industries that produce and supply inputs such as hand tools used in both ASM and agriculture should be created and supported to generate more competitive jobs that will serve as other means for women to make a living. Access to innovative financing for the ASM sector should also be tailored towards the needs

170 *Maame Esi Eshun*

and interests of WAMs. The positive impact of women's empowerment extends beyond the household level but contributes to sustainable livelihoods and economic growth at the national level. The multiplier effect reflects in their families' improved health, nutrition and children's education. Furthermore, it opens up windows of opportunity in economic, peace and political engagement.

Global peacebuilding initiatives and the role of policy makers

The high probability of minerals-related conflicts resurgence in Africa should be an opportunity for peacebuilding initiatives to emphasise the role of WAMs in peacebuilding, by integrating ASM into the peacebuilding agenda. Peace advocates should frequently deliberate on peace and security issues in post-conflict and fragile African countries, informed by the perspective and analyses of women miners as well. Local women miners should also be invited to participate in peacebuilding discussions with their various country or special representatives.

Consistently strengthening and enforcing existing laws, policies and action plans that advocate for women's rights and inclusion in peacemaking processes is a step to addressing the issue of limited political will. An international task force (this could start from the UN through the African Union) approved by countries should monitor women's rights (including WAMs) and inclusion in country strategy, policies and decision-making processes. Donors and foreign aid policies should aim at making the rights and participation of women at all phases of peace and state rebuilding an international requirement in obtaining even aid specifically tied to addressing mining-related issues and related sectors. Such strategies could target countries that undermine women's role and contribution in peacebuilding processes to encourage them to conform to such international standards by recognising women's rights and priorities.

Acknowledgements

This chapter is based on a research paper and panel discussion on "Women, Artisanal Mining and Peacebuilding in Africa: A Call to Action," which was published and hosted by the Wilson Center and Africa Programme under the Southern Voices Network for Peacebuilding Scholarship programme. Both research paper and panel discussion were made possible through the generous support and a grant from the Carnegie Corporation of New York.

Notes

1 In 2015, the United Nations Conference on Trade and Development said Africa's oil, gas and mining sectors must create more direct and indirect jobs to drive prosperity.
2 "Artisanal mining in Africa: Where women are mining for economic independence," an article written by Nicole Findlay, available at: https://carleton.ca/fass/story/artisanal-mining-in-africa/.

Women, artisanal mining and peacebuilding 171

3 http://studentredaksjonen.weebly.com/gjesteartikler/women-and-peacebuilding.
4 Conversation with Ghada Abdelrahman, cited from UN Environment's article on "Women as agents of peace in natural resource conflict in Sudan," available at: www.unenvironment.org/news-and-stories/story/women-agents-peace-natural-resource-conflict-sudan.
5 Weasua Women in Peacebuilding Initiative, Diamonds for Peace Liberia Staff, available at: https://eng.diamondsforpeace.org/weasua-women/.

References

African Union. 2009. *Africa Mining Vision.* Addis Ababa: African Union.
AMDC. 2015. *African Women in Artisanal and Small-scale Mining.* Addis Ababa: African Minerals Development Centre/African Union.
Amedzrator, L. M. 2014. "Breaking the Inertia: Women's Role in Mediation and Peace Processes in West Africa," *KAIPTC Occasional Paper No. 38.* Accra: Kofi Annan International Peacekeeping Training Centre.
Bailey, R., Ford, J., Brown, O., and Bradley, S. 2015. *Investing in Stability: Can Extractive-Sector Development Help Build Peace?* London: Chatham House.
Bakia, M. 2014. *Artisanal and Small-Scale Gold Mining in East Cameroon: Policy and Livelihood Implications.* Paper presented at the Annual Conference of the Centre of African Studies, 24–25 April, University of Edinburgh.
Berman, B. N., Couttenier, M., Rohner, D., and Thoenig, M. 2017. "This mine is mine! How minerals fuel conflicts in Africa," *American Economic Review* 107(6), 1564–1610.
Buxton, A. 2013. *Sustainable Markets Responding to the Challenge of Artisanal and Small-scale Mining: How Can Knowledge Networks Help?* London: International Institute for Environment and Development.
Collins, N., and Lawson, L. 2014. *Investigating Approaches to Working with Artisanal and Small-scale Miners: A Compendium of Strategies and Reports from the Field.* Brisbane/ Perth: International Mining for Development Centre.
Environmental Law Institute. 2014. *Artisanal and Small-scale Gold Mining in Nigeria.* Washington, DC: Environmental Law Institute.
Fortune, F. 2008. *UNIFEM: Supporting Women's Engagement in Peacebuilding and Preventing Sexual and Gender Based Violence in Post Conflict – Community Led Approaches.* Washington, DC: Search for Common Ground. Available at: www.sfcg.org/wp-content/uploads/2014/08/LBR_BL_Oct08_UNIFEM-Supporting-Womens-Engagement-in-Peacebuilding.pdf
Grown, C. 2015. *How Mining Affects Women in the DRC.* Geneva: World Economic Forum. Available at: www.weforum.org/agenda/2015/09/how-mining-affects-women-in-the-democratic-republic-of-congo/
Hayes, K., and Perks, R. 2012. "Women in the artisanal and small-scale mining sector of the democratic Republic of the Congo," in P. Lujala and S. A. Rustad (Eds.) *High-Value Natural Resources and Post-Conflict Peacebuilding.* London: Routledge.
Hentschel, T., Hruschka, F., and Priensten, M. 2003. *Artisanal and Mining Challenges and Opportunities.* London: World Business Council for Sustainable Development.
Hinton, J.,Veiga, M., and Beinhoff, C. 2003. "Women and artisanal mining: Gender roles and the road ahead," in G. M. Hilson (Ed.) *The Socio-Economic Impacts of Artisanal and Small-Scale Mining in Developing Countries.* London: CRC Press.
Hruschka, F., and Echavarria, C. 2015. *Rock-Solid Chances for Responsible Artisanal Mining.* Envigado, Colombia: Alliance for Responsible Mining.

172 *Maame Esi Eshun*

International Labour Organization (ILO). 2007. *Girls in Mining: Research Findings from Ghana, Niger, Peru, and United Republic of Tanzania*. Geneva: Bureau for Gender Equality, ILO.

Kameri-Mbote, P. 2006. "Gender issues in land tenure under customary law," in Collective Action and Property Rights (CAPRi Briefs), *Land Rights for African Development: From Knowledge to Action*. Geneva: CAPRi / UNDP, 11–13.

Labonne, B. 2009. "Artisanal mining: an economic stepping stone for women," *Natural Resources Forum* 20(2), 117–122.

Mai, N., and James, N. 2015. *The Role of Women in Peacebuilding in South Sudan*. Policy Brief. Juba: The Sudd Institute.

Mbugua, J. K. 2015. "Women, Natural Resources Management and Peace building in Turkana County," Occasional Paper Series 6, No. 1. Nairobi: International Peace Support Training Centre.

Orina, H. 2014. *Gender and Conflict Resolution Practices in Post-Conflict Burundi: Interactions between Macro- and Micro-processes of Norms Change*. Washington, DC: Georgetown University Library.

Pankhurst, D. 2000. "Women, gender and peacebuilding," *Centre for Conflict Resolution Department of Peace Studies Working Paper* 5. Bradford: University of Bradford.

Perks, R. 2011. "Towards a post-conflict transition: Women and artisanal mining in the Democratic Republic of Congo," in K. Lahiri-Dutt (Ed.) Gendering the Field. Towards Sustainable Livelihoods for Mining Communities. Canberra: Australian National University Press, pp. 177–195.

Sigsgaard, M. 2016. South Sudan. *Africa Yearbook*, 12, 357–365.

Strachan, A. L., and Haidar, H. 2015. Gender and Conflict: Topic Guide. *GSDRC, University of Birmingham*, 26.

UNEP. 2013. *Women and Natural Resources: Unlocking the Peacebuilding Potential*. New York: United Nations Environment Programme, UN Women, United Nations Peacebuilding Support Office, United Nations Development Programme.

USAID. 2014. *Minerals and Conflict: A Toolkit for Intervention*. Washington, DC: Office of Conflict Management and Mitigation, USAID.

Waisath, W., et al. 2014. *Closing the Gender Gap: A Summary of Findings and Policy Recommendations*. Los Angeles: WORLD Policy Analysis Center.

Zuckerman, E., and Greenberg, M. 2005. "The gender dimensions of post-conflict reconstruction: An analytical framework for policymakers," *Gender, Peacebuilding, and Reconstruction* 12(3), 70–82.

12 A role analysis of women in the fight against terrorism in Nigeria

Grace Atim

Background

Terrorism is a serious menace that has bedevilled the Nigerian State. The origin of this problem in Nigeria stems from ideological, religious and ethnic chauvinism, where tribal and religious groups at some point take up arms against each other. The problem has been compounded by a governance crisis and high unemployment, as well as high levels of poverty, hunger, sickness/diseases, abductions, kidnapping and corruption in a country that is otherwise well blessed with human and mineral resources. These Hydra-like problems account for the emergence, development and intensity of terrorism in contemporary Nigeria. Against this backdrop, the chapter examines the role of women in the fight against terrorism, since they occupy the centre stage on the development ladder of the Nigerian state. For elaborate analysis and discussion, the chapter, therefore, establishes dimensions in which women fight terrorism in Nigeria. It establishes that women actively discourage their children, husbands and other loved ones from engaging in terrorist acts. They also conduct peaceful demonstrations, while others engage terrorist groups in physical combat (for example, women hunters in north-eastern areas where Boko Haram are entrenched). The chapter highlights that, in as much as they play these crucial roles, women are not recognised by the Nigerian state when mapping out counter-terrorism strategies. The chapter, therefore, recommends that the Nigerian authorities acknowledge the positive contributions made by women and include them in all strategies for counter-terrorism. For this war to be won successfully, women must play a full part in the fight.

Introduction

The fight against terrorism in Nigeria has long been considered the exclusive duty of men, who are always seen at the forefront, while the vital roles of women are ignored. However, women have been directly involved in, and affected by, violent conflicts, riots and many wars in Africa. For example, 30% of fighters in the Lord's Resistance Army (LRA) during the Northern Uganda conflicts in the 1980s were female (McKay 2007:390), while some abducted

174 *Grace Atim*

girls were given as "wives" to LRA commanders. Aside from being fighters in frontline combat, some with command positions, girls and young women also carried out supportive tasks such as preparing food, spying, carrying loot and moving weapons (McKay and Mazurana 2004: 75). In Eritrea's liberation wars for independence, women constituted about 25–30% of the Eritrean People's Liberation Front (EPLF), which defeated the Ethiopian armed forces (Klingebiel et al. 1995). Examples of women as combatants can be seen in virtually all of the African countries that have been involved in armed conflict. In Nigeria, the Boko Haram terrorist group made use of women and girls as spies, suicide bombers, wives, cooks and in other roles.

Women have been central to successes in countering terrorism and violent extremism. However, sadly, most African societies have seen women as weaker vessels and, as such, excluded them when it comes to issues of conflict management and resolution, as well as counter-terrorism roles. The exclusion of women in such important matters is a violation of their human rights and should be challenged. This goes in line with the International Convention on the Eradication of all Forms of Discrimination against Women (CEDAW). Therefore, the purpose of this chapter is to analyse the role of women in the fight against terrorism in Nigeria. This is because such roles are not appreciated by many people, including the government. The chapter has six parts, beginning with this introduction, followed by a review of the conceptual discourse on terrorism, a discussion of a theoretical framework, and the emergence, development and intensity of terrorism in Nigeria, the contributory roles of women in the fight against terrorism in Nigeria and, finally, a conclusion with recommendations.

Conceptual discourse on terrorism

In order to fully appreciate women's roles in responding to terrorism, it is important to spend some time clarifying the concept. Further, it is important to acknowledge that although the conceptual discourses are quite complex, the simple truth is that terrorism affects women more than it does men. Defining terrorism is a tedious and complex task. This is because a suitable and universally acceptable definition remains elusive, arising from the fact that different bodies, organisations and government agencies have different definitions to suit their own particular roles, purposes or biases. However, an attempt has been made in this chapter to capture some of the arguments that surround this concept to drive home the understanding of this important concept. Since the massacre at the 1972 Munich Olympics, the United Nations (UN) has battled to come up with a universally accepted definition of terrorism, and in 2001 produced a partial definition of the concept (Gregor 2014: 2), suggesting that violent acts can be categorised as terrorism if:

> … they are resulting or likely to result in major economic loss, when the purpose of the conduct, by its nature or context, is to intimidate a

Nigerian women fighting against terrorism   175

population, or to compel a government or an international organisation to do or abstain from doing any act.

The UN admitted its inability to capture the totality of this concept when on 1 December 2010 the head of the UN Counter-Terrorism Committee Executive Directorate said that "the fact that there was not a universal definition of terrorism presented a challenge" (Gregor, 2014: 2). However, an avalanche of definitions of terrorism has been examined over time by academics, psychologists, medical practitioners, government agencies and politicians.

Walter Laqueur (1987: 72) examines terrorism as "the illegitimate use of force to achieve a political objective by targeting innocent people." This definition had reinforcement in Fernando Reinares, who distinguishes three traits that define terrorism. Firstly, he asserts it is an act of violence that produces widespread disproportionate emotional reactions such as fear and anxiety which are likely to influence attitudes and behaviour. Secondly, he asserts that the violence is systemic and rather unpredictable and is usually directed against symbolic targets. And, thirdly, he asserts that the violence conveys messages and threats in order to communicate and gain social control (Reinares, cited in Schmid et al. 1988). This definition has been summed up by Schmid as "peacetime equivalent of war crimes" (Kelkar 2017).

Arnold et al. (2003: 49, italics original) enrich this chapter by providing a medical dimension of terrorism when they assert that terrorism is:

> *The intentional use of violence – real or threatened – against one or more non-combatants and/or those services essential for or protective of their health, resulting in adverse health effects in those immediately affected and their community, ranging from a loss of well-being or security to injury, illness, or death.*

The definition puts more emphasis on the psychological effects on victims and regards threatened violence as significant as actual violence. The definitions strive to be an accurate reflection of the reality of terrorism and avoid terms which may imply bias or an emotional response to terrorism.

Terrorists themselves also justify their acts with preferred terms like freedom fighter, guerrilla, insurgent and revolutionary. It is on this premise that Hoffman submits that terrorist groups evoke more acceptable images of themselves by the use of favourable descriptors or definitions, such as "freedom and liberation," "armies" or other military organisational structures, "self-defence movements" and "righteous vengeance" (Arnold et al. 2003). Through such words they justify their destructive conscience.

The United State Department of Defense gives this chapter a succinct but all-encompassing definition of terrorism when they assert that: "Terrorism is the calculated use of unlawful violence to inculcate fear, intended to coerce or to intimidate government or societies in pursuit of goals that are generally political, religious, or ideological" (Ityonzughul, 2016: 491). The strength of this definition for this chapter lies in the fact that it underscores terrorism as a

Theoretical framework

calculated attempt rather than something that happens by mistake or chance. The definition also underscores the fact that the use of unlawful force is also applied by terrorist groups. Terrorists have their own motives for the attacks, and they carry out such acts to actualise their selfish goals.

Theoretical framework

The understanding of terrorist activities in Nigeria in the context of this chapter is premised on two theoretical frameworks, namely, the "Relative Deprivation" theory (an ancient Greek theory) and the "Social Conflict" theory. These theories assist in understanding terrorism in Nigeria. In turn, this will facilitate a more in-depth appreciation of the role of women in addressing terrorism in the country.

One of the great Greek philosophers, Aristotle, posited that the idea behind revolution is driven by a sense of relative inequality (Bature, 2016: 481). Aristotle, cited in Richardson (2011: 5), justifies this argument on the premise that

> the principal cause of revolution is the aspiration for economic or political equality on the part of the common people who lack it and the aspiration of oligarchs for greater inequality than they have: i.e. a discrepancy in both instances between what people have of political and economic goods relative to what they think is justly theirs.

From a psychological dimension, Gurr (1970: 87) summarises the above analysis simply as a "Frustration–Aggression Mechanism." His explanation of the phenomenon is that anger induced by frustration is a motivating force that disposes humans [men] to aggression, irrespective of its instrumentalities. Gurr also asserts that people are more likely to revolt when they lose hope of attaining equitable societal values and the intensity of discontent/frustration varies with the severity of depression and inflation.

From the foregoing, the Relative Deprivation theory rightly explains one dimension of terrorism in Nigeria. This is because a greater percentage of Nigerians are discontented with Nigerian democratic governance as a result of hunger, poverty, unemployment, HIV and AIDS, the scourge of malaria and other diseases, all amid abundant mineral resources. It is from this perspective, too, that Cyril Obi (2008: 7) rightly argues that the high expectations of the people that democracy would reverse decades of poverty, corruption and underdevelopment have not been met. This, in essence, has created feelings of alienation and deprivation, and the impulse to form rebel groups that undertake senseless terror attacks on the innocent and the governed.

To further reinforce this contention, although from a different dimension, is the Social Conflict theory, which posits that a society's social life is determined in the main by social production: that is, what is produced, and how the produce is shared. The theory explains numerous conflicts in Nigeria, including those informed by ethnic, political, religious and economic dimensions, among others. The theory, therefore, sees violent attacks by terrorist groups in Nigeria from contradictions inherent in human activities in the course of material production. Yecho (2006: 118) laments the role of social structure and urges us to give particular consideration to:

> Those material bases of society, the nature of the social system, religious organisations, the structure of social consciousness, the ideology and socio psychological orientation of the members of the society, views of the ruling classes and various social groups and the rivalry between the various groupings within the ruling circles.

It is the contention of the conflict theoretical paradigm that terrorist activities should be examined and analysed from the perspective of political and historical materialism. Accordingly, the theory postulates that political formation is a historical entity that encompasses and penetrates all social formations, including class structures. It would be genuinely misleading to assume that terrorist groups operate independently. They operate alongside such variables such as economic, political, religious and ethnic lines. However, whether religious or political, terrorist groups work towards achieving and enhancing economic domination in Nigeria for their supporters. Against this background, it is astute to state at this juncture that terrorism is also used as a mask for the privileged class, allowing political elites to perpetrate violent attacks in order to further their economic and political self-interests. Therefore, to understand the origin, dimensions and modus operandi of any terrorist group in Nigeria, one would need to situate it from the socio-economic, political, religious and ethnic structures of Nigerian society.

The emergence, development and intensity of terrorism in Nigeria

Understanding the emergence, development and intensity of terrorism in Nigeria lays the foundation for appreciating women's contributions towards overcoming its effects in the country. The history of terrorism in Nigeria can be traced to ideological, religious or ethnic chauvinism. This is because the territorial amalgamations that formed Nigeria (1906 and 1914), imposed by British imperial power, created an incompatible marriage destined to collapse in the near future. Scholars justify this hypothesis on the basis that these colonial amalgamations did not recognise geographical disparities or heterogeneous ethno-religious and socio-cultural divides that were clearly incompatible. Having enforced the amalgamation of these peoples, with diverse socio-cultural forms and backgrounds, instability was inevitable, as highlighted by O'Connel (cited in Ikpanor and Gbamwuan 2015: 123):

> The boundaries of African nations were drawn arbitrarily by the colonial masters and that the ethnically and political diverse peoples grouped

178   *Grace Atim*

together under these artificial boundaries were only held together by the force of a powerful authoritarian and external colonial power. That, these ethnic categories and cleavages re-asserted themselves very powerfully as the competition for state power and other public resources intensified just before and after independence. And that, the political elites who inherited power from the departing colonial rulers, having themselves been tutored with the authoritarian tradition of the colonial state and having assumed leadership of their respective states via ethnic tickets; lacked the competence, democratic skills and managerial ability to handle conflicts associated with heterogeneous societies and relied on corruption and the politics of primordial tendencies to perpetuate themselves in power.

Therefore, immediately after Nigeria's independence, this colonial marriage began to experience, among other things, daunting political, socio-cultural, and ethno-religious challenges. The emergence of terrorist activities in contemporary Nigerian society today can be accounted for by looking at this history. For example, the Niger Delta Volunteer Force (NDVF) of 1965, planned and coordinated by Isaac Boro, the Movement for the Emancipation of the Niger Delta (MEND), the Oodua People's Congress (OPC), the Movement for the Actualisation of the Sovereign State of Biafra (MASSOB), and suchlike, at one point or another terrorised the Nigerian state (Gbamwuan 2016: 423). Ogundiya (2009) gives further names of ethnically oriented terrorist groups in Nigeria from 1997 and beyond.

The proliferation of terrorist groups along ethnic lines in Nigeria is problematic, given the fact that they always pose a challenge for democratic governance. The reason for discussing these groups is because their agitations in whatever cause they believe and pursue have elements of terror and violence leading to damage to properties and loss of lives, and constitute a threat to the security and safety of the people. These groups have mounted assaults against the Nigerian state by directly attacking either the representatives of the state, such as security personnel, or targeting its economic well-being by paralysing oil exports through pipeline vandalisation, kidnapping foreigners, or even engaging the military in battle. One of the terrorist actions of MEND, for example, was the 1 October 2010 bombing in Abuja. It is strange how MEND was able to penetrate the security network in the capital city and detonate a bomb without detection (Gbamwuan, 2016: 426). Although most scholars categorise these groups as militants, they use terror to achieve their objectives and they also form the basis for contemporary terrorism in Nigeria.

Another group that also demonstrates an element of terror is the OPC, which operated in the south-west of Nigeria. Their activities were aimed at advancing the Yoruba people's interests and to bring all Yoruba under one umbrella. To achieve this, the OPC battled with other ethnic groups and also had confrontations with the police (Ogundiya, 2009: 39). Despite all these conflicts unfolding, Nigeria was not identified as a terrorist state by the international community. However, at the time of writing, the widespread activities of Boko Haram had placed the Nigerian state on the list of those nations facing the greatest threat of terrorism. Boko Haram's actions in Nigeria have compelled international observers to rank Nigeria as the third most terrorist-conflicted country in the world, below Afghanistan and Iraq (Global Terrorism Index (GTI) 2017). The GTI report also indicates that Boko Haram was among the four deadliest terrorist groups in the world, namely ISIL, Boko Haram, al-Qaida and the Taliban (Global Terrorism Index (GTI) 2017: 72).

The Boko Haram group was originally formed in 2002 by Mohammed Yusuf who, in his statement to Aljazeera News, blatantly asserted that: "Democracy and (the) current system of education must be changed, otherwise this war that is yet to start would continue for long." The spate of terrorist attacks committed by Boko Haram only came sharply into focus in July 2009, when the extremist militants carried out a series of attacks across three states in the northern Nigerian states of Yobe, Kano and Borno. This series of attacks resulted in the deaths of approximately 5,000 civilians in the course of the brutal operation. Boko Haram's terrorist activities have ravaged the entire north-eastern part of Nigeria and some states in the Middle Belt, including the Federal Capital Territory (FCT), Abuja. The impact of this terrorism is felt by all citizens, though the most traumatised are women and children, who are the more vulnerable members of society. For example, some women were forced into marriage to terrorists. Others were raped and contracted various sexually transmitted diseases, or brutally killed, or made to trek many kilometres in the bush without food or water. It is in line with this knowledge and understanding that this chapter appraises the role of women in the fight against terrorism in Nigeria.

Women's contribution to the fight against terrorism in Nigeria

Although women's participation in peacebuilding and development initiatives is often not appreciated or valued in Nigerian society, their roles and efforts in the fight against terrorism cannot be overemphasised. This is because the same factors that motivated men into terrorism are also responsible for integrating women into terrorist groups. Such factors, as argued by Naureen et al. (2013: 3), include; grievances about socio-political conditions, grief over the death of a loved one, real or perceived humiliation on a physical, psychological or political level, a fanatical commitment to religious or ideological beliefs, an intention to derive economic benefits, or a desire to effect radical societal change, among numerous others. Against this backdrop, women have played decisive roles in the fight against terrorism in Nigeria. At home, they played motherly roles to discourage the inclination to terrorism in their children, husbands and other loved ones. Naureen et al. (2013: 4) noted that:

> Women can be powerful preventers and participate in innovative efforts to inform, shape and implement policies and programs to mitigate the effects

of conflict and violent radicalisation. Within families, their traditional roles allow them to shape familial and social norms and promote increased tolerance and nonviolent political and civic engagement. Even in societies where it may appear that women are not empowered, they may wield emotive influence within families and communities, and their voices may be especially compelling when they speak out as victims or survivors of terrorist attacks.

The traditional roles ascribed to women in Nigerian societies as wives, mothers and nurturers, therefore, empower them to become the custodians of cultural, social and religious values. As they are uniquely positioned to transmit these ideals to the next generation, many women actively deflect family members and children from engaging in terrorist activities. Akwembe (2016) reinforces this by arguing that:

> As mothers they have a role within the family, specifically in the formation of children's character. If every mother or woman does a good job of bringing up her children, teaching them good morals, godliness, this will prevent the children from engaging in violent and extremist behaviours, thereby limiting the advent of them becoming terrorist or vulnerable to such. In the community, women have access to information that can go a long way to counter terrorism. They have capacity to handle problems in a less violent manner than men.

To substantiate these facts, a report highlighted how the Women Without Walls Initiative (WOWWI) in partnership with Women Without Borders (WWB) participated in a project known as "Mothers School" in Jos, Nigeria. Here, 147 women, most of whom were housewives and mothers, were trained to be the first line of security for their homes, families and communities at large (Akwembe, 2016). This training was carried out in five unstable communities and the impact was tremendous, as the confidence of the women – who were formerly kept out of what was known as the "men's world" of tackling security issues – was built up and they suddenly realised that they too were part of the fight against terrorism.

Another crucial role Nigerian women are playing in the fight against terrorism can be examined through the lens of peaceful protest organised under the umbrella of such organisations such as the Women Without Walls Initiative (WOWWI) and Christian Women for Excellence and Empowerment in Nigerian Society (CWEENS), among others. WOWWI, for example, held a protest march of 100,000 people with the famous slogan "Bring Back Our Girls" (BBOGs), a platform initiated by Obiageli Ezekwesili to call the world's attention to the menace of Boko Haram in Nigeria. The BBOGs was a reaction by the women following the abduction by Boko Haram of 276 Chibok schoolgirls in Borno State, Nigeria, in 2014 (Ibanga, 2015). It is in this light that women came out onto the streets in Nigeria and across the globe asking

Nigerian women fighting against terrorism 181

for the safe return of these girls. Nancy King (2017: 8) captures the efficacy of BBOGs protest:

> The Bring Back Our Girls (BBOGs) protesters became a leading advocate for the immediate rescue of this vulnerable, innocent and defenceless group of young girls who were seeking education as a means of empowerment. The BBOGs stepped out in protest and also raised their voices against what they considered the lack of quick intervention of the government and, more specifically, the social neglect of the security units in confronting the terrorist group Boko Haram who had laid claim to abducting the girls, who were final year students of a government secondary school at Chibok, Borno State, North East Nigeria.

Boko Haram's abduction of the schoolgirls in 2014 was a signal of the weakness of government to provide safe, secure and enabling learning environments for vulnerable schoolgirls, thus raising a moral question as to the premium value attached to girl-child education in Nigeria.

Another reaction by women was seen from a Nigerian artist, Sarah Peace, who created a public art installation in Epping Forest, north-east of London, UK, representing the abducted Chibok girls with black veils (Ibanga, 2015). Also, the First Lady of Nigeria, Aisha Muhammadu Buhari, and Mrs Dolapo Osinbajo, the Vice President's wife, met with the mothers of the abducted girls to discuss the way forward. On the other hand, CWEENS provided a safe house for victims of terrorism and assisted with legal aid where necessary. All of these were tremendous efforts by women in the fight against terrorism in Nigeria.

Furthermore, Nigerian women also served as combatants in the fight against Boko Haram terrorism. They supported the Nigerian security agencies in rescue operations. The exploits of women hunters cannot be easily forgotten at this point. For example, the crucial role played by Aisha Bakari Gombi cannot be overemphasised, the _Guardian African Network Nigeria_ (2017) newspaper describing her gallantry in this way:

> Bakari Gombi is Muslim but also believes in traditional spirits. One of her rituals is to douse fellow hunters with a secret potion to protect them from bullets. The 38-year-old leads a command of men aged 15–30 who communicate using sign language, animal sounds and even birdsong. "Boko Haram know me and fear me," says Bakari Gombi whose band of hunters has rescued hundreds of men, women and children … I'm waiting for a call authorising me to go back to rescue those women and children from Daggu, but I don't know if they will give us more arms.

Hamsat Hassan, another woman hunter who fought Boko Haram bravely, explained the reason she became a terrorist fighter. She explained that: "I couldn't fire a gun when I was asked to join the Hunters' Association in a town also called Gombi, but all I knew was that I wanted [revenge on] the

182   *Grace Atim*

people who abducted my sister" (*Guardian African Network Nigeria* 2017). These two gallant female hunters were among other women hunters who vowed to root out Boko Haram terrorists. They were poorly equipped and underpaid, but they fought selflessly in the war against Boko Haram's terrorism.

Finally, the exploits of Civilian Joint Task Force (CJTF) would have not been achieved without the relentless efforts of women. The CJTF boasts between 50 and 100 women members whose responsibilities include conducting pat-downs of women in churches, mosques and other public places, gathering intelligence, and arresting suspected female insurgents. The north-east has experienced many attacks by Boko Haram and, through the efforts of the female CJTF members, several other attacks have been prevented through successful intelligence gathering. Peace Direct (2017) captured the essence of this argument:

> In an exposé with female CJTF, members recounted their experiences in intelligence gathering, detecting Boko Haram members, and acting as bait. According to the women, they search women before they enter public places such as mosques, weddings or other festivals, most importantly because of the Islamic religious and cultural system which forbids non-related men from entering women's homes, the female CJTF members easily help in arresting female Boko Haram members in their abodes.

The women CJTF members played roles that would have been difficult for its male members. Their efforts contributed greatly to the successes recorded by the military in the fight against Boko Haram extremist groups.

A critique of women's representation in leadership in Nigeria and implications for counter-terrorism

This chapter has highlighted the extent to which women are involved in the fight against terrorism in Nigeria. A succinct appraisal of their participation in decision making could be made at this juncture: Nigerian women have been totally neglected in all facets of social influence. When decisions are being made on crucial matters that concern the state, women are totally ignored. This is because of some traditional African misconceptions that women are less powerful, weaker or not as capable as men, despite their valuable contributions throughout history. This overarching patriarchy means Nigerian women are not well represented in decision-making processes. Figures from the National Bureau of Statistics show the most significant representation of women among high-ranking government administrators with decision-making powers was 17.1% in 2011 for the position of directors-general and 19.1% for permanent secretaries. In the National Parliament in 2015, women constituted only 8.3% of members of the upper house of assembly; 7.2% in the lower house of assembly. In addition, women made up 26.2% of judges; 5.6% in local government; and 9.8% of councillors. At the state level, only 5 women were deputy governors and Nigeria is yet to have a woman governor in any of the 36 states. In the military and paramilitary, women are very scarce and have less influence because of the nature of the assignments given to them, most of which are office related. Women are, therefore, excluded from mainstream physical combat against terrorist groups. This explains why, out of thousands of CJTF personnel in 2017, only about 50–100 were women. The above figures make it clear that women are not economically, socially or politically empowered in Nigeria. They are neglected when important decisions that affect them are being made. Hence, their contributions to counter-terrorism efforts in Nigeria go unacknowledged.

Proposals

The war against terrorism can be a success when women are involved and empowered. Moreover, sociologists like Zeinabou Hadari, who worked for over two decades on the promotion of women's rights and leadership in Niger, once said: "every step forward for women's rights is a piece of the struggle against fundamentalism" (Mlambo-Ngcuka 2015). If women are empowered, this will go a long way to boost the fight against terrorism in Nigeria. This is because empowered women are the foundation of resilient and stable communities that can stand firm against radicalisation. This view has been supported by Alaa Murabi, a Libyan human rights defender, who also asserted that "women peace builders are leading the fight against extremism by challenging its root causes" (Mlambo-Ngcuka 2015).

Furthermore, while women have an important role in the family, governments should also encourage women's participation in the police, armed forces and in special anti-terrorist units. This is because women often notice small, yet vital, things that their male counterparts overlook, and they have the same level of competence, if not better. Unfortunately, only very few women are involved in special units in Nigeria, Africa, and across the world. According to Timo Smit and Kajsa Tidblad-Lundholm (2018: iv), "Approximately 4% of the military personnel and 10% of the police that are currently deployed in UN peace operations are female." These numbers are far too low to make a real impact. Clearly, more women in security infrastructures and a greater focus on women's role in counter-terrorism could help to end senseless killings by extremist groups in Nigeria, Africa and elsewhere in the world. As in many other instances of women's participation in the security sector, this would bring a positive dimension to the counter-terrorism efforts.

Finally, it is the suggestion of this chapter that women should be involved when government policies on counter-terrorism are being made. This is because they have a reservoir of knowledge on the root causes of terrorism and are key stakeholders in the quest for peace and security. Such knowledge and commitment would go further to strengthen the existing government policies on counter-terrorism.

184 *Grace Atim*

Conclusion

This chapter has analysed the role of women in the fight against terrorism in Nigeria. Women's roles in the fight against terrorism span from the home to the battlefield. At home, they are the first people to suspect that their family members and other loved ones might be drawn to joining terrorist groups. Therefore, women have the opportunity to use their influence to nip terrorism in the bud. Furthermore, their roles in peaceful mass protests and demonstrations, which attract international attention to the activities of terrorists, constitute another crucial dimension in which women fight terrorism in Nigeria. Finally, as combatants, women perform well as intelligence personnel. They also conduct pat-downs of women in churches, mosques and other public places in the fight against terrorism. Despite all these efforts, Nigerian women are not empowered and are neglected in Nigerian society. Their value is grossly underestimated as a result of the perceptions about them in Nigerian and African societies in general. The chapter, therefore, calls for an urgent review and acknowledgement of women's critical role in the overall response to terrorism in Nigeria.

References

Arnold, J. L., et al. "A proposed universal medical and public health definition of terrorism," *Journal of Medicine*, 18(2), 2003, 47–52.

Akwembe, A. "The role of women in counter-terrorism in Nigeria," *SlideShare*, 2016. Available at: www.slideshare.net/chantalabam/the-role-of-women-in-counterterrorism-in-nigeria-69345795, accessed 3 August 2020.

Bature, E. "The nexus of poverty, terrorism and development in Nigeria," in O. Chukwuma (Ed.) *Leadership and Military Complex Operation Series*. Kaduna: Nigerian Defence Academy, 2016, p. 481.

Gbamwuan, A. "Civil–military relations in Nigeria: A search towards combating Boko-Haram terrorism," in O. Chukwuma (Ed.) *Leadership and Military Complex Operation Series*. Kaduna: Nigerian Defence Academy, 2016, pp. 423–426.

Global Terrorism Index (GTI). Sydney: Institute for Economics & Peace, 2017. Available at: http://visionofhumanity.org/app/uploads/2017/11/Global-Terrorism-Index-2017.pdf, accessed 27 July 2020.

Gregor, B. "Definition of terrorism: Social and political effects," *Journal of Military and Veterans' Health*, 21 (2), 2014, 26–30.

Guardian African Network Nigeria, "Meet Aisha, a former antelope hunter who now tracks Boko Haram," 8 February 2017. Available at: www.theguardian.com/world/2017/feb/08/antelope-hunter-boko-haram-nigeria, accessed 30 May 2019.

Gurr, T. *Why Men Rebel*. Princeton, NJ: Centre for International Studies, 1970.

Ibanga, O. "The role of women in countering terrorism in Nigeria." Paper presented to the United Nations on 9 September 2015.

Ikpanor, E. I., and Gbamwuan, A. "Revisionism on the 'One North' template in the Nigerian project: The predicament of central Nigeria," in C. S. Orngu et al. (Eds.) *Ethnic Minority Agitations and Political Development in Nigeria*, Vol. 1. Abuja: Donafriq Publishers, 2015.

Ityonzughul, T. T. "Nigeria's war on terror: An assessment of the challenges in the fight against Boko Haram," in O. Chukwuma (Ed.) *Leadership and Military Complex Operation Series*. Kaduna: Nigerian Defence Academy, 2016.

Kelkar, K. "When it comes to defining 'terrorism,' there is no consensus," *PBS News Hour Weekend*, 26 February 2017. Available at: www.pbs.org/newshour/nation/defining-terrorism-consensus, accessed 2 August 2020.

King, N. "Promoting strategic women's engagement for social change through dramatics of protest performance: Bring Back Our Girls (BBOG) as paradigm." Jos: University of Jos, Theatre and Film Arts Department, 2017.

Klingebiel, S. I., et al. *Promoting the Reintegration of Former Female and Male Combatants in Eritrea*. Berlin: German Development Institute, 1995.

Laqueur, W. *The Age of Terrorism*. London: Weidenfeld & Nicolson, 1987.

McKay, S. "Girls as 'weapons of terror' in northern Ugandan and Sierra Leonean fighting forces," *Studies in Conflict and Terrorism* 28(5), 2007, 385–397.

McKay, S., and Mazurana, D. *Where Are the Girls? Girls in Fighting Forces in Northern Uganda, Sierra Leone and Mozambique: Their Lives During and After War*. Quebec: Rights and Democracy, 2004.

Mlambo-Ngcuka, P. "Women are the best weapon in the war against terrorism," 2015. Available at: https://foreignpolicy.com/author/phumzile-mlambo-ngcuka, accessed 3 August 2020.

Naureen, F., Liat, S., and Rafia, B. *The Roles of Women in Terrorism, Conflict, and Violent Extremism: Lessons for the United Nations and International Actors*. Washington, DC: Center on Global Counterterrorism Cooperation, 2013.

Obi, C. *No Choice, but Democracy: Prising the People out of Politics in Africa?* Claude Ake Memorial Papers No. 2. Uppsala: Nordic Africa Institute, 2008.

Ogundiya, I. "Domestic terrorism and security threats in the Niger Delta region of Nigeria," *Journal of Social Science* 20(1), 2009, 37–39.

Peace Direct. "The role of women in Countering Violent Extremism: the Nigerian experience with Boko Haram," *ReliefWeb*, 20 March 2017. Available at: https://reliefweb.int/report/nigeria/role-women-countering-violent-extremism-nigerian-experience-boko-haram, accessed 30 May 2019.

Richardson, C. *Relative Deprivation Theory of Terrorism: A Study of Higher Education and Unemployment as Predictors of Terrorism*. Senior Honors Thesis, Politics Department, New York University, 2011.

Schmid, A. P., Albert, J., and Jongman, A. J. *Political Terrorism: A New Guide to Actors, Authors, Concepts, Data Bases, Theories and Literature*. New Brunswick, NJ: Transaction Books, 1988.

Smit, T., and Tidblad-Lundholm, K. *Trends in Women's Participation in UN, EU and OSCE Peace Operations*, Policy Paper. Stockholm: Stockholm International Peace Research Institute, 2018.

Yecho, J. I. "An overview of the Tiv-Jukun crises," in T. T. Gyuse and O. Agene (Eds.) *Conflict in the Benue Valley*. Makurdi: Centre for Peace and Development Studies, 2006, pp. 113–129.

13 "Not all heroes wear caps"

Women and peacebuilding in the public sphere in Zambia through a narrative of Susan Sikaneta

Nelly Mwale

Background

Despite growing calls for women's recognition and participation in peacebuilding in Zambia, women have not only continued to be marginalised but also the few extant women's contributions to peacebuilding have remained undocumented. Grounded in gender and peacebuilding as an approach orientation and informed by narrative research in which data were collected through document analysis and recorded interviews, this chapter trails Susan[1] Sikaneta's contribution to peacebuilding in the public sphere. The chapter shows that Susan contributed to peacebuilding through her long service in Zambia's public and diplomatic service until her retirement early in 2019. Apart from serving as Ambassador of the African Union (AU) and the first Executive Secretary of the AU at the Southern African regional office in Malawi from 2002 to 2005, she was also High Commissioner of Zambia to Sweden and India in 2012 and to Ethiopia from 2013 to 2019.

During her tenure as a diplomat to Ethiopia, and as permanent representative at the AU Peace and Security Council, Susan was the chief proponent of the development of the AU Master Roadmap on silencing guns by the year 2020. She also spearheaded the implementation of the African Amnesty Month for the surrender and collection of illicit firearms and other light weapons, scheduled for September every year, as a recommendation from Zambia (the AU sponsored Zambia's Amnesty Month activities in 2018). Besides supporting Zambia's participation in missions of peacebuilding in coordination with the UN and EU to discuss the resolution of conflicts in the Central African Republic, the Democratic Republic of Congo, Libya, Mali, Burundi, and South Sudan, she vigorously championed women as peacemakers. Seen from the perspective of engendering peacebuilding, the chapter argues that Susan's narrative, while symbolising heroines without caps, represents what women can do in peacebuilding and how women can be beacons of peace at the local, national and regional levels.

Introduction

During the 2017 International Day of the United Nations (UN) Peacekeepers commemorations in Lusaka, Minister of Defence Davis Mwila and the UN resident coordinator Janet Rogan called for women's inclusion in peacebuilding activities (Musika 2017). This was because the role of women in peace negotiations had not been fully developed despite some positive strides to achieve gender equality, such as the introduction of a 30% quota system for women to encourage their participation in peacekeeping and the national defence force, and the establishment of the Gender Desk to foster gender mainstreaming at the Ministry of Defence.

This chapter explores the contribution of women to peacebuilding in Zambia through the example of a professional woman outside the defence forces. Such an exploration was deemed significant because while gender and peacebuilding has gained popularity in global scholarship, it has only attracted media attention and received little scholarly engagement in the Zambian context. Most importantly, this gender dimension largely dwells on the contribution of "women in uniform and caps" (in the security sector) in peacekeeping missions. For example, the narratives of women in peacekeeping missions were largely associated with peacebuilding in the public sphere to the neglect of other women not in caps (part of the uniform associated with the defence personnel). Such women in uniform include Captain Barbra Musonda (*Daily Mail*, 21 September 2018), Major Michelle Kayanda (BBC News, 6 October 2018), Major Ketty Chikwekwe (BBC News, 24 August 2018) and Charity Chanda (United Nations-African Union joint Peacekeeping Mission in Darfur (UN-AUMID) News, 8 March 2018) among others.

The motivation for this chapter was also sparked by lapses in the discourses of peacebuilding in Zambia that were also largely associated with the theme of the country's contribution to the liberation struggles in the region since the 1960s (Good 1987; Macmillan 2014). For example, Smith-Hohn (2009: 9) observed that in the 1960s and 1970s, Zambia was instrumental in the liberation struggles in neighbouring countries for which a price was paid in the form of reprisal raids by Rhodesian, South African and Portuguese forces. Nyamazana et al. (2017: 8) also observed that Zambia chose to support the liberation struggle and consequently hosted refugees or freedom fighters from five of its eight neighbouring countries (Angola, Democratic Republic of Congo (Zaire), Mozambique, Zimbabwe and Namibia).

Apart from Zambia's involvement in peacebuilding during the liberation struggles, notions of peacebuilding in the public sphere were further characterised by the country's hosting of refugees and engagement in peacekeeping missions. Nyamazana et al. (2017: 8) noted that after all of Southern Africa was liberated from colonialism, Zambia continued to host refugees on humanitarian grounds (including taking in refugees from far afield; namely, the Great Lakes region and the Horn of Africa), while the UN ranked Zambia as one of the exemplary countries in terms of contributing troops to peacekeeping missions in Africa and other parts of the world ravaged by war and conflicts (Phiri 2019). As at 31 May 2018, the country had contributed a combined total number of 1,011 military, police and staff officers to various UN peacekeeping missions; namely, the United Nations Multidimensional Integrated Stabilisation Mission in the

188   *Nelly Mwale*

Central African Republic (MINUSCA), United Nations – African Union Mission in Darfur (UNAMID) and the United Nations Mission in South Sudan (UNMISS) ("UN thanks Zambia over peacekeeping troops" 2018).

This chapter trails the gender and peacebuilding interface in Zambia within the wider frame of Zambia's contribution to peacebuilding in a context that had not been at war. This was achieved by exploring the contributions of women to peacebuilding in Zambia by trailing Susan Sikaneta's narrative in the public sphere in order to exemplify the contribution of women not in uniform to peacebuilding. In so doing, the chapter does not claim that Susan was the only woman making a contribution to peacebuilding, as many other women have also had roles in peacebuilding. Instead, the interest lies in providing a stepping-stone towards an understanding of the contribution of women not in uniform to peacebuilding in contemporary times in a context like Zambia. The insights in this chapter are informed by findings from a narrative research in which data were collected through document analysis and recorded interviews in the public sphere on representations of Susan Sikaneta. Through the gender and peacebuilding as an approach perspective, the chapter argues that Susan's narrative, while symbolising heroines without caps, signified what women are doing in peacebuilding and that they are beacons of peace at the local, national and regional levels. The chapter proceeds by highlighting the adopted gender and peacebuilding orientation and situates gender and peacebuilding in wider scholarship before contextualising women and peacebuilding in Zambia. Thereafter, the chapter offers a brief biography of Susan and highlights the representations of Susan's contributions to peacebuilding in the public sphere, and finally draws conclusions on the heroine without a cap.

Gender and peacebuilding orientation

The gender and peacebuilding orientation adopted in this chapter is informed by Munro (2000), who argued that when gender is combined with peacebuilding, it illuminates three connotations: namely an approach, analytical tool and a goal. Gender and peacebuilding as an analytical tool emphasises using gender analysis in the experiences of men and women during conflict and peace, needs assessment and gender relations. To the contrary, gender and peacebuilding as a goal is underpinned by the thinking that the attainment of peace and establishment of gender equality leads to greater gender equality and peace respectively (Wright 1998, Munro 2000). Ultimately, when gender and peacebuilding are viewed through the prism of a goal, the goal is oriented towards the attainment of gender equality and peace.

This chapter, however, adopts gender and peacebuilding as an approach orientation that entails (en)gendering peacebuilding because peacebuilding is gendered, based on differing perceptions and approaches according to one's gender (Munro 2000). This orientation emphasises that women do play an important and largely unrecognised role in peacebuilding. As such, engendering peacebuilding is anchored on mainstreaming gender equality. In practice,

Women and peacebuilding in Zambia   189

this entails broadening peacebuilding to bring out the important voices and activities of women with the goal of sustainable peace and gender equality (Woroniuk 1999; Munro 2000). Therefore, gender and peacebuilding as an approach was adopted because the focus of the study informing this chapter was on uncovering the contribution of women to peacebuilding in the Zambian context, as exemplified by a narrative of an outstanding woman peacebuilder not in uniform.

Situating gender and peacebuilding in wider scholarship

Suffice to mention that there is growing acknowledgement of the interconnectedness of gender and peacebuilding, as conflict affects women's lives in ways that differ from the impact on men. For example, Agbalajobi (2010) noted that while men in communities under attack tended to abandon public spaces to avoid being attacked or taken hostage, women's burdens were increased as they held communities together in the absence of men and that women as symbols of community and ethnic identity could become targets of extensive sexual violence.

Similarly, there is agreement in scholarship on the roles that women have played in peacebuilding. For example, Schirch and Sewak (2005) revealed roles of women in peacebuilding mainly related to being activists and advocates for peace, peacekeepers and relief aid workers, mediators, trauma healing counsellors, policymakers, educators and participants in the development process. By this, women addressed conflict non-violently by pursuing democracy and human rights, contributing to reducing direct violence, transforming relationships, addressing the root of violence and building the capacity of their communities and nations to prevent violent conflict (Schirch and Sewak 2005; McKay and Rey 2001; Issifu 2015). Other roles were related to women's group activities. For example, Alaga (2010) reported that women's groups organised themselves to participate in peacebuilding initiatives and processes through the provision of survival necessities (food, medical care), building bridges of reconciliation across the conflict divide and initiating community dialogue.

There has thus been a growing trend of analysing women's roles in peacebuilding. This has been partly attributed to international and national resolutions. For example, Alaga (2010) attributed the growing popularity of women's role in and potential for peacebuilding in global, regional and national discourses to the unanimous adoption of the landmark Resolution 1325 on Women, Peace and Security by the United Nations Security Council on 31 October 2000. In doing so, the critical role women could play in preventing and resolving conflicts, negotiating peace, participating in peacekeeping and in humanitarian response and post-conflict peacebuilding was recognised.

Suffice it to note that while gender and peacebuilding was largely mainstreamed after the UN resolution, peacebuilding was further popularised after it emerged that in a report from the former UN Secretary-General Boutros-Ghali, he used the concept to refer to "action to identify and support

190   *Nelly Mwale*

structures, which will tend to strengthen and solidify peace in order to avoid a relapse into conflict" (Boutros-Ghali 1992: 11). In this chapter, peacebuilding also relates to those initiatives which foster and support sustainable structures and processes that strengthen prospects for peaceful coexistence and decrease the likelihood of the outbreak, recurrence or continuation of violent conflict (Luc and Paffenholz 2001: 62). It also encompasses both immediate and longer-term objectives that deconstruct the structures of violence and construct the structures of peace.

Contextualisation of women and peacebuilding in Zambia

While often contextualised in areas that have experienced conflicts in the form of war, the discourse on women and peacebuilding in Zambia is framed in a context that has had no experiences of war and largely deemed as a beacon of peace in the region. As the 2016 Country Gender Profile for Zambia[2] observed, Zambia was not a country with conflict, but a host country for refugees. Zambia's contribution to peacebuilding through hosting refugees stretches back to the 1960s when the first Angolan refugees crossed the border into the western part of Zambia. The Angolan refugees were fleeing from the ongoing war for independence from their Portuguese colonial masters (Chanda 1995: 24). Apart from political will, Zambia's geographical position surrounded by war-torn neighbours who were fighting for liberation during the 1960s and 1970s rendered the country a safe haven. Thus, having hosted other refugees in Southern Africa, Kenneth Kaunda, the first president, was distinguished by his dedication and support for the independence struggles in the region and consequent commitment to the refugee issue that followed (Brosché and Nilsson 2005).

In addition, the refugees that have resided in the country for a long time have been classified as former refugees (people of concern) due to the with-drawal of their refugee status. This was ignited by the government's attempt to integrate refugees under the Solution Alliance, whose goal was to attain local integration of former refugees with host communities (Country Gender Profile for Zambia[3] from October 2015 to March 2016).

As regards the national policy context, Zambia's Vision 2030 advances the aspirations of the country on peace through principles such as peaceful coex-istence that underscore commitment to peaceful diplomacy, domestic politics and a positive stance towards peacebuilding (2016 Country Gender Profile for Zambia[4]). Other guiding pieces of legislation that address peace include the Defence Act, Zambia Police Act (Police Act revised in 1999) and Prisons Act.

At the regional and international levels, Zambia signed the Protocol to the African Charter on Human and People's Rights on the Rights of Women in Africa and adopted UN Security Council Resolution 1325 (UNSCR 1325), which requires member countries of the UN to promote women's equal involvement in peace and security, protect women in conflicts and prevent sexual violence and gender-based violence (GBV).

Women and peacebuilding in Zambia 191

A brief biography of Susan in Zambia's public sphere

Susan Sikaneta was born on 27 December 1948 in eastern Zambia. To start with, she was represented as a product of mission education and an example of a woman who had achieved academically at a time when educational attainment was male dominated. Having done her primary education at Mindolo Ecumenical Centre in Kitwe, she went to Chipembi Girls School in 1963 for her secondary schooling (Kapatamoyo 2005). After her completion of secondary education in 1967, she proceeded to the newly established University of Zambia in 1968 where she studied for a bachelor's degree in business and public administration. She graduated in 1972.

Susan was also portrayed as a woman with a long career in the public service. Upon graduation from the University of Zambia, she joined the National Assembly as a general clerk where she worked from 1973 to 1978, becoming the Senior Training Officer and Head of the Personnel and Administrative Department. She later joined Zambia Consolidated Copper Mines (ZCCM) in Lusaka and had to resign with regret soon after because her then husband Arthur Yoyo was transferred to Kitwe. Her long career in the diplomatic service began in 1978 when she joined the Ministry of Foreign Affairs. As soon as she joined this ministry, she was sent for further studies at the University of Namibia, where she obtained a post-graduate diploma in International Relations. In an interview with Kapatamoyo (2005), Susan added that she was next sent to Germany to study diplomacy courses, essentially becoming a trained foreign service officer. The further studies enabled her to serve at the Ministry of Foreign Affairs from 1978 to 1982 as Principal Political Officer.

Between 1982 and 1988, she worked with the Anti-Corruption Commission as Senior Investigations Officer and then as Assistant Director at the Research Bureau (Ministry of Foreign Affairs Press Statement, 19 November 2012). It was at this time when the government established a department for Women Affairs under Mama Chibesa Kankasa at Freedom House and asked Susan to assist Mrs Kankasa.

In 1988, she returned to the Ministry of Foreign Affairs as Deputy Permanent Secretary with the additional task of overseeing political affairs until her transfer to State House to act as Senior Private Secretary of President Kaunda up to 1990, the end of Kaunda's term (Kapatamoyo 2005). During this time, she was appointed Chairperson of the Commission of Inquiry to look into the administration of the prison service. Susan was also appointed chairperson to work out conditions of service for foreign service officers, resulting in the formulation of the first rules and regulations for Zambians working in foreign service.

After the 1991 wave of political change, President Frederick Chiluba recalled and appointed Susan as Permanent Secretary in the Ministry of Information and Broadcasting Services. Having served for 3 years in that ministry, she was transferred to the Cabinet Office as Permanent Secretary for Special Duties attached to the office of the secretary to cabinet.

192 *Nelly Mwale*

Apart from her long public service, Susan was further depicted as a long-serving woman in diplomatic service. This began with her entry into the AU during the time that Susan served under Levy Mwanawasa's presidency. Having assumed the presidency in 2002, President Mwanawasa appointed her as Permanent Secretary for Management Development Division (MDD) at the Cabinet Office with the core purpose of restructuring the civil service (Phiri 2002).

> Apparently that time the heads of state had just established a regional office for Southern Africa in Malawi and they wanted an executive secretary, I went for interviews and two months later in January 2003 I was offered the job.
>
> (Kapatamoyo 2005)

This marked Susan's career trajectory that ushered her into the platforms that facilitated her contributions to peacebuilding until her retirement in early 2019.

Susan and peacebuilding in the public sphere

Susan can be appreciated as having contributed to peacebuilding at different levels in the public sphere. For example, Susan was portrayed as advocating for stability by tapping into religion as a resource for peacebuilding at the family and national levels. This was illustrated while serving as Information and Broadcasting Permanent Secretary and officiating at a women's leadership workshop at Lilayi Lodge in Lusaka. She urged women to work hard and dedicate their work to God if they were to excel as leaders in all areas and that that the church had a critical role to play in promoting unity and stability in the nation (*Times of Zambia*, 27 August 1999). This resonated with the emerging discourses of religious peacebuilding in which it has been acknowledged that considerable spiritual and theological resources for peacebuilding could be drawn from religion (Dubois 2008).

Appleby (1996) also argued that religious traditions were vehicles for peacebuilding because of their existing networks and religious education through which peace builders could share best practices and inculcate religious teachings on peace respectively. Susan's call for the church to promote unity and stability was also related to the remarks by Rugyendo (2005), who argued that the church leaders had a pivotal role in the promotion of equality, justice and peace in the area of gender in his analysis of the contribution of religion towards the promotion of gender and peacebuilding in Africa. The church could therefore use religion to respond to societal concerns (Mwale and Simuchimba 2018) because, as Ter Haar and Ellis (2006) argued, religious resources produce knowledge that could be beneficial to a community for developmental purposes.

In addition, Susan can be viewed as having contributed to peacebuilding in Zambia through her involvement in the hosting of refugees. For example, in 2008, while serving in the Ministry of Home Affairs, Susan supported the country's hosting of refugees from Angola by emphasising and upholding the commitment to the international protection of refugees in accordance with the conventions on refugees, to which the state was party.

> ... the borders with the Democratic Republic of Congo (DRC) will remain open to asylum seekers who are victims of persecution and war ... the borders will remain open to ordinary migrants but the ministry has put up contingency measures to ensure that asylum seekers entering Zambia were disease free.
>
> (*Times of Zambia*, 1 November 2008)

The prominent portrayal of Susan was that of her contribution to peacebuilding as a diplomat. She was renowned not only for her ambassadorship to the AU but also her service as Zambian High Commissioner. For example, she was the first Executive Secretary of the AU at the Southern African regional office in Malawi from 2002 to 2005 and High Commissioner of Zambia to Sweden and India in 2012; and to Ethiopia in 2013 to 2019. During her tenure as Ambassador to the AU in Malawi, she advocated for peace on the African continent so as to enhance economic development. For instance, during the commemoration of the African Freedom Day in 2005, Susan noted that Africa's vision, among other things, was to maintain peace, security and stability as a prerequisite to economic development (*Times of Zambia*, 25 May 2005). This resonated with gender and peacebuilding as an approach orientation that argues that women are more concerned with positive peace, such as advancing conditions of social justice, economic equity and ecological balance (Munro 2000). Susan's advocacy for peace not only added a gendered voice to the continent's strides for peace, but also provided an example of how women could break cultural obstacles and be part of the continental peacebuilding conversations. Among the obstacles to women's participation in peacebuilding are those identified by Puechguirbal (2005), ranging from lack of time, status, resources and political experience, plus exposure to the burden of traditions.

As permanent representative to the AU from 2016 to April 2019 (during Zambia's 3-year tenure), Susan contributed to peacebuilding by lamenting the lack of an African representative to the UN. This was perceived as a gross injustice for the African continent on the UN Security Council 70 years after the institution was established (*Daily Nation*, 8 May 2015). This formed the bedrock of the Livingstone summit that had been called by heads of state in order to foster progress for the full AU summit, where the proposals from the C-10 committee meeting in Livingstone were submitted.

In addition, during her tenure as a diplomat to Ethiopia and as permanent representative at the AU Peace and Security Council, she was the chief proponent of the development of the AU Master Roadmap on silencing guns by the year 2020.

> ... the country used its tenure to push for a number of issues such as the development of the AU Master Roadmap on Silencing the Guns by the

194   *Nelly Mwale*

> year 2020, which was crafted in the Zambian capital of Lusaka ... as soon
> as Zambia became a member of the AU Security Council, silencing guns
> by 2020 was one of the issues it brought to the council.
>
> (*Xinhua News*, 4 April 2019)

Susan also spearheaded the implementation of the African Amnesty Month
for the surrender and collection of illicit firearms and other light weapons,
scheduled for September every year, as a recommendation from Zambia (the
AU sponsored Zambia's Amnesty Month activities in 2018).

> Another major achievement during Zambia's tenure in the Security Council
> was to push for the implementation of the "Africa Amnesty Month" for
> the surrender and collection of illicit weapons, which is designated for
> September every year.
>
> (*Xinhua News*, 4 April 2019)

The AU duly declared September of each year until 2020 as "Africa Amnesty
Month" in line with African and international best practices. This declaration
was made during the 29th Heads of States and Government Summit of 2017,
where Zambia's President Edgar Lungu presented a Master Roadmap to the
summit on the Practical Steps to Silencing the Guns in Africa by 2020. (The
Master Roadmap on Silencing the Guns in Africa by 2020 was crafted in
November 2016, during a retreat of the Peace and Security Council that was
held in Lusaka.)

Susan's engagement in this advocacy role furthered the strides for positive peace associated with women (Munro 2000). Susan pledged Zambia's
commitment in ensuring that the Roadmap to Silencing Guns in Africa was
achieved by advocating for peaceful ways of dealing with disputes as opposed to
guns on the African continent (Sakala 2018). These efforts were acknowledged
by other countries such as Zimbabwe, which praised Zambia for its role in
silencing the guns.

Besides supporting Zambia's participation in missions of peacebuilding in
conjunction with the UN and European Union (EU) to discuss resolution of
conflicts in the Central African Republic, the Democratic Republic of Congo,
Libya, Mali, Burundi, and South Sudan, Susan vigorously championed women
as peacemakers. She did so because of the recognition that there could be
no sustainable and lasting peace without the active involvement of women
(The Business Year 2017). Her stance confirmed the conclusions drawn by
Peuchguirbal (2005) that without the participation of women, there could not
be any sustainable peace.

Given that female representation in peacekeeping and protecting lives in
challenging security environments had remained low, Susan advocated for
initiatives supported by the AU to empower women and involve them in
peacebuilding. The result of this advocacy was the 2004 Solemn Declaration
on Gender Equality in Africa adopted by the heads of state. This called on

Women and peacebuilding in Zambia

governments to ensure the full and effective participation and recognition of women in peacebuilding, including the prevention and management of conflict and post-conflict reconstruction in Africa (The Business Year 2017). Furthermore, governments were called upon to appoint women as special envoys and special representatives of the African Union (The Business Year 2017). Part of the result of this initiative was Zambia's attainment of the UN target of recruiting women for 15% of military peacekeeping posts and 20% of police peacekeepers by 2020. Consequently, Zambia was considered a leader in ensuring the involvement of women peacekeepers by spearheading the Female Engagement Teams training (*Daily Mail*, 21 September 2018). These contributions revealed the strides made to engender peacebuilding and the positive peace associated with women in the gender and peacebuilding as an approach orientation (Munro 2000).

Susan: Heroine without a cap

Susan retired in early 2019. As a mother of four, she considered her biggest achievement in life to be the raising of her children. "…despite all the achievements, looking at my children and seeing them become the responsible adults they have become will always remain my greatest achievement in life" (Kapatamoyo 2005). This confirms the point that there is no necessary contradiction between women's peacebuilding work and their role as mothers. Based on the contributions of Susan to peacebuilding at the national and international levels, and informed by gender and peacebuilding as an approach, the chapter argues that the gender and peacebuilding discourse in Zambia needs to capture the strides made by women not in uniform. This is because Susan's narrative pointed to engendering peacebuilding in ways that bring out the voices and contributions of women in peacebuilding.

In addition, while her contributions could easily be linked to the different positions she held in her career, from Kenneth Kaunda's, Frederick Chiluba's, Levy Mwanawasa's, Rupiah Banda's, Michael Sata's to Edgar Lungu's presidencies, her narrative in the public sphere also pointed to how gender and peacebuilding is shaped by a woman's context. The chapter agrees with Myrttinen et al. (2014) who argued that gender identities in peacebuilding are social, cultural and political constructs that depend on a range of other factors such as class, age, profession, urban or rural setting, kinship and marital status. In this case, Susan's contributions to peacebuilding were largely shaped by professional factors and her context. Her early access to education equipped her for the task ahead, as well as her determination to succeed. This pointed to the complex nature of peacebuilding that is often embodied and in turn a product of its context.

Susan's contributions also signified an example of a woman who overcame structural barriers in order to rise to the top and contribute to a gendered peacebuilding discourse at national and international levels. As opined by O'Reilly et al. (2015), women in leadership positions pushed for broader

196 Nelly Mwale

inclusion and gender provisions in peacebuilding. This, therefore, confirmed Mazurana and McKay's (2007) examples of women's peacebuilding activities that illustrated how women played a very active and crucial role in peacebuilding and reconstruction at the local, regional, national and international levels. As such, the chapter views Susan as a symbol of a woman peacebuilder in the Zambian context.

Conclusion

The chapter trailed the narrative of Susan Sikaneta in the public sphere as a reaction to the growing calls for women's recognition and participation in peacebuilding in Zambia on the one hand, and the undocumented women's contributions to peacebuilding outside the defence wing in the Zambian context on the other hand. The chapter revealed that Susan contributed to peacebuilding through her long service in Zambia's public and diplomatic service. Apart from serving as the ambassador of the African Union (AU) and the first Executive Secretary of the AU at the Southern African regional office in Malawi, she was also High Commissioner of Zambia to Sweden and India in 2012 and Ethiopia in 2013 to 2019. The chapter showed how, through her positions, Susan advocated for peacebuilding and women's active and meaningful participation in peacebuilding. Through the prism of gender and peacebuilding as an approach orientation, the chapter argues that Susan's narrative, while symbolising heroines without caps, represents what women are doing in peacebuilding and how women could be beacons of peace at the local, national, and regional levels.

Notes

1 This chapter will use her first name and not the surname.
2 Japan Development Service Co. Ltd. 2016. *Country Gender Profile: Zambia. Final Report*. Commissioned by the Japan International Cooperation Agency (JICA). Available at: www.jica.go.jp, accessed 8 July 2019.
3 Ibid.
4 Ibid.

References

Agbalajobi, D.T. "The role of African women in conflict resolution and peacebuilding," in R. Bowd and A. B. Chikwanha (Eds.) *Understanding Africa's Contemporary Conflicts*, Institute for Security Studies Monographs, No. 173, 2010, 233–253.
Alaga, E. "Challenges for women in peacebuilding in West Africa," *Africa Institute of South Africa Policy Brief No. 18*, 2010, 1–9.
Appleby, R.S. "Religion as an agent of conflict transformation and peacebuilding," in C. Crocker, F.O. Hampson and P. Aall, Eds., *The Challenges of Managing International Conflict*. Washington, DC: United States Institute of Peace Press, 1996, 821–840.

Women and peacebuilding in Zambia 197

Boutros-Ghali, B. *An Agenda for Peace: Preventative Diplomacy, Peace Making and Peacekeeping*. New York: United Nations, 1992.

Brosché, J., and Nilsson, M. *Zambian Refugee Policy: Security, Repatriation and Local Integration*. Uppsala: Department of Peace and Conflict, 2005.

Chanda, R. "The demographic impact of refugees in Zambia," in N. Mijere (Ed.) *African Refugees and Human Rights in Host Countries*. New York: Vantage Press, 1995, pp. 33–49.

Dubois, H. "Religion and peacebuilding," *Journal of Religion, Conflict and Peace* 1(2), 2008, 393–405.

Good, K. "Zambia and the liberation of South Africa," *Journal of Modern African Studies* 25(3), 1987, 505–540.

Issifu, A.K. "The role of African women in post-conflict peacebuilding: The case of Rwanda," *Journal of Pan African Studies* 8(9), 2015, 63–78.

Kapatamoyo, M. "Ambassador Susan Sikaneta's Journey to the African Union," *Times of Zambia*, 24 March 2005.

Luc, R., and Paffenholz, T. *Peace Building: A Field Guide*. London: Lynne Rienner Publishers, 2001.

Macmillan, H. 2014. "The University of Zambia and the liberation of Southern Africa, 1966–90," *Journal of Southern African Studies* 40(5), 2014, 943–959.

Mazurana, D., and McKay, S. "Gendering peacebuilding," in D. J. Christie., R. V. Wagner and D. A. Winter (Eds.) *Peace, Conflict and Violence: Peace Psychology for the 21st Century*. Englewood Cliffs, NJ: Prentice Hall, 2007, 341–349.

McKay, S., and Rey, C. "Women's meanings of peacebuilding in post-apartheid South Africa," *Peace and Conflict: Journal of Peace Psychology* 7(3), 2001, 227–242.

Munro, J. *Gender and Peacebuilding*. Prepared for Canadian International Development Agency, 2000.

Musika, C. "Engage women in peacebuilding-chama." *Daily Mail*, 7 June 2017.

Mwale, N., and Simuchimba, M. "125 years of Catholicism in Zambia: The history and mission of the church in the provision of university education," *Oral History Journal of South Africa* 6(1), 2018, 1–16.

Myrttinen, H., Naujoks, J., and El-Bushra, J. *Re-thinking Gender in Peacebuilding*. London: International Alert, 2014.

Nyamazana, M., Grayson, K., Funjika, P., and Chibwili, E. "Zambia refugees economies: Livelihoods and challenges." Geneva: United Nations High Commissioner for Refugees, 2017.

O'Reilly, M., Suilleabhain, A. O., and Paffenholz, T. *Reimagining Peacemaking: Women's Roles in Peace Processes*. New York: International Peace Institutes, 2015, 11–13.

Phiri, C. "UN ranks Zambia top in peacekeeping," *Zambia Reports*, 22 February 2019.

Phiri, R. "Mwanawasa Shakes up Civil Service," *The Post Newspaper*, 22 January 2002.

Puechguirbal, N. "Gender and peacebuilding in Africa: Analysis of some structural obstacles," in D. Rodríguez, and E. Natukunda-Togboa (Eds.) *Gender and Peacebuilding in Africa*. Ciudad Colón: University of Peace, 2005, pp. 1–12.

Rugyendo, M. "The Contribution of religion towards the promotion of gender and peace building: Case study, Christianity." in D. Rodríguez, and E. Natukunda-Togboa (Eds.) *Gender and Peacebuilding in Africa*. Ciudad Colón: University of Peace, 2005, pp. 127–140.

Sakala, J. "Africa Amnesty Month for surrendering illegal weapons," *Times of Zambia*, 31 August 2018.

Schirch, L., and Sewak, M. "The role of women in peacebuilding," *Global Partnership for the Prevention of Armed Conflict*. Utrecht: European Centre for Conflict Prevention, 2005.

Smith-Hohn, J. *A Strategic Conflict Assessment of Zambia*, Institute for Security Studies Monographs, No. 158, 2009.

Ter Haar, G., and Ellis, S. "The role of religion in development: Towards a new relationship between the European Union and Africa," *European Journal of Development Research* 18(3), 2006, 351–367.

The Business Year. "A Place to Live for," diplomacy interview, 2017. Available at: www.thebusinessyear.com, accessed 2 July 2019.

"UN thanks Zambia over peacekeeping troops," *Lusaka Times*, 9 July 2018.

Woroniuk, B. *Gender Equality and Peacebuilding: An Operational Framework*. Prepared for Canadian International Development Agency, 1999.

Wright, J. "Conclusions: Problems and prospects in peacebuilding," in A. Griffiths (Ed.) *Building Peace and Democracy in Post Conflict Societies*. Halifax: Centre for Foreign Policy Studies, Dalhousie University, 1998.

Xinhua News. "Zambia's AU Security Council tenure ends," 4 April 2019.

14 "Swimming against the current"

Queen Labotsibeni, the epitome of effective peacebuilding in Eswatini[1]

Sonene Nyawo

Background

Peacebuilding is an amorphous concept, defined differently depending on context. Though originally conceived of in terms of post-conflict recovery efforts in war-torn countries, the chapter uses the term peacebuilding more broadly in the context of a non-violent conflict between Emaswati and European settlers over the land, amongst other issues. It presents a scenario of a Liswati female politician who in the 36 years of her reign, beginning in 1889, employed peacebuilding processes to settle both internal and external disputes. Furthermore, the chapter argues that Labotsibeni's ascension to the throne was rather atypical, as Swazi patriarchal hierarchies would not have allowed a woman in her situation to occupy such a political position. The patriarchal nature of the Swazi society has remained intact down the centuries, and it constructs women as passive citizens subordinated to male dominion. Power is unequally distributed between women and men and the majority of women do not have a voice in public decision making and peacebuilding processes. Instead, their participation in peacebuilding is limited to micro-level activities, constrained within the poles marked by patriarchy. However, the chapter asserts that, by emulating the character of the Queen Labotsibeni, who was an outstanding social reformer and an astute politician, Emaswati women can derive the strength to swim against the tide of cultural barriers and make their voices heard in peacebuilding and decision-making processes.

Introduction

Conflict and unrest expand in scope and scale across the globe. The 2018 Global Peace Index (GPI) (Institute for Economics & Peace 2018) reveals a world in which tensions, conflicts and crises that emerged in previous decades remain unresolved, resulting in a gradual and continual fall in peacefulness. The report identifies 13 countries that score "very high" and 16 that score "very low" across three domains of safety and security, ongoing conflict and militarisation. Among the 163 independent states and territories ranked by their level of peacefulness, 92 countries had declined while 71 had improved.

200　*Sonene Nyawo*

The report further reveals that global peacefulness has deteriorated by 2.38% in the past 10 years, and that more than one-third of armed conflicts are civil wars with international powers involved. Nations in Africa are no different from others elsewhere in the globe, as over the years Africans have been ravaged by conflict, which has torn apart the social fabric of the continent and also weakened the solidarity and human characteristics of the Africa society (Pina 2006). This has resulted in destabilization, displacement and infrastructural destruction, which have a gender-specific impact on the affected population (Dore-Weeks 2010). The GPI does make reference to sub-Saharan Africa, which is the region where the country of focus in this chapter is located. Countries where the intensity of internal conflict has increased are listed as the Democratic Republic of the Congo (DRC), Togo, and Lesotho, with the DRC in particular experiencing a significant increase in violence and rebel activity throughout the country. It is noted in this world measure of global peacefulness that, over the past decade, 42 countries have experienced an escalation in the intensity of their internal conflict, twice the number of countries that have improved. With regards to Eswatini, the snapshot of the Global Peace Index reveals peace to be "high," but that does not mean that the country is conflict free. It does experience its own tensions over a diversity of viewpoints but not at the same magnitude of political tension as elsewhere. Some political analysts attribute the passive nature of the Swazis to radical change in their attachment to their culture, protected by their king in his capacity as the custodian of tradition (Jones 1993).

In terms of comparison of the genders, it is mostly the women that are causalities of the costly destruction of war in Africa: it is women who are raped; it is women who constitute the majority of the world's refugees and internally displaced persons (Enloe 1990). However, as noted by Kaya (2016), protecting the world from the destructive cost of war requires not only international communities but also women, who must work together to prevent the outbreak and spread of violent conflict. Although in patriarchal societies power is unequally distributed between women and men, and the majority of women do not have a voice in local or national decision-making processes, women do play an important but largely unrecognised role in peacebuilding. This chapter, however, discusses Queen Labotsibeni, an outstanding social reformer and an intellectual of unusual commitment (Jones 1993), who, through peacebuilding, consolidated Swazi nationhood during turbulent times, while also protecting its sovereignty and culture from foreign encroachment. Peacebuilding ultimately supports human security, wherein people would be free of fear, want and humiliation, yet Labotsibeni went beyond this and, among other things, successfully regained tracts of land that her husband King Mbandzeni had lost to European settlers. Furthermore, she successfully resolved disputes between white settlers and the Swazis, and those between the Swazis themselves, thus ensuring security to every resident. Also, despite strong opposition from her advisers, she secured government support to establish the first non-Christian school for Swazi children to receive education.

Women and peacebuilding

Scholars generally agree that peacebuilding is an amorphous concept, leading to it being defined differently in various contexts. Whilst most definitions restrict the scope of peacebuilding to post-conflict interventions, common to all is the idea that it seeks to improve human security by ensuring that people are safe from harm and they have access to law and justice. It also strives to protect people from political decisions that may adversely affect them and offer them access to better economic opportunities and improved livelihoods (Khodary 2016).

Peacebuilding approaches and methods are varied and diverse but, as mentioned above, they all ultimately work to ensure that people are safe from harm, have access to law and justice, and are included in the political decisions that affect them, have access to better economic opportunities, and enjoy better livelihoods (Moghadam 2005). Though originally conceived in the context of post-conflict recovery efforts in war-torn countries, the chapter uses the term peacebuilding more broadly in the context of conflicts between Emaswati and European settlers over the land, and between concessionaires who clashed over land grants for livestock grazing and minerals. This understanding of peacebuilding is in line with Khodary's definition that peacebuilding is a "range of measures targeted to reduce the risk of lapsing or relapsing into conflict by strengthening national capacities at all levels for conflict management and to lay the foundation for sustainable peace and development" (2016: 499).

Generally, women are under-represented in peace processes as core actors and when they do participate, their role is limited. However, through local and international resolutions that support women's advocacy, a gender-perspective is integrated into conflict transformation and peacebuilding efforts so that women's contributions can be seen as crucially important and their voices heard. Resolutions that mark a major breakthrough for women's participation in peace processes include the United Nations Security Council Resolutions (UNSCR) 1325 and 1820, which build upon many other interventions, such as the United Nations Convention on the Elimination of all Forms of Discrimination Against Women (CEDAW), the Beijing Declaration and Platform for Action, and the Windhoek Declaration (Henrizi 2015). However, as noted by Kaya (2016), in spite of all this progress, women are still not systematically involved in peace processes and obstacles to their participation are numerous. These range from lack of time, status, resources, political experience and exposure to the burden of traditions.

In contexts where women suffer political repression, they utilise civil society to pressure for gains, rather than the male-dominated political system (Pina 2006). Civil society organisations mobilise many people and decision makers to pressurise for women's fair representation in peacebuilding forums. Illustrating this point on civil society as an important space for women's advocacy, given that access to the political structures is restricted, Henrizi (2015) cites Iraq as an example. She argues that the 25% quota for women in the parliament is just to ensure that women are represented numerically, but does not lead to them

202 *Sonene Nyawo*

having any real impact on decision making. Instead, women find the NGOs to be places for meaningful political agency, in that they create a safe space for women to air their grievances and articulate their ideas.

O'Reilly et al. (2015) make an important observation on what debars women's meaningful involvement in peacebuilding. They submit that between 1992 and 2011, only 2% of chief mediators and 9% of negotiators in peace processes were women. They argue that a leading barrier to women's participation is that the goal is often merely to end violence, where women play a small part, and that if the focus were instead on building peace, women would play a more prominent role. O'Reilly et al. (2015) further state the importance of including women in peacebuilding as being that their involvement makes it more likely for an agreement to be reached and it increases the probability that the peace agreement will last longer.

Patricia Justino, Rebecca Mitchell and Catherine Müller (2016) conducted a study where they analysed women's involvement in peacebuilding processes in post-conflict contexts in places such as Afghanistan, Nepal, Sierra Leone and Liberia. Their findings were that women, both individually and as part of women's groups, do contribute to peacebuilding processes in numerous ways. For instance, they would mediate disputes among themselves and among other members of the community; promote women's involvement in power positions in communities; and support women's access to justice. They were also found to start productive activities such as cooperative farming and livelihood training, and they conduct community campaigns such as promoting children's attendance at school. According to Justino et al. (2016), these roles were as intended by United Nations Security Council Resolution 1325 and subsequent peacebuilding initiatives promoted by international, national and local organisations. However, the study strongly posits that despite women's efforts to create for themselves safe spaces to come together to support each other in peacebuilding activities, substantial cultural, social and economic barriers continue being a hindrance. Enloe (1987) confirms this observation by stating that women's involvement in formal peacebuilding agendas is being frustrated by the persistence of harmful cultural and social norms and patriarchal values. She claims that women would feel insecure, intimidated and defeated in gender-skewed political contexts.

Swazi culture and women's active participation in politics

As alluded to above, culture is a significant obstacle to women's political engagement and participation, and this has led many women to abandon politics or activism (Khodary 2016). Women are pressurised by social institutions, including family, school and church, to conform to traditional gender roles, pervasive use of negative stereotypes, and other patriarchal norms that set boundaries for all genders. Women, therefore, tend to shun active participation in politics because they have been socialised to believe that their domain is the home and politics is a male domain. Ntawubona (2013) attributes women's limited occupancy of political positions to the limited nature of participation in political activities. With reference to parliamentary elections, she asserts that by not participating in activities such as campaigning and attending meetings, access to power centres such as parliament and councils, where selections of decision makers and representation are made, women's chances of occupying political seats and decision making positions become limited (Ntawubona 2013: 45). These boundaries that control the social space of a woman are, by and large, set by culture (see also Oduyoye 2001; Nnaemeka 2003; Nyawo 2014).

A study on women's representation in the 2008 and 2013 parliamentary elections in Swaziland by Nyawo and Mkhonta (2016) confirms this observation. The findings were that Swazi women remain largely on the margins of the political process in Swaziland, despite the government's declaration of commitment to promote equality between men and women in decision-making positions. Formidable obstacles to women's effective participation and equitable representation in government bodies, especially the legislature, were highlighted by the study. The role and place of women in politics, it is argued, has been shaped by powerful socialisation forces. Swazi culture and traditions impose restrictions on women's participation, since the rule and command function is ascribed to men, and women are considered to be subordinate to men. Parliament is viewed as "a masculine decision-making territory" where important decisions concerning the country's governance have to be made predominantly by men. The women's tendency to shy away from parliament is therefore consistent with the assumption that decision making in Swazi society is a male preserve. Because of the patriarchal nature of Swazi society, men would be reluctant to allow their wives to venture into politics or to seek public office. Apart from these cultural impediments, the women's meagre financial resources also impede their political participation. They need money to finance political campaigns in order to compete with their male counterparts. But, men would always win the election race because they have more avenues to raise finance and are able to outspend women competitors (Nyawo and Mkhonta 2016).

Concerns on gender disparities and dimensions in these parliamentary elections were raised by the Commonwealth Election Observer Mission to Swaziland, using the provisions of Section 84 and Section 86 of the Constitution as baseline, which seek to ensure effective participation and fair representation of women in the political process. In its assessment of participation and representation, the Commonwealth Observer Mission noted a decline in women's representation in Parliament during the 2013 elections, compared with the 2008 elections, despite the country's commitment to increase women's representation in the legislative chamber to at least 30%. It was observed that only one woman candidate had won a seat in parliament at the conclusion of the 2013 general elections, representing a significant drop from the five women who won seats during the 2008 elections. It was a similar outcome in the 2018 elections, when only three women made it to parliament.

The cited parliamentary elections, amongst other political processes, underscore that mechanisms like culture have taught Swazi women that the man is

204 Sonene Nyawo

the ruler in all social units and that the woman, as a subordinate, must support male leadership at all costs. It is for that reason that those who find themselves in leadership, either by choice or by default, experience antagonism, especially from other women (Nyawo and Nsibande 2014). As scathingly put by Ntawubona (2013: 57), "women believe that any woman who joins politics is stubborn and unmanageable and defies the social customs and traditions that restrict women to the home." The attitudes of these other women remind any woman leader that she is a misfit in a man's world, and she defies culture and the "normal" behaviour of a woman. This pervasive ideology of male superiority, as Whitehead (2012) described it, shapes women's views about themselves and their capabilities. Culturally, a woman must remain a minor throughout her life. She is always under the guardianship of a male: from childhood she is attached to her father; at marriage to her husband; when widowed to her late husband's brother or a close agnate; and at work to her male boss (Ngcobo 2007; Nukunya 1998). Connell (2000) refers to this stereotypical mentality as "hegemonic masculinity." Connell defines it as a cultural dynamic by which a particular gender claims and sustains a leading position in social life. Women in political leadership positions are, therefore, victims of the hegemonic masculinity discourse which constructs gender identities in settings such as schools, politics, families, friendships and work.

Namariba and Kamanzi (2013), in their exploration of culture, discuss gender asymmetries in terms of the power cube framework, which presents power as having forms, levels and spaces. They argue that in most African societies there are invited, closed and claimed spaces that people carve for themselves. Invited spaces are those where there are opportunities for involvement and consultation by authorities; closed spaces are those where decisions are made by a set of actors behind closed doors, without any pretence of broadening the boundaries for inclusion; and claimed spaces refer to those spaces which relatively powerless or excluded groups create for themselves (Namariba and Kamanzi 2013: 85–86).

However, there are women who rise against the tide that is anchored on male-dominated political and socio-cultural norms, which all work together to keep them secluded from political activities and official peace negotiations. This chapter, therefore, discusses a Liswati woman leader, visionary and strategist who in the 36 years of her reign, which began in 1889, used official diplomacy, mediation and negotiation strategies to regain tracts of land that her husband, the king, had lost to European colonisers and by employing peacebuilding skills managed to establish security, stability and peaceful coexistence between Swazis and the European settlers (Jones 1993; Watts 1922). Furthermore, the chapter argues that Labotsibeni's ascension to the throne was somewhat atypical, as Swazi traditional laws did not allow a woman to occupy such a leadership position. Against the patriarchal nature of the Swazi society, which has remained intact down the centuries, Labotsibeni used her peacebuilding and leadership abilities to consolidate the nation during turbulent times.

Who is Queen Labotsibeni?

Labotsibeni Mdluli, also known as Gwamile or "Mgwami" (c. 1858–1925) was the Queen Mother and Queen Regent of Swaziland from 1899 to 1921. She is a notable female politician and religious personage in the history of Swaziland. She is described as having had a marvellous memory, with an exceptional ability to unravel the most intricate disputes between the Swazi and British colonialists (Kuper 1963). She is also remembered for her shrewdness in passing judgments (Nyawo 2017). As Queen Mother or *Indlovukazi* (She-elephant) she was, in terms of the unwritten constitution of Swaziland, a dual monarch with political influence equal to that of the king, and with the supernatural power to make rain. Thus, Swazis at that time boasted about her rain-making powers. When Swaziland and neighbouring areas experienced droughts, she would be visited by large deputations to implore her to make rain. They would bring with them many black cattle for ritual performances. There were instances where she would refuse to make rain and larger and more desperate deputations would beg her for weeks (Watts 1922).

Swaziland, now known as Eswatini following King Mswati III's announcement on its change of name in 2018, is a small country with a population of 1.2 million locked between South Africa and Mozambique, and it is one of the last surviving "absolute" monarchies. The name was coined about 1850 when European hunters and traders first came to the country during the reign of King Mswati I. It was from his name that the word was made up (Watts 1922). When King Mswati died there was serious infighting over the claim to the throne such that older chiefs had to seek assistance from Boers, and together they appointed King Mbandzeni, Labotsibeni's husband, as the preferred candidate to assume the throne (Kuper 1947). King Mbandzeni's reign ushered in a new era where the country experienced European invasion. These were Boer farmers and elephant hunters from Transvaal and Natal, who approached the king seeking permission to graze their cattle and sheep in his fertile grounds. Mbandzeni valued the friendship of the white farmers, who would also pamper him with gifts like guns, horses and greyhounds. He also faced pressure from the neighbouring Zulus, who wanted to invade the country, so "the white belt of farmers would protect him from them" (Watts 1922: 21).

The many white farmers who made inroads into the country bought farms, and they made Swaziland their permanent homes. This is the period that Watts refers to as the "concession boom," where applicants would persuade Mbandzeni to put his mark on papers, which ceded to them ownership of great tracts of land that had minerals like gold and tin (Watts 1922: 25). By the time of his death in October 1889 he had granted numerous overlapping and conflicting land concessions, and a variety of equally contentious monopolies, including one that purported to give its holder the right to collect "the king's private revenue" (Macmillan, 2007). Critics alleged that many of these were granted in exchange for greyhounds and gin, but a good deal of money

206   *Sonene Nyawo*

changed hands, much of it finding its way into the pockets of corrupt white advisers, including the egregious and venal Theophilus "Offy" Shepstone, the eldest son of Sir Theophilus Shepstone (Siyinqaba 1984). Mbandzeni died prematurely and unexpectedly in 1889.

Queen Labotsibeni, whose second name Gwamile means "the indomitable one," was brought to power as Queen Mother at the death of her husband, upon the appointment of her eldest son Bhunu as royal heir in 1890, at the age of 15. Although Swazi society is patrilineal, its rule is a dual monarchy, under which the incumbent king reigns jointly with his mother (Jones 1993). Labotsibeni then became Queen Regent to her grandson Mona in 1899, and relinquished rule with Mona's coronation as Sobhuza II in 1921. Her ascension to the throne was rather unusual, as Swazi traditional norms did not allow a woman in her situation to rule. According to laws of Swazi succession, a king must not be followed by a son who has blood siblings, yet already Labotsibeni was a mother to four children. It was rather her keen perceptions, early exposure to royal politics, and her capacity to manipulate certain foes into becoming her greatest admirers that enabled her to hold the fort (Macmillan 2007; Booth 1993; Kuper 1947). According to Ginindza (1996), she was chosen because of her outstanding intelligence, ability and character, and political acuity. Despite having no formal education, her wisdom, her perception, her wit, and her determination led her to become a force to be reckoned with. Her influence even went beyond Swaziland, as she was involved in the affairs of the South African Native National Congress (SANNC), now ANC, to the extent that she founded and financed its communication organ, the *Abantu-Batho* newspaper in 1921 (Mokoatsi 2017), whose first editor, Cleopas Kunene, had been her secretary and interpreter. Thus, she was honoured during the International Women's Day on 8 March 2017 as one of the "forgotten" African women who played a significant role in the fight against colonialism.

Labotsibeni's role in disputes

Anthropologist Hilder Kuper described Labotsibeni as an assertive and brave young woman who had a shrewd understanding of her social position, and a deep insight into the politics of the period (Kuper 1947). In dealing with conflicts, she had the able support of her son Malunge, Bhunu's younger brother, whom she had previously preferred over Bhunu as king; however, Malunge refused to usurp his brother's birthright (Booth 1993; Jones 1993). Watts refers to her as the old queen that had a clear understanding of the political intrigues, and notes that both Swazis and European settlers took note of her rare ability to solve conflicts. He then cites Lord Milner and Lord Selborne amongst many settlers, who he says spoke highly of Labotsibeni's marvellous memory, as well as her ability to unravel the most intricate disputes (Watts 1922: 34).

She played a leading role in opposition to the third Swaziland convention of 1894, which provided for the establishment of a Transvaal protectorate over Swaziland in February 1895. According to Jones (1993), the British and the

Boers disagreed over the fate of Swaziland, as both Britain and the Republic pressed Swaziland to accept new administration. This administration would replace a tripartite arrangement involving Great Britain, the Transvaal, and the Swazi nation that had been set up in 1890 (Macmillan 2007). Labotsibeni received at her residence representatives of the Transvaal, Vice-President N. J. Smit and Commandant-General Piet Joubert, as well as the Republic's Special Commissioner in Swaziland, J. C. Krogh, and successive British consuls in Swaziland, namely James Stuart and Johannes Smuts. It was at this time that Labotsibeni emerged as a remarkably intelligent, articulate and astute spokesperson for national political affairs. She dominated the discussions concerning the royal family's ability to rule, and its vehement opposition to the continued residence in the country of Theophilus Shepstone Junior, the Swazi nation's erstwhile adviser (Jones 1993). Her successful discussions with officials on these political concerns, according Jones (1993: 401), led the *Times of Swaziland* to heap praise on Labotsibeni in April 1899, saying that;

> she is the ruler. In spite of her years she is a hale and hearty woman, alert and active, and displays untiring zeal in the political government of the Swazi nation. She marches with a royal bearing and appearance, not only the wise men, the councillors, but the king himself is awe stricken.

Although Bhunu, her eldest son had been installed as *ingwenyama* or king, with the title Ngwane V, in February 1895, Labotsibeni retained considerable authority. As stated earlier, she was, in terms of the unwritten constitution of the country, a dual monarch with political influence equal to that of the king, and with the supernatural power to make rain. Her position was strengthened by the reckless behaviour of Bhunu, who was also implicated in the murder of Labotsibeni's senior headman, Mbhabha Nsibandze, and two other headmen. The Transvaal administration sought to bring him to trial, and he escaped to the British colony of Natal (Siyinqaba 1984). He later returned to Swaziland under British protection and a commission of inquiry imposed a fine on him, holding that he had allowed disorderly behaviour within his kingdom. Britain and the Transvaal then combined to add a protocol to the Swaziland convention that purported to reduce his status from king to paramount chief, and removed his powers of criminal jurisdiction (Marwick 1966). This new development further gave Labotsibeni a solid grip on the levers of power over the nation.

At the outbreak of the second Anglo-Boer War in October 1899, the Transvaal's Special Commissioner J. C. Krogh and the British Consul Johannes Smuts withdrew from Swaziland. General Piet Joubert wrote to Bhunu, indicating that the South African Republic was leaving Swaziland in his hands. After the withdrawal, he resumed full authority over his kingdom, but he did not live long enough to enjoy untrammelled power. Labotsibeni now became Queen Regent as well as Queen Mother and acted in the name of Bhunu's son, Mona, also known as Nkhotfotjeni, who was chosen to succeed him at the age of 6 months; he eventually became paramount chief, and later King

208   *Sonene Nyawo*

Sobhuza II. This era also saw Labotsibeni being a mediator in disputes between concessionaires. Boer–British tensions crystallised around their respective economic interests. According to Kuper (1947), Boers dominated in agriculture whilst the British controlled mining and trade. Land and mineral rights frequently overlapped, and this territorial coincidence of dual interests was made a bitter political issue (Kuper 1947: 25), which required Labotsibeni's intervention.

Throughout most of the 3-year South African War, although the country was supposedly a neutral territory, both sides maintained contact with Labotsibeni (Jones 1993). During this period, while leaning towards the British, she sought to preserve Swaziland as a neutral space and maintained a diplomatic relationship with the South African Republic's forces (Watts 1922). As the war came to an end, Labotsibeni and the Swazi council hoped for the establishment of a British protectorate. They were disappointed by Lord Milner's initial decision that Swaziland should be administered through the Transvaal. Labotsibeni and her council protested strongly against the terms of the Swaziland order in the Council of 1903 and the Swaziland Administration Proclamation of 1904, which set up the machinery of government under a resident commissioner. Prince Malunge, instructed by Labotsibeni, led a Swazi deputation to meet Milner's successor as high commissioner, Lord Selborne, in Pretoria in 1905, to protest over these and other issues. Selborne himself paid a visit to Swaziland in September 1906 (Marwick 1966). On that occasion he announced that the administration of Swaziland would, in view of the imminent restoration of self-government to the Transvaal, be transferred to the high commissioner. Subsequent to Labotsibeni's pressure on the white administration, Swaziland became a high commission territory, like Bechuanaland and Basutoland, though it was never formally declared to be a British protectorate.

As stated earlier, Mbandzeni lost a lot of land to Europeans as concessions, and he had regrets as Swazis were now subjected to a type of economic warfare eventually sanctioned by powerful European governments. According to Kuper (1947:24), at the end of his life "Mbandzeni saw his heritage dwindling, his domain restricted by European boundary commissions, his power questioned by European governments. When he was near his death he mourned, 'Swazi kingship ends with me.'" But Swazi kingship did not go to the grave with him; Labotsibeni rose to power and claimed the Swazi political space. Through peacebuilding strategies, she protected the nation's sovereignty and culture from foreign encroachment. Marwick (1966) asserts that her selection to be queen was more of a question of expediency to deal with the new threat posed by the influx of European mineral and grazing concessionaires in Swaziland. Echoing these sentiments, Genge (1999: 160) argues that there was no better choice than Labotsibeni, given that Mbandzeni would often invite her to meetings with Europeans, and thus she accumulated a crucial repertoire of political knowledge about Swaziland.

As Queen Regent, Labotsibeni and her council protested unwaveringly against the terms of the 1907 land partition, which divided Swaziland between the Swazi nation, the white concessionaires, and the British crown. Robert Coryndon, who was brought in from north-western Rhodesia as resident commissioner in that year, sought to take a hard line with Labotsibeni and her supportive son Malunge, and their loyal faction. He was not, however, able to get support from his superiors for a plan to depose Labotsibeni and replace her with Mona, the infant heir (Siyinqaba 1984). After a year in office, Coryndon described Labotsibeni as "a woman of extraordinary diplomatic ability and strength of character, an experienced and capable opposition with which it [the administration] was for some time incapable of dealing" (Jones 1993: 402). Prince Malunge led a Swazi deputation to London, which met the colonial secretary, Lord Elgin, in February 1908. They got little or no redress on the land issue, apart from a disputed, and subsequently dishonoured, promise that they would be able to buy back the crown land. Three years after the return of the deputation, Labotsibeni and Malunge became, with the consent of Coryndon, the prime movers behind a national fund to buy back land lost to European settlers (Macmillan 2007). For some historians, such as Kuper, Labotsibeni strove to regain the rights of the Swazis lost to whites, through methods introduced by whites, within the framework of a domination she realised she could no longer overthrow by force (Kuper 1963: 13); hence the move to impose the cash levy on the Swazi in order to establish the *Lifa* (inheritance) fund to buy back the land.

Labotsibeni's political interactions with the Europeans made her realise the importance of education. Kuper (1963: 31) records her to have said, "the power of Europeans lies in money and in books ... we too will learn; we too will be rich ..." Her last major contribution, therefore, as Queen Regent, was her insistence, in spite of some opposition, that Mona, the heir to the throne, should receive the best education then available to a black person in Southern Africa (Jones 1993). She first established a government school for princes and sons of leading councillors, known as Zombodze Swazi National School. She aimed especially at educating the young king so that he could be able to peacefully negotiate back land lost to Europeans. After primary education, he was sent in 1916 to Lovedale, a school run by the United Free Church of Scotland at Alice in the Cape, which he attended for 3 years. In 1919 she decided that he should be withdrawn from school and prepared for his installation as king. She transferred authority to him at a ceremony on 22 December 1921, in a moving address, which was read and translated on her behalf by her secretary, Josiah Vilakazi (Jones 1993). To Labotsibeni, this was a dream coming true after a long struggle against cultural and colonial tides. Thus, she rested peacefully in 1925, having consolidated the Swazi nation during turbulent times.

Conclusion

Culture as an indispensable variable within gender discourse in Africa shapes and influences the experiences of African women (Oduyoye 2001). Culture uses social institutions such as the family to socialise children into society's

210　*Sonene Nyawo*

normative system of values and appropriate status expectations. Thus, it provides a stable emotional environment that cushions the male's ego against any harm and abuse. Conversely, such socialisation renders women powerless and docile and when internalised it generates submissive, compliant and self-effacing behaviours (Unger 1979: 35).

The chapter has discussed a patriarchal society where a woman overrides cultural expectations and social norms and she claims a space in the leadership structure of the Swazi nation. Labotsibeni strove to regain the rights of the Swazis lost to whites through negotiating and peacebuilding, and she successfully consolidated the people into a nation during the pre-industrial era in Swaziland. This proves that although patriarchy allows men to dominate, there are women who develop their own power to counter patriarchal norms and traditions. Thus, as Arat (1989) puts it, power must be understood as a shared and continuous process instead of an unchanging domination.

Prior to Labotsibeni becoming Queen Mother, the Mdluli clan to which she belonged had no history of providing queens to royalty. However, her grip on the levers of power and her aristocratic self-perception fashioned the history of her clan into becoming a "power house," even in the present Eswatini. She also moved against the cultural tide and became Queen Mother despite the fact that, according to traditional norms of succession, she did not qualify because she already had four children. She did not conform to expectations of the patriarchs who control female sexuality, whereby a Queen Mother should have only one son, amongst other qualifications. Such expectations would normally brainwash women to construct their personhood around their ability to procreate, especially male children. As Nganga (2011) has noted, women internalise all the dynamics of the male-dominated social hierarchy, which subsequently shape their self-conceptualisations such that they can only be appropriately defined by male children. In that way, men are able to reproduce themselves through social institutions, norms, values, traditional and religious cultures, so that their legacies would thrive down through the generations (Nyawo 2014). These inequalities, as further noted by Nganga (2011: 16), are very subtle, making it difficult for women to find their way out of them. Clifford (2001: 16), elaborating on the impact of the subtle social conditioning, asserts:

> It reinforces women's reluctance to develop a sense of personal worth. Studies show that women, far more than men, tend to have low self-esteem … many women spend much of their time trying to figure out what other people want of them, especially what male "significant others" want.

The chapter has demonstrated that there are women peacebuilders who conquer all of the cultural impediments that mark their boundaries within the poles of patriarchy. Such women as Queen Labotsibeni can be used as a point of reference in empowering other women to rise against the patriarchal current and contribute meaningfully to political peacebuilding.

Note

1 Eswatini was formerly known as Swaziland. In April 2018, King Mswati III announced that the country, hitherto known as Swaziland, would henceforth be called Eswatini, and its citizens would now be known as Emaswati. For the purposes of this chapter, which discusses a historical occurrence in the 19th century, the name Swaziland is frequently used, and the people are referred to as the Swazi or Swazis.

References

Arat, Y. *The Patriarchal Paradox: Women Politicians in Turkey*. London: Associated University Presses, 1989.

Booth, A. *Swaziland: Tradition and Change in a Southern African Kingdom*. Boulder, CO: Westview Press, 1993.

Clifford, A. M. *Introducing Feminist Theology*. Maryknoll, NY: Orbis Books, 2001.

Connell, R. W. *The Men and the Boys*. Berkeley, CA: University of California Press, 2000.

Dore-Weeks, R. *Post Conflict Countries, Women's Political Participation and Quotas: A Research Brief*. Background Paper for the Report of the Secretary-General on Women's Participation in Peacebuilding. New York: UN Peacebuilding Support Office, 2010.

Enloe, C. "Feminist thinking about war, militarism, and peace," in Beth B. Hess and Myra Marx Ferree (Eds.) *Analysing Gender: A Handbook of Social Science Research*. Newbury Park: Sage, 1987, pp. 526–547.

Enloe, C. "Women and children: Making feminist sense of the Persian Gulf War," *Village Voice*. September 25, 1990.

Genge, M. Power and Gender in Southern African History: Power Relations in the Era of Queen Labotsibeni Gwamile Mdluli of Swaziland. Unpublished PhD thesis, Michigan University, 1999.

Ginindza, T. "Labotsibeni/Gwamile Mdluli: The power behind the Swazi throne, 1875–1925," *Annals of the New York Academy of Sciences*, 1996, 135–158.

Henrizi, A. "Building peace in hybrid spaces: Women's agency in Iraqi NGOs," *Peacebuilding* 3(1), 2015, 75–89.

Institute for Economics & Peace. *Global Peace Index 2018: Measuring Peace in a Complex World*. Sydney: Institute for Economics & Peace, 2018. Available at: http://visionofhumanity.org/reports, accessed 15 July 2019.

Jones, H. M. *A Biographical Register of Swaziland to 1902*. Pietermaritzburg: University of Natal Press, 1993.

Justino, P., Mitchell, R., and Müller, C. Women Working for Recovery: The Impact of Female Employment on Family and Community Welfare after Conflict, 2016. New York: UN Women. Available at: www.researchgate.net/publication/319320489_Women_Working_for_Recovery_The_Impact_of_Female_Employment_on_Family_and_Community_Welfare_after_Conflict, accessed 15 July 2019.

Kaya, Z. "Women, Peace and Security in Iraq: Iraq's National Action Plan to implement Resolution 1325," *LSE Middle East Centre Report*, 2016. Available at: http://eprints.lse.ac.uk/67347/1/WPSIraq.pdf

Khodary, Y. M. "Women and peace-building in Iraq," *Peace Review* 28(4), 2016, 499–507.

Kuper, H. *An African Aristocracy*. London: Oxford University Press, 1947.

Kuper, H. *The Swazi: A South African Kingdom*. San Francisco: Holt, Rinehart and Winston, 1963.

212   Sonene Nyawo

Macmillan, H. "Labotsibeni (c. 1858–1925), queen mother and queen regent of Swaziland," *Oxford Dictionary of National Biography*. Oxford: Oxford University Press, 2007. doi:10.1093/ref:odnb/94560

Marwick, B. A. *The Swazi*. London: Frank Cass and Company, 1966.

Moghadam, V. M. "Peacebuilding and reconstruction with women: Reflections on Afghanistan, Iraq and Palestine," *Development* 48(3), 2005, 63–72.

Mokoatsi, T. "Pioneers: Swazi Queen Labotsibeni," *The Journalist*, 2017. Available at: www.thejournalist.org.za/pioneers/pioneers-swazi-queen-labotsibeni

Namariba, J., and Kamanzi, A. "Rearranging the patriarchal value system through women's empowerment: An experience from Tanzania," in Mansah Prah (Ed.) *Insights into Gender, Equity, Equality and Power Relations in Sub-Saharan Africa*. Addis Ababa: Fountain Publishers, 2013.

Nganga, T. W. *Institutions and Gender Inequality: A Case Study of the Constituency Development Fund in Kenya*. Addis Ababa: OSSREA Publications, 2011.

Ngcobo, L. "African motherhood myth and reality," in O. Tejumola and A. Quaysin (Eds.) *African Literature: An Anthology of Criticism and Theory*. Malden: Blackwell Publishing, 2007.

Nnaemeka, O. "Nego-feminism: Theorising practicing and pruning Africa's way." *Journal of Women in Culture and Society* 29(2), 2003, 357–385. doi: 10.1086/378553

Ntawubona, J. "Women's political participation in Uganda: A case study of Mbarara Municipality," in M. Prah (Ed.) *Insights into Gender Equity, Equality and Power Relations in Sub-Saharan Africa*. Addis Ababa: Fountain Publishers, 2013.

Nukunya, G. K. *Tradition and Change in Ghana, An Introduction to Sociology*. Accra: Ghana University Press, 1998.

Nyawo, S. "*Sowungumuntfu ke nyalo*" "You Are Now a Real Person": A Feminist Analysis of How Women's Identities Are Constructed by Societal Perceptions on Fertility in the Swazi Patriarchal Family. Unpublished doctoral thesis, University of KwaZulu-Natal, Pietermaritzburg, 2014.

Nyawo, S. "Are prayers a panacea for climate uncertainties? An African traditional perspective from Swaziland," *The Ecumenical Review* 69(3), 2017, 262–374.

Nyawo, S., and Mkhonta, P. "Reflections on women's political participation and representation in the post constitutional era (2005–2015)," *UNISWA Research Journal* 28, 2016, 1–13.

Nyawo, S., and Nsibande N. "Beyond parity: Gender in the context of educational leadership in Swaziland," *UNISWA Research Journal*, Special Volume 27, 2014, 45–58.

Oduyoye, M. A. *Introducing African Women's Theology*. Sheffield: Sheffield Academic Press, 2001.

O'Reilly, M., Súilleabháin, A. Ó., and Paffenholz, T. *Reimagining Peacemaking: Women's Roles in Peace Processes*. New York: International Peace Institute, 2015, 11–13. Available at: www.ipinst.org/wp-content/uploads/2015/06/IPI-E-pub-Reimagining-Peacemaking.pdf

Pina, A. D. *Women in Iraq: Background and Issues for US Policy*. CRS Report for Congress, No. RL32376. Fort Belvoir, VA: Defense Technical Informations Center, 2006. Available at: https://apps.dtic.mil/dtic/tr/fulltext/u2/a458958.pdf

Siyinqaba. 1984. "The Swazi monarchy," *Africa Insight* 14(1), 14–16.

Unger, R. *Female and Male: Psychological Perspectives*. New York: Harper & Row, 1979.

Watts, C. C. *Dawn in Swaziland*. Aberdeen: The University Press, 1922.

Whitehead, A. "Gender ideology and religion: Does a masculine image of God matter?" *Review of Religious Research* 54, 2012, 139–156.

15 *Pray the Devil Back to Hell* as a resource for appreciating African women's contribution to peacebuilding

Anna Chitando

Introduction

The chapter examines the extent of women's participation in peace and security, and their potential to influence and engage in peace negotiations in cultural and patriarchal contexts. This chapter utilises the movie *Pray the Devil Back to Hell* as a basis/resource for African women's participation in the continent's peacebuilding endeavours. The movie depicts women who speak with one voice as they bring out everyday meanings of peace and security. Nonetheless, there is never a neat struggle as portrayed by the women's movement in the movie. Therefore, in its discussion, the chapter highlights some of the challenges African women face in peacebuilding, which are understated in the movie.

The arts play an important role in communicating key truths in society. Literature, music, dance, theatre and film, poetry, among others, are valuable platforms for raising awareness of major issues that trouble society. They can also be employed to propose solutions to the matters that concern society. For example, African women's writings have been very helpful in bringing to the fore the problem of patriarchy and the marginalisation of women in society (Chitando 2012). In *Secrets of a Woman's Soul*, Shaba (2005) shows how patriarchy puts women in danger, as men often have both financial and cultural power. African women writers have been able to alert society to address women's issues. African women musicians have also been actively involved in drawing attention to women's issues (Jenje-Makwenda 2013).

The arts have also been utilised to bring out the role of African women in peacebuilding. Although not focusing specifically on women, Mtukwa (2015) illustrates how informal peacebuilding processes must be accorded space in Africa. Women, who are mostly left out of the formal peacebuilding processes, have been utilising informal peacebuilding processes in Africa. This chapter focuses on the importance of the movie *Pray the Devil Back to Hell* in the context of appreciating African women's contribution to peacebuilding. The chapter's first section focuses on African women's exclusion from peacebuilding. This is followed by a summary of the movie *Pray the Devil Back to Hell*. The chapter

214 Anna Chitando

assesses the potential of the movie to serve as a resource for African women's contribution to peacebuilding in the third section. The chapter concludes with a call for more artistic works to raise and deepen awareness of women's critical role in peacebuilding in Africa.

Understated and underappreciated: Women in peacebuilding in Africa

The story of African women remains highly complex, confirming the dynamic nature of African women's struggles (Bouilly et al. 2016). African women scholars and activists bemoan the tendency to project African women as helpless victims who are waiting for feminist saviours from other parts of the world. Rightly, they insist that such a defeatist stance perpetuates the colonising trope that has dominated the study of Africa in general and African women in particular. African women scholars have argued that negative images of African women in Western feminism disempower the very women that Western feminists seek to liberate. Also, African women scholars draw attention to the notable progress that has been made in African women's struggles (Ahikire 2014).

Analysing the unequal power relations between Western feminists and "third world" (Global South) women, Chandra Mohanty (1984: 335) asserts strongly that Western feminists have, unfortunately, adopted a homogenising approach:

> An analysis of "sexual difference" in the form of a cross-culturally singular, monolithic notion of patriarchy or male dominance leads to the construction of a similarly reductive and homogeneous notion of what I call the "Third World Difference" − that stable, ahistorical something that apparently oppresses most if not all the women in these countries. And it is in the production of this "Third World Difference" that Western feminisms appropriate and "colonize" the fundamental complexities and conflicts which characterize the lives of women of different classes, religions, cultures, races and castes in these countries. It is in this process of homogenization and systemitization of the oppression of women in the third world that power is exercised in much of recent Western feminist discourse, and this power needs to be defined and named.

Such approaches have led African women scholars to insist on the agency of African women. They have consistently argued that African women possess the agency to change their situation in life. From the precolonial, colonial and now postcolonial periods, African women have not relied on the generosity of foreigners or men to act in empowering ways. If anything, African women have always drawn from within and among themselves to shake off the chains of oppression and to shape their own destiny.

Women have been particularly strategic in peacebuilding in Africa, although their distinctive contributions have often been underappreciated. They have been actively involved in bringing peace and development in their families and communities, although the focus has been predominantly on men. Due to social construction that tends to regard activities and processes involving men as more important, male peacemakers have received greater acknowledgement. Not surprisingly, the volume *Africa's Peacemakers* (Adebajo 2014) is dominated by men. However, this has not deterred African women from engaging in peacebuilding. Two of the three women featured in *Africa's Peacemakers* (out of 15) are directly relevant to this chapter. These are the Liberian women Leymah Gbowee and Ellen Johnson Sirleaf Gbowee (Liberia's and Africa's first woman president) who were joint winners of the 2011 Nobel Peace Prize.

In keeping with global trends, men's roles in peacebuilding in Africa tend to receive greater attention. This goes hand in glove with the patriarchal construction of public space, which positions men as public actors and restricts women to the domestic space. Most of the formal peace deals that have been brokered on the continent have been presented as agreements between different sets of *men*. The photographs of such grand events are usually all-men affairs, with women tucked far away in the background. However, this is a misrepresentation of reality, as women have always been actively involved in struggles for peace, both formally and informally. In defiance of many oppressive factors, African women have contributed towards peace at different levels. The persistence of negative forces means that this is an ongoing struggle. Pailey (2019: 1) expresses it well when observing that,

> African women have had to overcome constraints imposed on them not only by patriarchy, but also by histories of slavery, colonialism, structural adjustment, land dispossession, militarism, and neoliberalism. They have often been subordinated in the domestic or private sphere, with gendered values and norms then undermining their agency in the public sphere. Although African women have managed to secure some political, socio-economic, and cultural rights, resources, and representation, this has certainly not been the panacea for achieving full equality of citizenship or gender justice.

In the area of peacebuilding, the major focus has tended to be on women's greater vulnerability to sexual and gender-based violence during wars and armed conflict in Africa. Although this is a legitimate concern, it has the danger of perpetuating the stereotypes associated with Africa in general, and African women in particular. This stereotype presents the African woman as a perpetual victim of violence, never taking the initiative herself and having to rely on foreign agents to save her from her terrible situation. This overlooks the agency of African women (see below) that needs to be centralised in analysing African

216 *Anna Chitando*

women's experiences. Scholars must also revise the tendency to make African experiences of universal human experiences, such as pain, uniquely African (see, for example, Norridge 2013: 3). Associating Africa with pain negates the reality that human beings everywhere experience pain. Why should an impression be created that "African pain" is unique? As a result, this chapter seeks to place emphasis on Liberian (and African) women's active role in peacebuilding in Africa.

Summarising *Pray the Devil Back to Hell*

One of the most vivid illustrations of African women's involvement in peacebuilding is the movie *Pray the Devil Back to Hell* (hereafter, *Pray the Devil*). Numerous reviews of the movie have been published. These include Alaga (2011), Prasch (2011) and Hilkovitz (2014). Therefore, this chapter will not be elaborate in its description of the movie. In summary, the movie recreates the powerful story of women in Liberia and their search for peace in their country. The women came together to eventually contribute towards the end of the Second Liberian Civil War (1999–2003) that was fought between the then president, Charles Taylor, and the rebels. It is a riveting account of the horrors of war, the vulnerability of women and girls and the intransigence of most men.

Although focusing on a women's mass movement, namely, the Women of Liberia Mass Action for Peace Campaign, there are some leading personalities. These include Leymah Gbowee (later a joint winner of the Nobel Peace Prize in 2011, as noted above), Asatu Bah Kenneth, Vaiba Flomo, Janet Bryant-Johnson, Etty Weah and Etweda "Sugars" Cooper (Badoe 2008: 133). As the rebels ravage the countryside and bring the war to Monrovia, the capital city, the women organise for peace. Initially set up as a Christian women's group, the group expands to include Muslims and others.

Pray the Devil is a captivating account that captures the struggles that women face in times of war. Although men too are victims of war, the impact of war on women is mostly greater (Shteir 2013). The movie enables one to understand the strategies adopted by the women activists as they sought to force the protagonists to attend the Accra Peace Conference in neighbouring Ghana. They showed impressive organisational skills in building an interfaith mass movement, put on white clothes to symbolise their struggle for peace and took up strategic positions in order to gain Taylor's attention.

The movie provides vivid footage of the women's activities, including dramatic moments of confrontation and frustration. These include Gbowee's daring act of speaking truth to power while addressing Taylor, as well as the rebels' threats of physical violence during the stand-off at the peace talks in Ghana. It also carries heart-warming scenes of jubilation when peace is finally achieved. *Pray the Devil* is a balanced and informative movie, which is helpful for understanding the contribution of African women to peacebuilding. Although it focuses on a single process in a specific African country, it offers

Pray the Devil Back to Hell 217

material that enables an appreciation of the broader issues of African women and peacebuilding.

Key ideas from *Pray the Devil* and African women's role in peacebuilding

The movie offers very practical ideas as to African women's contributions to peacebuilding. It shows the mobilisation of women at the grassroots level and follows the mass movement as it grows into a formidable force. *Pray the Devil* confirms the commitment that women possess when they focus on a specific task

Women's agency

The movie exemplifies the agency that women possess and exercise in the face of numerous stumbling blocks. The peace activists do not sit idly and wait for the war to finish them off. They do not succumb to fatalism, but take concrete steps to protect their children, themselves and those dear to them (consistently, the interviewees prioritise the well-being of their children, ahead of their own). The collective action taken by women from different socio-economic classes and religions demonstrates the power of unity among women. The tendency by donors to emphasise the gap between "elite" and "grassroots" African women (Okech and Musindarwezo 2019: 257–258) runs the risk of demobilising African women. Foreign donors in general and African men, especially, are uncomfortable when African women forge a united front. Unity is strength, as many African proverbs confirm.

It was through unity and maximising their talents that different women brought to the Mass Action for Peace Campaign that enabled the resistance to succeed. *Pray the Devil* brings out the power of women from diverse backgrounds acting together for a common cause. Women's peacebuilding abilities are demonstrated as they use various strategies to persuade the militants on both sides to silence the guns in Liberia. The women are highly strategic as they put together effective strategies that enable them to achieve their set objectives. This is consistent with observations in other settings. For example, reflecting on women's contributions to peacebuilding in Jos, Plateau State, in north central Nigeria, Ilesanmi observes that "… women's positions transcend being passive victims in armed conflict and war situations to being active agents of peace" (2017: 188).

Most reports on women and conflict in Africa and other places tend to focus on women's vulnerability. As the chapter will illustrate below, this is a legitimate concern. However, one problem with this approach is that it takes away women's agency. In different scenes, women are seen as decisive individuals who bring together their capabilities in order to contribute towards the overall goal. There is no participant who is rendered less important, as each one has a role to play. They are all driven by the quest for peace. The women in *Pray the*

218 *Anna Chitando*

Devil illustrate the value of the "Capability Approach," where concepts of heterogeneity, agency and public deliberation (Marovah 2015) are central.

Equally important in *Pray the Devil* is the use of motherhood as a strength in African women's peacebuilding. One is here aware of the ambivalent status of motherhood in African feminist and womanist debates. Some African feminists contend, consistent with a strand within Euro-American feminism, that putting a premium on motherhood runs the risk of curtailing women's access to the public space. On the other hand, there are some African feminists and womanists who maintain that motherhood remains key in Africa. For instance, Prasch (2015), has studied how Gbowee and other Liberia Mass Action for Peace activists deployed motherhood to achieve their goal of winning peace. Therefore, it is important for scholars to have more open approaches towards concepts and positions and allow the possibility of surprises in different contexts. This will enable African feminism and womanism to avoid the dangers that come with fundamentalism. In short, there will be contexts where motherhood is a resource in African women's peacebuilding endeavours, and there will be other contexts where it will be a liability. To declare only one position is to fall into fundamentalism.

Acknowledging women's experience of violence

Giving priority to African women's agency in peacebuilding should not be placed on the same plane as ignoring African (and all other) women's experiences of violence during war. Scholars such as McKay (1998), Mazurana (2012), their joint work (McKay and Mazurana 2004), Lubunga (2016) and others have provided detailed analyses of women's experiences of violence during armed conflicts. *Pray the Devil* recounts the stories of rape that women and girls experienced in the civil war in Liberia. The senseless violence perpetrated by the combatants had women and girls as collateral damage. Sadly, the silencing of the guns never translates immediately into peace, as the chapter shows below. This is expressed by Liebling-Kalifani et al. (2011: 3) in the following passage:

> The fourteen years of armed conflict saw not only the destruction of Liberia's social and economic infrastructure, but high levels of brutality by all factions. These included widespread killings, rape, sexual assault, abduction, torture, forced labour, recruitment of child soldiers. As a result, related to their experiences of violence and torture during the conflict the population is suffering from a wide range of psychological, alcohol/drug related addiction, surgical problems and for women, urgent gynaecological problems.

Pray the Devil is a painful reminder of the rape and sexual abuse that women experience in contexts of war. It serves to encourage African women to bring their all to the task of peacebuilding. The movie goes a long way in clarifying why many African women are peace activists. They do not engage in

Pray the Devil Back to Hell   219

this undertaking out of looking for some thrills in dangerous places. They take up the task because of the existential risks posed by war in their midst. The narratives of women's experience of sexual and gender-based violence in *Pray the Devil* serve as a clarion call for African women to invest in peacebuilding as a matter of urgency.

The personalities leading the struggle for peace in *Pray the Devil* are flesh-and-blood women. They are not superwomen characters who are fearless and arrive on time to take out the bad guys. The women in *Pray the Devil* express fears about their own safety and worry constantly about the safety of their children and loved ones. This is because peacebuilding work is political. When peace is won, the warmongers lose. Therefore, the warmongers are in the business of sponsoring and continuing war and violence. They loot, plunder, violate, dominate and thrive on chaos. As the experiences of women human rights defenders globally (Amnesty International 2019) and in Africa confirm, resisting tyranny and violence comes at a cost. Young women peacebuilders in Africa are constantly negotiating threatening and dangerous contexts (Chitando 2019: 2).

Pray the Devil serves to shine light on how women and girls in Africa continue to be at the receiving end of violent conflict. The urgency demonstrated by the women in the movie provides insights into similar movements in contemporary society, such as the #BringBackOurGirls Campaign, which gathered momentum in the wake of the abduction of the Chibok girls in Nigeria by Boko Haram (see, for example, Chiluwa and Ifukor 2015). The harrowing narratives in *Pray the Devil* are a reminder that the struggle does not belong to the annals of history, but that it is a persistent and ongoing struggle that takes different forms, in different contexts, at particular historical periods.

Peacebuilding work is done by regular women

One of the most striking aspects about the women in *Pray the Devil* is that they are "regular or day-to-day" individuals. Here, one is deliberately avoiding the term "ordinary" because of its negative connotations. One is aware that the term "ordinary" creates the impression that there is a category of "extraordinary women" who are supposed to be qualitatively superior to "ordinary women." The leaders and activists in the women's mass movement for peace are down-to-earth women. They include housewives, market women, women from religious organisations, from various professions and stations in life. Gbowee, later to become a Nobel Peace Prize winner, is simply one who is at the front of a movement of equals.

While training, funding, exposure, networking and other dimensions are important to successful peacebuilding by women, *Pray the Devil* confirms that nothing beats dedication. The women's sense of revulsion at the loss of their children, the abuse they experienced and the carefree attitude of the men on both sides of the conflict drives them more than anything else. Women who are doing peacebuilding work in Africa are motivated by the commitment to peace and security. All the other considerations and benefits that might accrue come as a bonus.

United Nations Security Council Resolution (UNSCR) 1325 (Paragraph 1) seeks to increase women's participation in peacebuilding and encourages member states:

> "to ensure increased representation of women at all decision-making levels in national, regional and international institutions and mechanisms for the prevention, management and resolution of conflict". It furthermore: calls on all actors involved, when negotiating and implementing peace agreements, to adopt a gender perspective, including, *inter alia*: the special needs of women and girls during repatriation and resettlement and for rehabilitation, reintegration and post-conflict reconstruction; measures that support local women's peace initiatives and indigenous processes for conflict resolution, and that involve women in all of the implementation mechanisms of the peace agreements.

The most appealing aspect of UNSCR 1325 cited above is its commitment towards ensuring that women of different social classes, including those from the often-marginalised indigenous communities, are included in peacebuilding. As the influence of the Global North continues to be felt in all parts of the globe and the so-called evidence-based, scientific approach seeks to dominate, the role of indigenous approaches to peacebuilding becomes critical. It is not only the "experts" from the Global North, or their counterparts who have formal educational qualifications from universities, who can contribute towards peacebuilding. *Pray the Devil* is a timely reminder that, given the opportunity, *every* woman has a contribution to make.

African women, religion and peacebuilding

In *Pray the Devil*, religion and spirituality play an important role in the mobilisation of women. Specifically, Christian and Muslim women collaborate across the formal doctrinal lines to achieve a common goal. Religion emerges as a strategic resource in peacebuilding in *Pray the Devil*. Cognisant of the reality that religion has often been used to justify terror (as is the case with Boko Haram in Nigeria), many peace activists are hesitant to allow religious actors to be part of peacebuilding efforts. It is also true that religion is often divisive and does not always provide an effective platform for bringing activists together.

Pray the Devil invites a rethinking of the role of religion in peacebuilding in Africa. The activists in the movie draw inspiration from their religions and they can resist the warlords because of their faith. It is also religion that gives them a sense of purpose, even when their efforts appear to be going to waste. Religious spaces such as churches and mosques act as networking zones for sharing strategies and for mutual encouragement. The collaboration across religions generates and sustains the idea that there is a superior force behind

Pray the Devil Back to Hell   221

the engagement. The power of symbolism was confirmed by the women who dressed in white. Religion can, therefore, be a strong factor in peacebuilding in Africa.

African spirituality can also be seen in the women's threat to strip naked. Some African women writers such as Yvonne Vera (1993) have demonstrated the spirituality associated with African women's bodies. In *Pray the Devil*, the men, usually very stubborn and disrespectful, fully recognise the symbolism and consequences of women stripping naked as an expression of anger. Razak (2016) has described the sacredness associated with African women's bodies in a convincing manner. This dimension has a role to play in women's peacebuilding in Africa.

A note on some challenges

Women's peacebuilding work in Africa and globally faces several challenges. Unfortunately, *Pray the Devil* understates some of these challenges. The result is that although the movie is helpful in giving key ideas regarding African women's contribution to peacebuilding, there is the danger that movie-goers can overlook some of these challenges. The chapter shall now draw attention to four of the key issues.

Persistence of patriarchy and post-conflict violence against women and girls

Pray the Devil is largely a celebratory movie. It narrates the brave story of dedicated women who risk everything and succeed against men who were preoccupied with power. Viewers are left with a sense of contentment, as good triumphs over evil. However, and this is not the problem of the movie; in reality the story beyond the movie is more complicated. Women's experiences in most post-conflict settings are that sexual and gender-violence continue, even as they take new forms. This is confirmed in the following extract from Shilue and Fagen (2014: iii):

> Although Liberia recently celebrated ten years of relative peace, the postwar DDR programs left most of the youth without prospects for a better future. Liberian women, and in particular, rural women and displaced women living in the border areas, continue to experience various forms of human rights abuses, marginalization and exclusion. Incidences of violence incurred during 14 years of war have continued to manifest in continued widespread cases of rape, domestic violence and other forms of gender-based violence.

The cessation of hostilities does not result in an end to sexual and gender-based violence. For many women, there is always the threat of being "on the road again" (Nyamubaya 1986) to face the same challenges that they faced

222 *Anna Chitando*

during the armed conflict. In Nyamubaya's poetry, getting back "on the road again" expressed the frustration that the promise of independence and freedom (in Zimbabwe, where she had served as a field commander during the armed liberation struggle) had not been realised. In many different African countries, the end of armed conflict has not translated into peace for many women.

Going beyond *Pray the Devil*, it is necessary for all the stakeholders to maintain the search for women's security after conflict. Women's active involvement in peacebuilding must translate to women's security after conflict. This can be achieved by ensuring that women are at the table during peace negotiations, not as observers, but as decision makers as well. The recommendations made by the Global Network of Peacebuilders (2019) regarding the need to focus on long-term goals, women's decision making, role of local women, full inclusion of different categories of women and the call for increased funding must be taken seriously.

Women as conflict instigators and combatants

Pray the Devil minimises the problematic theme of women as conflict instigators and combatants. In Liberia, as in various other conflicts in Africa, some women took up arms and were involved in many different ways. Some armed women perpetrated violence against men and women (Shulika 2016: 8). The discussion on African women's agency implies that women have the capacity to become active in combat in African conflicts. However, this is often a difficult discussion because of the social construction of women in general and African women in particular.

In *Bombshell: Women and Terrorism*, Mia Bloom (2011) describes the activities of women terrorists in different parts of the world. In Nigeria, Boko Haram has recruited and uses female suicide bombers (Markovic 2019). Admittedly, many of the women are forced. However, others take the decision to join the rebels. This dimension is particularly difficult for feminists to discuss, as it does not give a positive view of women. African women peacebuilders ought to face the issue of women who are implicated in violence. They need to adopt a realistic and effective approach for their work to be effective.

Role of men

The men in *Pray the Devil* are, overwhelmingly, a terrible lot. They are warmongers, corrupt, intransigent and unreasonable. It is women who initiate all the positive steps. There are only a few good men in the movie, including the Nigerian mediator who challenges the Liberian men to get serious during the long peace negotiations in Accra. The challenge regarding the role of men in women's peacebuilding is not limited to the portrayal of men in the movie. It is a longstanding issue in feminism and womanism in their various forms. For some radical feminists, men are the problem. Therefore, women have no business in collaborating with the oppressor. For Africana womanism, however, it is important for women to collaborate with men for women to thrive (Hudson-Weems 2004)

It is possible that a new era of more effective collaboration with younger African men, who are reflecting on feminism, is beckoning (see, for example, Chiweshe 2018). Younger African feminists are also reflecting on the potential of working with progressive men (Makama et al. 2019). Although men are portrayed negatively in *Pray the Devil*, it might be strategic for African women peacebuilders to reflect on the possible role that men can and do play in the struggle for peace, security and development in Africa. What cannot be negotiated, however, is the welfare, security and leadership of women. Men in Africa must learn to accept that women have the capacity to lead.

Conclusion

African women's participation in peacebuilding is a remarkable story of agency and strategic planning. *Pray the Devil* recounts one particularly successful story, in which women in Liberia challenged the male protagonists to choose the path of peace rather than war. It serves as a powerful testimony to the mobilising power of day-to-day African women for peacebuilding. Armed with determination, the women coordinated their activities up the point of forcing the alpha males locked in a senseless war to come to the negotiating table. This story of women's triumph is, sadly, also the story of women's marginalisation. Although Liberia has the distinction of having provided Africa's first woman president and women played a major role in peacebuilding, women continue to face sexual and gender-based violence as well as patriarchal oppression. *Pray the Devil*, however, remains an important entry point towards understanding African women's contribution to peacebuilding. It can be used in mobilising women activists and in teaching and training, as it captures African women's agency effectively. Other artistic genres, including theatre for development, music, literature (including children's literature) can also be harnessed to show women's capacity to contribute to peacebuilding in Africa.

References

Adebajo, Adekeye (Ed.). 2014. *Africa's Peacemakers: Noble Peace Laureates of African Descent.* Cape Town: Centre for Conflict Resolution.

Ahikire, Josephine. 2014. "African feminism in context: Reflections on the legitimation battles, victories and reversals," *Feminist Africa*, 19, 7–23.

Alaga, Ecoma. 2011. "Security sector reform and the women's peace and activism nexus in Liberia," in Olonisakin Funmi and Awino Okechi (Eds.) *Women and Security Governance in Africa.* Cape Town: Pambazuka Press.

Amnesty International. 2019. *Challenging Power, Fighting Discrimination: A Call to Action to Recognise and Protect Women Human Rights Defenders.* London: Amnesty International.

Badoe, Yaba. 2008. "Review: *Pray the Devil*. Gini Reticker and Abigail Disney; Fork Films; USA," *Feminist Africa* 10, 133–135.

224 *Anna Chitando*

Bloom, Mia. 2011. *Bombshell: Women and Terrorism.* Philadelphia: University of Pennsylvania.

Bouilly, Emmanuelle, Ophélie Rillon and Hannah Cross. 2016. "African women's struggles in a gender perspective," *Review of African Political Economy* 43(149), 338–349.

Chiluwa, Innocent, and Presley Ifukor. 2015. "'War against our children': Stance and evaluation in #BringBackOurGirls campaign discourse on Twitter and Facebook," *Discourse and Society* 26(3), 267–296.

Chitando, Anna. 2012. *Fictions of Gender and the Dangers of Fiction in Zimbabwean Women's Writings on HIV and AIDS.* Harare: Africa Institute for Culture, Dialogue, Peace and Tolerance Studies.

Chitando, Anna. 2019. "From victims to the vaunted: Young women and peacebuilding in Mashonaland, East Zimbabwe," *African Security Review* 28(2), 110–123. doi: 10.1080/10246029.2019.1662462

Chiweshe, Malvern. 2018. "African men and feminism: Reflections on using African feminism in research," *Agenda* 32(2), 76–82.

Global Network of Women Peacebuilders. 2019. *Building and Sustaining Peace from the Ground Up: A Global Study of Civil Society and Local Women's Perception of Sustaining Peace.* New York: Global Network of Women Peacebuilders.

Hilkovitz, Andrea. 2014. "Beyond sex strikes: Women's movements, peace building, and negotiation in *Lysistrata* and *Pray the Devil Back to Hell,*" *Journal for the Study of Peace and Conflict*, 124–134.

Hudson-Weems, Clenora. 2004. *African Womanist Literary Theory.* Trenton, NJ: Africa World Press.

Ilesanmi, Omotola A. 2017. "Women's agency and peacebuilding in Nigeria's Jos crises," in Toyin Falola and Olajumoke Yacob-Haliso (Eds.) *Gendering Knowledge in Africa and the African Diaspora: Contesting History and Power.* London: Routledge.

Jenje-Makwenda, Joyce. 2013. *Women Musicians of Zimbabwe: A Celebration of Women's Struggle for Voice and Artistic Expression.* Harare: Storytime Promotions.

Liebling-Kalifani, Helen et al. 2011. "Women war survivors of the 1989–2003 conflict in Liberia: The impact of sexual and gender-based violence," *Journal of International Women's Studies* 12(1), 1–21.

Lubunga, Esther. 2016. "The impact of conflict in the Democratic Republic of Congo on women and their response to peace-building," *Stellenbosch Theological Journal* 2(2), 347–364.

Makama, Refiloe, Rebecca Helman, Neziswa Titi and Sarah Day. 2019. "The danger of a single feminist narrative: African-centred decolonial feminism for Black men," *Agenda* 33(2), 61–69.

Markovic, Vesna. 2019. "Suicide squad: Boko Haram's use of the female suicide bomber," *Women and Criminal Justice* 29(4–5), 283–302.

Marovah, Tendayi. 2015. "Using the capability approach to conceptualise African identity(ies)," *Phronimon*, 16(2), 42–57.

Mazurana, Dyan. 2012. "Women and girls in non-state armed opposition groups," in Carol Cohn (Ed.) *Women and Wars: Contested Histories, Uncertain Futures.* Cambridge: Polity Press.

McKay, Susan. 1998. "The effects of armed conflict on girls and women," *Peace and Conflict*, 4(4), 381–392.

McKay, Susan, and Dyan Mazurana. 2004. *Where Are the Girls? Girls in Fighting Forces in Northern Uganda, Sierra Leone and Mozambique: Their Lives During and After the War.* Montreal, Quebec: Rights & Democracy.

Mohanty, Chandra Talpade. 1984. "Under Western eyes: Feminist scholarship and colonial discourses," *boundary 2*, 12(3), On Humanism and the University I: The Discourse of Humanism. (Spring–Autumn, 1984), 333–358.

Mtukwa, Tendai. 2015. "Informal peacebuilding initiatives in Africa: Removing the table," *African Journal of Conflict Resolution* 15(1), 85–106.

Norridge, Zoe. 2013. *Perceiving Pain in African Literature.* New York: Palgrave Macmillan.

Nyamubaya, Freedom. 1986. *On the Road Again: Poems During and After the National Liberation of Zimbabwe.* Harare: Zimbabwe Publishing House.

Okech, Awino, and Dinah Musindarwezo. 2019. "Building transnational feminist alliances: Reflections on the post-2015 Development Agenda," *Contexto Internacional* 4(2), 255–272.

Pailey, Robtel N. 2019. "Women, equality and citizenship in contemporary Africa," in *Oxford Research Encyclopedia, Politics.* New York: Oxford University Press. doi: 10.1093/acrefore/9780190228637.013.852

Prasch, Allison M. 2011. "Media Review: *Pray the Devil Back to Hell,* produced by Abigail E. Disney and directed by Gini Reticker," *Women and Language,* 34(1), 105–107.

Prasch, Allison M. 2015. "Maternal bodies in militant protest: Leymah Gbowee and the rhetorical agency of African motherhood," *Women's Studies in Communication* 38(2), 187–205.

Razak, Arisika. 2016. "Sacred women of Africa and the African diaspora: A womanist vision of black women's bodies and the African sacred feminine," *International Journal of Transpersonal Studies* 35(1), 129–147.

Shaba, Lutanga. 2005. *Secrets of a Woman's Soul.* London: Athena Press.

Shilue, James S., and Patricia Fagen. 2014. *Liberia: Links Between Peacebuilding, Conflict Prevention and Durable Solutions to Displacement.* Washington, DC: Brookings Institution, Georgetown University.

Shteir, Sarah. 2013. *Gendered Crises, Gendered Responses: The Necessity and Utility of a Gender Perspective in Armed Conflicts and Natural Disasters: An Introductory Overview,* Civil-Military Occasional Papers. Canberra: Australian Government/Australian Civil-Military Centre.

Shulika, Lukong S. 2016. "Women and peacebuilding: From historical to contemporary African perspectives," *Ubuntu: Journal of Conflict and Social Transformation* 5(1), 7–31.

Vera, Yvonne, 1993. *Nehanda.* Harare: Bobab Books.

Index

Abonnema 131
Abuja 178–9
access to resources 166
action plans, *national* and *regional* 40, 44, 46, 161–2
Adichie, Chimamanda Ngozi 127
Adur, Winnie 57–8
advocacy 104, 168, 201
Africa's Peacemakers 215
African Amnesty Month 186, 194
African Charter 24, 39, 190
African Gender Institute (AGI) 7
African Peacekeeping Network (APN) 2
African studies institutes 7
African Union 22, 39–41, 44–6, 56, 86, 159, 170, 193–4; Master Roadmap 186; Special Envoy on Women, Peace and Security 40, 162
Agbaje, Funmilayo Idowu 10
Agbalajobi, D. T. 189
agency of African women 150–4, 214–18, 222–3; limits to 150–1
Agenda 2030 7, 64, 167
Agenda 2063 22–3, 31–2, 39
Ageng'o, Carole 102
agents of change 25
Ahonsi, Babatunde 132–3
aid policies 170
AIDS 59–60
Akwembe, A. 180
Alaga, E. 21, 189
Alma Ata Declaration (1978) 138
altruism 145–6
Anderlini, S. N. 22
Angola 11, 190–3
Appleby, R. S. 192
Arat, Y. 210
Aristotle 176
Arnold, J. L. 175

Arostegui, Julie 131
artisanal and small-scale mining ASM) 14, 158–71; formalising of activities in 161–4; uplift for women in 159
artistic genres 223
Atim, Grace vii, 14; *author of Chapter 12*
Atuhaire, Pearl Karuhanga vii, 12; *author of Chapter 5*
Audi, Robert 99

Ball, Jennifer 126, 128
Banda, Rupiah 195
banditry 88
Beauvoir, Simone de 1
Beijing Declaration and Platform for Action (1995) 21, 24, 38, 128, 201
best practices 27
Bloom, Mia 222
Boers 206–8
Boko Haram 53, 125, 131, 173, 178–82, 220, 222
Boro, Isaac 178
boundaries between countries, artificiality of 177–8
Boutros-Ghali, B. 189–90
Buhari, Aisha Muhammadu 181
Burundi 163, 168
Buxton, A. 161
buy-in 159

Castillejo, Clare 5
Catholic Commission for Justice and Peace (CCJP) 114
cattle rustling 88, 90
Cecile, Manorohanta Marie 89
CEDAW *see* Convention on the Elimination of All forms of Discrimination against Women

Index   227

challenges facing women concerned with peacebuilding 10–11, 22, 29, 31, 37, 39, 59, 104, 109, 193, 202–3, 221–2
chama 149
Chanda, Charity 187
"change agents" 168
Chikwekwe, Ketty 187
Chiluba, Frederick 191, 195
Chirongoma, Sophia vii, 13; *author of Chapter 8*
Chitando, Anna vii, 11, 15; *editor and author of Chapters 1 and 15*
Christina, P. 66, 72
church leadership 111–12
civic education 100
Civilian Joint Task Force (CJTF) 182–3
civil society organisations (CSOs) 25, 28, 43, 57, 61, 78–9, 92, 94, 201
civil wars 27, 38, 64
Clifford, A. M. 210
Cockburn, Cynthia 98
Cohen, S. 25
collaboration between women and men 223
collective actions 167
collective guilt 110
Collins, N. 162
Colonialism 113, 177–8, 214
community health volunteers (CHVs) 136–55
community health workers (CHWs) 14, 78–9, 92, 94; definition of 138
conflict diamonds and other conflict minerals 158, 160, 163
conflict resolution 14, 94, 100, 103–4, 108–9, 169, 174, 201
Congo, Democratic Republic of (DRC) 153, 159–60, 165, 200
Connell, R. W. 204
constitutional change 87, 99
Continental Result Framework (CRF) 40–1
Convention on the Elimination of All forms of Discrimination against Women (CEDAW) 24, 38, 70–2, 75, 174, 201
Convention on the Rights of Persons with Disabilities (CRPD) 130
Copenhagen conference (1980) 24
corporate social responsibility 163
Coryndon, Robert 209
Coulter, C. 25
counter-terrorism 173, 183–4

countries covered by peacebuilding research 8, 11
countries not recognising women's rights and priorities 170
Croatia 139–40
culture and cultural norms 11, 61, 149, 152, 159, 202, 209–10
Curle, Adam 97
customary law 166

dahalo 90
democracy 94, 99–100, 176
de la Rey, C. 152–3
D'Errico, N. 139–40, 153
development partners 77
De Witte, Marleen 99
diamond market 160
diasporas 60
disabilities, women with 13, 124–34
discrimination: double form of 50; gender-based 12, 31; and human rights 70
discriminatory laws 45, 47
dispute settlement 200; peaceful 194
doctoral studies 7
documentation of peacebuilding 15, 186, 196
donor funding 40–1, 46, 170
Dorina, B. 66, 72

Echavarria, C. 159
economic conditions 60
education 3, 7, 31, 60, 94, 100, 110, 165, 169, 179, 181, 209
elderly women 110–11, 116
elections and election violence 28, 45, 65, 83, 94, 102–3, 113–14, 142–3
Elgin, Lord 209
elite groups 177
Ellis, S. 192
emancipation of women 101
Emaswati women 15, 199–201
emotive influence within families 180
empowerment 13, 61, 92–4, 97, 104, 108–9, 121, 159, 162, 180, 183–4; economic form of 169–70
enabling factors for African women scholars 4–5
engagement, 5Ps of 128
Enloe, C. 202
Environmental Law Institute 159
Eritrea 174
Eshun, Maame Esi viii, 14; *author of Chapter 11*

228 *Index*

Eswatini 210; change of name from Swaziland (2018) 205
ethnic tensions 113, 152
European Union (EU) 194

Fagen, Patricia 221
Falola, Toyin 3
female genital mutilation (FGM) 75
femininity, boundaries of 54
feminism and feminist analysis 3, 6, 43, 98, 101, 127, 214, 222–3
Fisher, Denise 89
formal peace structures 151–4, 213–15; absence of women from 151, 154, 202
Freeman, Samuel Richard 99
Fubara-Manuel, Jessie viii, 13; *co-author of Chapter 9*
funding 151

gacaca courts 58–9
Galtung, Johan 25, 79
Gap Report (2004) 49–50
Gbowee, Leymah 9, 29, 43, 215
gender-based violence *see* sexual and gender-based violence
gendered nature of peacebuilding 153–4, 188
Gender Equality in Africa, Solemn Declaration on (2004) 194–5
gender norms and roles 12–13, 26, 38–9, 104–5, 149–50, 153, 159, 163–4, 168, 187–8, 199, 202–4, 210
Genge, M. 208
genocide 29–30, 58
Ghana 40–1, 45
Ginindza, T. 206
global initiatives on peacebuilding 170
Global Network of Peacebuilders 222
Global Peace Index (GPI) 199–200
global security concerns 5–6
Global Terrorism Index (GTI) 179
Gombi, Bakari 181–2
Gombi community 124, 127–34
governance, participation in 13
Goyol, Yilritmwa 5
grass-roots initiatives 26–32, 43, 66, 97, 104, 136–7, 154, 169
Greenberg, M. 168
Gukurahundi massacres (1982–87) 112–13
Guma, Maureen viii, 12; *author of Chapter 4*
gun control 88, 193–4
Gurr, T. 176

Habermas, Jürgen 99
Hadari, Zeinabou 183
harmony, social 109
Hasan, Hamsat 181–2
Hayes, K. 160
health care: as a bridge for peace (HBP policy) 138–9, 148–54; system of 145–7, 153–4
health and safety issues 161
Hendricks, Cheryl 2, 87
Henrizi, A. 201
Hentschel, T. 161
HIV 59–60
Hruschka, F. 159
Hudson, Heidi 154
Human Development Index (HDI) 69
human rights 21–2, 25, 70, 97, 114, 163, 174
human values 94

Ilesanmi, Omotola A. 217
implementation of new policies 179–80
inclusivity 21
iNdlovukazi 111
informal activity 148–9
Institute of Security Studies (ISS) 85
integration into peacebuilding 154, 166; into terrorism 179
interdisciplinarity 7
intergenerational communication 11
internally displaced peoples (IDP) 53–4, 200
International Crisis Group 59–60
International Labour Organisation (ILO) 161
Iraq 201
Isike, Christopher 130–1
Issifu, Abdul Karim 128
Izabiliza, J. 22

Jones, H. M. 206–7
Joubert, Piet 207
journalism 57
Justino, Patricia 202

Kamanzi, A. 204
Kaunda, Kenneth 190, 195
Kaya, Z. 200–1
Kayanda, Michelle 187
Kenya 13–14, 96–105, 136–55
Khodary, Y. M. 201
King, Nancy 181
Krogh, J. C. 207
Kunene, Cleopas 206

Index   229

Kuper, Hilder 206–9
kuripa ngozi ritual 110–11

Labotsibeni, Queen of Swaziland
   199–200, 204–10
land reform 113–14, 166, 200, 209
Laqueur, Walter 175
Lawson, L. 162
leadership positions, women in 6, 10, 45,
   58, 195–6, 203, 223; *see also* church
   leadership
Lederach, John Paul 97
legitimacy 147–8
Lesotho 200
Liberia 15, 27–9, 31, 44, 54, 59, 64–79, 160,
   166–9, 215–16, 223; conflict resolution
   processes 65–6; economic context 70–2;
   human rights and discrimination 70;
   legal frameworks and access to justice
   75–6; Peacebuilding Commission (PBC)
   66–7; population 69–70; Strategic
   Roadmap 68; violence against women
   and girls (VAWG) 73–5; women in peace
   and security 72
Liebling-Kalifani, Helen 218
Lindborg, Nancy 94
Literacy 60, 165
"local turn" in peacebuilding 137, 152
Lord's Resistance Army (LRA) 53, 173–4
Lungu, Edgar 194–5

MacCarthy, M. K. 23–4
Mac Ginty, R. 137, 152
Machakanja, Pamela 1
Machel, Graca 56
McKay, S. 152–3, 196
MacQueen, G. 139, 153
Madagascar 12–13, 83–94; Conseil
   des Sages 87; women's role in
   peacebuilding 89–91
maintenance of peace and security 15
Malawi 163
Mama, Amina 3
Mano River Women's Peace Network 45
marginalisation 3, 23, 29–30, 38, 146,
   213, 223
marriage 111; forced 91, 179
Marwick, B. A. 208
Maseno, Loreen viii, 13; *author of Chapter 7*
Mazurana, D. 196
Mbandzeni, King of Swaziland 200,
   205, 208
Mbugua, J. K. 165
mediation 103–4, 110–11, 202

Mexico conference (1975) 24
Millennium Development Goals (MDGs) 5
Milner, Lord 206, 208
mining *see* artisanal and small-scale mining;
   women artisanal miners
Mitchell , Rebecca 202
Mkhonta, P. 203
Mohamud, Leyla Osman 57
Mohanty, Chandra 214
Monrovia 68–9
motherhood 9, 53, 195, 218
Movement for the Emancipation of the
   Niger Delta (MEND) 178
Mozambique 11
Mpoumou, D. 22
Mtukwa, Tendai 213
Mueller-Hirth, N. 150
Mugabe, Robert 112–13
Müller, Catherine 202
Munich Olympics (1972) 174
Munro, J. 188
Murabi, Alaa 183
murder 110–11
Musonda, Barbara 187
Mutamba, J. 22
Muthuki, Janet Muthoni viii; *co-author of*
   Chapter 2
Mutisi, Martha 10
Mwale, Nelly viii, 14–15; *author of*
   Chapter 13
Mwanawasa, Levy 195
Mwila, Davis 186–7
Myrttinen, H. 195

Nairobi conference (1985) 24
Namariba, J. 204
Narrating War and Peace 3
narratives 102
Naureen, F. 179–80
Ndebele raids 112–13
Nepal 139–40
networking 11, 44–5, 149
neutrality in health care 146–7
Next Generation Social Sciences in Africa
   fellowship program 7
Nganga, T. W. 210
Ngwobia, Justina Mike viii, 13; *co-author of*
   Chapter 9
Niger Delta Volunteer Force (NDVF) 178
Nigeria 14, 53–4, 124–34, 173–84;
   Adamawa State 125; Justice, Peace and
   Reconciliation Movement (JPRM)
   124–7, 134; women's contribution to
   fight against terrorism in 179–82

230 Index

Njiru, Roseann viii, 14; *author of Chapter 10*
Nobel Peace Prize 29, 43, 215, 219
Nsibandze, Mbhabha 207
Ntawubona, J. 202–4
Nyamazana, M. 187
Nyamubaya, Freedom 222
Nyawo, Sonene viii–ix, 15, 203; *author of Chapter 14*

Obi, Cyril 176
official recognition for women's roles 14
Onsanti, Katherine 104
Oodua People's Congress (OPC) 178
operationalisation of new processes 32
oral tradition 93
O'Reilly, M. 195–6, 202
organisations concerned with peacebuilding 6–7
Orina, H. 164, 168
Osinbajo, Mrs Dolapo 181
Oxford Handbook of Women, Peace and Security 3

Pailey, Robtel 215
Palgrave Handbook of Global Approaches to Peace 2–3
Palva hut process 68
Pankhurst, D. 22
parliamentary representation of women 30, 57–8, 182, 203–4
patriarchal nature of society 1, 31, 36–8, 43, 52, 91, 105, 109, 121, 129, 164, 166, 182, 200–4, 210, 213, 215
Peace, Sarah 181
peace dividend 161
peace huts 59
peace processes 36–42, 58, 94, 103, 164, 169; women's involvement in 26, 202 (*see also* formal peace structures)
peacebuilding: African experiences of 27; broader view of 15, 189–90, 199, 201; complexity of 26, 195; definitions and concepts of 23, 96–7, 199, 201; as distinct from peacekeeping 96; four pillars of 23, from below 97–8; levels of 154; nature of 152; as a process 153, 199; through bridge-making 105
peacebuilding committees and peace meetings 150
peacefulness, extent of 199–200
Pentecostal-Charismatic preachers 100
Perks, R. 160
Persson, M. 25
political decisions affecting the people 201

political processes, women's engagement in 203–4
political will to promote the participation of women 165, 170
post-conflict situations 12–13, 96, 137, 139, 160, 165, 201
Potgieter-Gqubule, Fébé 10
poverty 60
Prasch, Allison 218
Pray the Devil Back to Hell (film) 15, 213–23
private sector institutions 78
Pro-Poor Agenda for Peace and Development (PAPD) in Liberia 69
psychological healing 13, 96
publications focusing on women and peacebuilding 5–6
Puechguirbal, Nadine 1, 193–4

Qorane, Nacima 55
quotas for women 10, 187

racial tensions 113, 152
rain-making powers 205
Rajoelina, Mialy 91
Ramsbotham, Oliver 97–8
Ranavalona I of Madagascar 90
Randriamalaza, Anjanirina Nadia 89
Rawls, John 99
Razafandrakoto, Gaby ix, 12–13; *author of Chapter 6*
Razak, Arisika 221
reconciliation processes 43, 114–15
refugees 187, 190–3, 200
regional economic communities (RECs) 39–40, 46
"regional particularities" 40
Rehn, E. 22
Reinares, Fernando 175
religious organisations and religious women 13, 96–105, 192, 220–1
remittances 161
researchers: initiatives providing support for 7–8; new directions for exploration by 10
rights for women 21, 24, 28–9, 43, 89, 170; equality with men's 29, 109
Rogan, Janet 186–7
Rugyendo, M. 192
rural communities 109, 163
Rwanda 27, 29–31, 44, 53, 56–8

Salah, Alaa 55–6
Sampson, Cynthia 97, 103–4
Santa-Barbara, J. 139, 153
Sata, Michael 195

Index   231

Schirch, L. 189
Schmid, A. P. 175
scholarly perspectives 4–5, 24–6, 187–90, 214
scholarship on peacebuilding, women's contributions to 3–5, 9–11, 15–16
security concerns 10, 84, 200–1, 222
Selborne, Lord 206, 208
self-awareness 10
Senegal 44
Sewak, M. 189
sex work 158
sexual exploitation and abuse (SEA) 12
sexual and gender-based violence (SGBV) 12, 31, 53, 55, 61, 73–5, 79, 90–3, 98, 101, 103, 132–3, 189–90, 215, 221, 223
sexually-transmitted infections (STIs) 37, 55, 179
Shaba, Lutanga 213
sharing experiences 11
Shepstone, Theophilus 206–7
Shilue, James S. 221
Shona people 110–13
Shulika, Lukong S. viii, 11; co-author of Chapter 2
Sierra Leone 44, 166
Sikaneta, Susan 15, 186, 188, 191–6; contribution to peacebuilding 192–3
Since Women Peace Network (SWPN) 28–9
Sirleaf, Ellen Johnson 22, 28–9, 65, 215
Smit, Timo 183
Smith-Holm, J. 187
Smuts, Johannes 207
social media 8, 54, 57, 94
social norms 180, 202
social risks 159
socialisation 9, 111, 202, 209–10
societal peacebuilding 166
socio-economic injustices 26
Somalia and Somaliland 55
South Africa 3, 10–11, 56, 152–3
South Sudan 58, 166
Southern Voices for Peacebuilding network 7
Specht, I. 25
spirituality 221
status of women 90–4, 101, 169, 182–3, 204
stereotyping 12, 31, 55, 57, 93, 182, 204, 215
sub-Saharan Africa 200
Sustainable Development Goals (SDGs) 5, 30
Swaziland 199–210; peacebuilding in 201–2

Tanzania 163
Tawiah, Esther ix, 9, 12; author of Chapter 3
Taylor, Charles 216
Ter Haar, G. 192
terrorism 14, 173; conceptual discourse and theoretical framework 174–7; definition of 174–6; in Nigeria 177–9; preferred terms for 175
think tanks 2
Tidblad-Lundholm, Kajsa 183
Togo 200
traditional societies and attitudes 93, 109–11, 180, 182
training opportunities 11–12, 44, 92, 151, 159, 165–9, 180
transitional justice 28, 58–9, 94
traumatisation 179
truth and reconciliation commissions (TRCs) 28, 67–8

Uganda 57–8
United Nations (UN) 6, 12–13, 174–5; Commission on the Status of Women (CSW) 24, 163; Decade for Women (UNDW) 24; Development Assistance Framework (UNDAF) 75; Development Fund for Women (UNIFEM) 26; Educational, Scientific and Cultural Organisation (UNESCO). 6; Entity for Gender Equality and the Empowerment of Women 163; Mission in Liberia (UNMIL) 28, 65, 68, 70; Office for West Africa and the Sahel (UNOWAS) 44; Peacebuilding Fund (PBF) 87–8, 166–7; Security Council (UNSC) 1, 5–6, 15, 24, 28, 36–40, 44, 46, 50–2, 65, 68, 72, 84–5, 109, 124, 127–9, 137, 162, 189–90, 193, 201–2, 213, 220; troops on peacekeeping missions 56, 183, 187 (see also Convention of the Elimination of All forms of Discrimination against Women; Convention on the Rights of Persons with Disabilities; Universal Declaration of Human Rights)
United States Department of Defense 175
Universal Declaration of Human Rights (1948) 22, 25
universities offering courses concerned with peacebuilding 77
Utas, M. 25
Uzodike, Ufo 130–1

value chains 169
Vera, Yvonne 221

232   *Index*

Vilakazi, Josiah 209
violence towards women 22, 25, 52, 73–5, 218–19; *see also* sexual and gender-based violence
visibility of women' participation 21, 98
volunteering 145–6, 155
vulnerability: associated with mining 159; of women and girls 217

Waki Commission 102
Wanyeki, Muthoni 103
war, impact of 24, 36, 84–5
war-related work, participation in 12
Watts, C. C. 205–6
Whitehead, A. 204
Wibben, A. T. R. 23–4
Windhoek Declaration 38, 201
Wolterstorff, Nicholas 99–100
women: benefits from involvement of 103; as combatants 89, 98, 173–4, 181–4, 188, 222; concern with health care 149–50, 153; concern with policy as well as research 9; distinctive perspectives of 37, 98, 101, 108, 121, 189, 193; experience of 101–3; peace-loving nature 25, 43; recent developments related to participation 21; special needs of 84; united and speaking for themselves 4; untapped potential of 111, 169
Women, Peace and Security (WPS) agenda 5, 44–7, 50–1, 84
women artisanal miners (WAMs) 158–71; participation in peacebuilding by 162–6; vulnerability of and risks run by 159–62
women-led processes 4; *see also* leadership positions
Women and Peace in Africa (2003) 6
Women in Peacebuilding Network (WIPNET) 28–9
Women Without Walls Initiative (WOWWI) 180
Women for Women International 23
"women's issues" 5

women's organisations 162, 166–9
women's situation rooms (WSRs) 45
working conditions 14
World Health Organisation (WHO) 130, 138–9

Yacob-Haliso, Olajumoke 11
Yecho, J. I. 177
Yoruba people 178
young women 49–62; actively joining armed groups 54; in the arts (music/dance/drama) 55–6; conclusions and recommendations on 61–2; in conflict areas 53–5; definition of 50; disengagement and later reintegration of 53–5; given as peace offerings 111; and the internet 56–7; justice system for 61; in parliament 57–8; participation by 12, 51–2, 55–6, 61; partnership with 52; protection of 52; and transitional justice 58–9
Youth, Peace and Security (YPS) agenda 50–1, 58
Yoyo, Arthur 191
Yusuf, Mohammed 179

Zambia 14–15, 186–96; absence of conflict within 190; involvement in peacebuilding 187–8; legislation addressing peace 190; Master Roadmap 193–4; *Vision 2030* 190; as a world leader in bringing forward women peacekeepers 195
ZANU PF 115
Zimbabwe 13, 108–21, 163, 222; enhancing women's participation in 120–1; legacies of violence in 112–15; National Peace and Reconciliation Commission (NPRC) 112; peacebuilding in the Midlands Province 115–21
Zimbabwe Trust 121
Zuckerman, E. 168
Zulu culture 111

Printed in the United States
By Bookmasters